SUPER LEAGUE

THE FIRST TEN YEARS

SUPER LEAGUE

THE FIRST TEN YEARS

PHIL CAPLAN & JONATHAN R. DOIDGE

TEMPUS

To Emma, Louisa, James and Zach;
the generation for whom Super League was invented.

Front Cover: Main Image: *Super League's most durable performer, Keith Senior has racked up more appearances (258) and tries (139) than any other player over the past ten seasons with Sheffield and Leeds.*
Portraits (left to right): *Kris Radlinski, a ten-year servant with Wigan Warriors and one of the most dependable, brave and nerveless custodians in the game.*

Chris Joynt is driven back in a tackle. Super League's quiet man led St Helens to Super League title wins in 1999, 2000 and 2002.

Bradford Bulls' inspirational skipper Jamie Peacock lifts the 2005 trophy, making history by leading his side to the summit from third spot.

The Super League hit man, Salford's Malcolm Alker, consistently the most prolific tackler in the game, downing an opponent a record 1,050 times in 2001.

Current Great Britain skipper Paul Sculthorpe began Super League as a teenager with Warrington, going on to become one of the code's most accomplished and respected performers at St Helens.
Back Cover: *Old Trafford welcomes the players of Bradford Bulls and Wigan Warriors for the 2003 Grand Final, the first decider at the 'Theatre of Dreams'.*

First published 2006

Tempus Publishing Limited
The Mill, Brimscombe Port,
Stroud, Gloucestershire, GL5 2QG
www.tempus-publishing.com

© Phil Caplan & Jonathan R. Doidge, 2006

The right of Phil Caplan & Jonathan R. Doidge to be identified as
the Authors of this work has been asserted in accordance with the
Copyrights, Designs and Patents Act 1988.

British Library Cataloguing in Publication Data.
A catalogue record for this book is available from the British Library.

ISBN 0 7524 3698 8

Typesetting and origination by Tempus Publishing Limited
Printed in Great Britain

CONTENTS

FOREWORD

BY PAUL SCULTHORPE

Super League has undoubtedly been a great boost for the game. For the players the move to summer has been doubly advantageous, not just out on the field but also in preparing to go into battle; while off it the profile of the sport has increased immensely.

Anyone who plays Super League has got to be a great athlete but there are those names that have stood out. No account of the era would be complete without mention of colleagues and rivals such as AndyFarrell, Kris Radlinski, Keiron Cunningham, James Lowes, Robbie Paul and Keith Senior – all mentioned within these pages – while coaches such as Shaun McRae, Brian Noble and of course Ian Millward have added their own splash of colour.

Those of us who provide the action are all aware that, as well being a great sport, Super League is now firmly established as part of the entertainment industry. Venues such as Headingley, Odsal and my home ground at Knowsley Road have become synonymous with pre-match entertainment and spectacle and it is great to see families enjoying themselves at those places and new stadiums like the Halliwell Jones in Warrington or the JJB at Wigan.

The quality of what is served up has come on leaps and bounds. That is down to full-time professionalism, which not only benefits players but also the coaches and everyone else involved in the extended backroom staff. The switch to summer has equally meant that we are now fortunate enough to have better conditions in which to display our skills.

From a personal point of view the abiding memories of the decade are those from three Grand Final wins with St Helens in 1999, 2000 and 2002. The occasion at Old Trafford is like nothing I've experienced and once you have been involved in something like that you just desperately want more of the same. Also, to be on the field when Chris Joynt scored his famous try in the play-offs against Bradford was incredible and something I will never forget. To think that your season is virtually over and for mates to then have the courage and instinctive ability to come up with an inspirational final play like that for the team is the reason why you put so much effort and preparation in, and the kind of thing you dream of when you set out.

There have been many other great moments in the competition since 1996, with Bradford in particular proving to be tremendous rivals, while the play-offs have undoubtedly added to the excitement and flavour since they were brought in.

My main hope for the future is that the administrators and officials can make a concerted effort to reduce the fixture list. Every year the increase in intensity becomes more physically demanding and draining and quality, rather than quantity, should always be the priority. Internationally we have improved, but this is the key area that will allow us to be at our best for the end-of-season Test matches.

Super League has been superb for me. I do something I love for a living, I consider myself very lucky to be involved and I would not wish to have played in any other era.

I am sure you will enjoy reading this account and detailed analysis of a memorable decade. Here's to the next ten years!

Paul Sculthorpe
Captain, Great Britain and St Helens
February 2006

The Authors

Phil Caplan, a third-generation watcher of the sport, began writing programme articles in the late 1980s and also provides regular match reports, interviews and columns principally for *Rugby Leaguer & League Express* and *Rugby League World*. He has experience as a radio summariser on the sport and is also media manager for the Rugby League Conference and a media officer for the Rugby League European Federation. This is his seventh book about the code.

Jonathan Doidge is a freelance sports journalist and broadcaster whose sporting passions are rugby league, cricket and horse racing. In addition to broadcasting and writing on the latter pair, he commentates on rugby league for BBC local radio, and writes about the sport for publications that include *Rugby League World* magazine and *Rugby Leaguer & League Express*.

Acknowledgements

Our sincere thanks go to the signature interviewees – Dean Bell, Gary Hetherington, Richard Lewis, Brian McDermott, Ian Swire and Vic Wakeling – who gave of their time selflessly and without restriction to convey a unique insight and perspective into events over the last ten years. We are also indebted to TEAMtalk for the use of their facilities, Stuart Charmak for his proofreading skills, Dave Williams at RLPhotos.com and Paul Sculthorpe for agreeing so readily to write the foreword. The support and encouragement of Holly Bennion, Rob Sharman and Stephen Holford at Tempus Publishing has been invaluable and we are extremely grateful to our respective families, along with Paula and Joe, for our indulgences. The *Rothmans Rugby League Yearbooks* and annual reviews produced by League Publications have been invaluable sources of information. Every effort has been taken to attribute all references; if anything has been omitted it is entirely unintentional.

ONE

RUGBY REBRANDED

'Super League will represent a dramatic sea change in approach, a quantum leap in thinking. Life is changing. We have to change with it. You can't stop history developing.' – Maurice Lindsay

What Freddie Banquet started, Jamie Peacock finished. The Paris Saint-Germain centre's kick-off officially heralded the arrival of Super League in March 1996 – just over a hundred years after the formation of the code – in front of an inquisitive crowd, numerous anxious administrators and a generally sceptical media. Ten seasons later, the Bradford Bulls and Great Britain captain lifted the trophy after his side's historic run to the Grand Final, their success acclaimed by a third consecutive sell-out crowd at Old Trafford. Such a wholesale transformation of a mainstream sport – which involved soul searching, redefinition and no little in-fighting along the way – is a fascinating odyssey, a tale of modernisation, sacrifice and rectification. In some ways it was a fitting mark that the tenth title was contested between Bradford and their arch derby rivals, neighbours Leeds Rhinos. The two West Yorkshire giants – who made history by becoming the first sides to face each other in consecutive last-night deciders – epitomised the changing face of a sport celebrating a decade in a new promised land.

Their initial contrasting reactions to the concept said much about the debate and upheaval that surrounded Super League's introduction that, at the distance of ten fateful seasons, can now be evaluated and analysed. Bradford so characterised the image and stereotype frequently portrayed of the sport that they were defiantly named 'Northern' so as to leave even those with just a passing interest in the game in no doubt as to their roots. Reinvigorated as the Bulls, they were the trailblazers who embraced the switch to summer and the consequent need to develop a new core support base better than any other and, in many ways, provided a role model for all modern sporting organisations. Leeds, on the other hand, frequently dubbed 'the Manchester United of rugby league' – before the Red Devils remembered how to win things – because of their consistent ability to underachieve when it came to gathering the landmark trophies despite signing arguably the best players, initially treated the radical conversion with almost a disdain before becoming the best-supported rugby club of either code in Britain. To virtually everyone involved – players, fans and even club officials – the advent of Super League appeared to come from out of the blue; a blindside move that even the most fastidious of coaches could not have planned or devised a strategy to defend against. At the time the overwhelming feeling was of breathless alteration and upheaval but in retrospect the portents were already present, both in the early history of the game and the increasing influence of business motives and imperatives associated with professional sport in the late twentieth century.

Elite sport cannot be formulated, or exist, in a vacuum; it is a product of the society and its values that spawn it and is seldom without precedent. While Super League talked at the outset of expansion and taking the game to a new nationwide public, a look at the venues for the inaugural Test series' against the touring New Zealand 'All Golds' in 1908 and then the Kangaroos a year later reveals that they included Chelsea, Cheltenham, Park Royal in the capital, St James' Park in Newcastle and Villa Park, Birmingham. Not so much breaking new ground then as revisiting it with a different ethos and will. In trying to explain or uncover the underlying motives and reasons for rugby league's transformation, it is too simplistic to look for single-issue explanations. In the age of the sound bite and headline, the rise of Super League is marginalised and pigeonholed by instilling it with a one-reason tag. In the common parlance of the time, the arrival of the competition was merely the sport 'selling its soul' to the increasing might of satellite television in the guise of Rupert Murdoch's Sky network. Aside from the fact that his organisation had already held the rights for televising the championship for four seasons by then and had shown the regular rounds of the competition on a weekly basis for the first time in the code's history, their monetary influx facilitated change rather than merely instigating it. Similarly, in 1895, when the Northern Union split from the Twickenham-based governing body, the perceived dispute was seen to be over 'broken time' payments for players and the consequent advent of professionalism but, again, while that was the defining symptom it was not the sole cause. There are considerable parallels between the two hugely significant eras that place Super League in its proper context. Both came about because of societal advances that acted as external forces for change combined with the desire and need for the game itself to undergo a metamorphosis, which was predominantly led by the clubs and their players. What comes through from such analysis is that in both eras the game was 'ripe for the picking' and a full understanding of the 1995 revolution cannot be gained without reference to its antecedents of a century before. Rugby League has always been the great sporting anomaly and enigma. The self-styled 'people's game' or 'greatest game', it generally remained an unsung mystery in the British nation's sporting consciousness; occasionally ridiculed, often patronised and frequently characterised as a mud-splattered, backwater northern English, working-class, industrial game. In truth it has been generally acknowledged to be one of the most visionary of sports with, for example, the advent of the big screen for televised games, the additional ten-metre penalty for dissent, the trialling of two officials and the 'on-report' facility among its often-coveted innovations.

Despite this, in over a hundred years of rich, contentious history it has rarely been able, or perhaps more importantly willing, to shake its parochial image. Born out of perceived prejudice, it has always carried a chip on its shoulder. The strength of its powerbase – in the industrial towns, villages and cities of Yorkshire, Lancashire and Cumbria – has also become its great-est weakness with constant division among officials and administrators over whether their game should be shared and appreciated by a mass, nationwide audience. While desirable economically, such a move would have meant that numerous 'little empires' would have become usurped. The cultural identity of the sport, so intimately wrapped up in the history of places like Featherstone, Whitehaven and Keighley, has been both a security blanket and insulation against outside interference. Since the sport's formation and through its subsequent guises, administrative self-interest has coloured stra-tegic policy making.

Nevertheless, the action remains captivating, popular – average attend-ance figures place it as the second-most-watched spectator sport in the country – and much admired, particularly among players of other team sports who laud league's exponents for their professionalism of prepara-tion and all-round athleticism. From its inception, Northern Union relied upon the attraction and support of the fans for its existence and growth but it also tended to polarise the patrons. As new clubs like Goole, South Shields, Ebbw Vale and Coventry were admitted at the turn of the century, the followers of the evolving pastime were cast as either 'expansionists' or 'traditionalists', in conflict about whether broadening the base and appeal of the game served to distil its very essence. Those divisions are clearly still evident at the start of the twenty-first century and are even more pertinent in the modern environment of sport as business.

Conversely, what divides can also bind and when rugby league has been systematically threatened from outside influences keen to see it discredited or marginalised, those radically differing factions find a single, common voice that harks back to its distinctive heredity. When BBC Radio Five Live ran a morning phone-in in 2001 predicting the demise of the thirteen-a-side game, just as Super League seemed to be firmly establishing itself, host Nicky Campbell reported that the general response had been one of the largest and most vocal for any of their daily topics of political debate.

What Super League has done is given the sport a true platform on which to establish its own real identity and a stage where the on-field drama finally takes precedence and can, and invariably does, sell itself. Like the Bulls, who with their 2005 success took their fourth title and thereby rivalled St Helens as the most successful team of the era, rugby league as a whole has rebranded itself and not simply by moving its traditional playing season from winter to summer, which was a quantum leap. To survive and prosper following that almighty upheaval alone would have been praiseworthy but, arguably better than any other, the sport has responded to the demands of the modern leisure industry while still retaining a feel for its community. Subjectively, how well it has achieved that overall depends upon personal club loyalties, with some of the code's most historic names – such as Swinton, Hunslet and Batley – currently out on a limb. That, though, is the same in all top-class sports nowadays; it is unlikely, for example, that Huddersfield Town will again be the pre-eminent force in soccer as they were in the 1920s. As the much-used sporting aphorism goes, 'tradition alone does not pay the bills'. There are always casualties in business, some due to a changing economy, others self inflicted but, like it or not, rugby league is subject to the laws of an intensely competitive modern marketplace for sport if it is to have the higher profile the majority believe it deserves and it requires to survive. If it is forced to operate within such parameters, its progress can be measured by subjecting it to acknowledged 'Key Performance Indicators'. In virtually all of them, Super League – the shop window by which the sport is judged and generally invested in from the outside – scores very favourably.

Attendances are on an increasingly upward spiral, Super League X producing a host of new milestones. In 2005, a record total of 1,493,084 spectators yielded a record average of 8,887 at the 168 matches played, which were also the best figures since the reintroduction of two divisions in 1973. In the last full winter season of 1994/95 the average in the top division was 5,543 while the average total for each round of six matches in Super League X was 53,324, as opposed to 39,426 in the inaugural summer season of 1996. There were a record sixty-eight Super League attendances of 10,000 or more with Bradford and Leeds posting five-figure-plus crowds at all of their fourteen home matches. A record-equalling seven clubs out of twelve had at least one 10,000-plus attendance with Wigan, Warrington, Hull, St Helens and Huddersfield joining the Bulls and Rhinos. Six times the 20,000 barrier was broken, three of those occasions coming at Headingley as Leeds claimed a new seasonal-high average of 17,006 since the 1973 restructure and the highest figure at their historic venue for fifty-three years. The season also included the record aggregate for one round with 69,830 at the six clashes in round seven in late March, which included a Super League record of 25,004 for the Wigan *v.* St Helens derby on Good Friday at the JJB Stadium.

Sponsorship income for the title rights and at individual club level has also increased. In the lead up to the 2006 campaign St Helens and Hull, for instance, both announced record deals with significant new partners, Earth Finance and P&O Ferries, both nationally recognised names who will – quite literally in the latter case – carry the sport to a wider public. The financial imperatives for both companies gives a key insight into the changing business dynamic and profile between Super League and its backers. According to Saints' chief executive Sean McGuire, 'Because of the nature of Earth's business, it is possible that we can work with them on an affinity programme, which will generate significantly big additional revenues of which we will get a big slice.' Similarly, Hull's head of marketing, James Rule commented, 'P&O Ferries are internationally recognised and it is a tremendous coup not just for Hull FC but for rugby league in general to have such a prestigious brand within the game. A partnership of this magnitude is indicative of the development Hull have achieved both on and off the field of play in 2005 and the ambition we have to take the club to a new level. A key factor in the development of our brand has been the passion and loyalty of our fan base. P&O Ferries have recognised that quality and view it as a key attribute of our relationship. I am sure Hull fans will welcome a partnership with an organisation that has such strong historical ties with the city.'

While it would be naive to give the impression that all of the Super League clubs' finances were rosy, again the indicator shows that under the new summer structure they are improving. In his end-of-season update in December 2005, Rugby Football League operations director Nigel Wood noted that more clubs were getting their finances in order. 'No more than three Super League clubs are in profit but the level of losses has come down significantly,' he reported. Much of that is down to television revenue and again the signs are encouraging for the code. The second deal done in the

Super League era, after the initial cash transfusion, in February 2004 is another highly significant KPI. While the figures relating to the agreements are more closely guarded these days, the game as a whole was one of the few sports to increase its overall income in the latest round of negotiations. While the value per match of soccer, television's principal sporting product, was reduced, the RFL reported a fifteen per cent increase in the worth of its properties with Sky purported to have signed a £53 million five-year deal and the BBC a new three-year option believed to be in excess of £2 million per season. The BBC agreement included enhanced coverage of the sport's legally protected 'crown jewel', the Powergen Challenge Cup final, which as a result was moved to the late August Bank Holiday week-end to give the domestic league season a more logical flow. Such enhanced monies were only possible because of continued increases in television ratings, which Nigel Wood indicated were up by thirty per cent in 2005. In further applying commercial principles to the leisure industry that Super League is intimately bound up in, Beech and Chadwick, in *The Business of Sport Management* (FT Prentice Hall, 2004), note, 'The essence of sport is competitive, seasonal, event-based activity, and, as a direct result, organisations seek indirect or more regular income streams through activities such as merchandising. With more and more commercialisation, direct revenue forms a smaller percentage of total revenue. The uncertainty of outcome in matches forms the basis of a sport's attractiveness.'

Through the adoption of squad numbering, which has led to a huge increase in the sale of replica shirts, and the addition of initially derided team suffixes, which has opened up new ranges of merchandise, the Super League clubs have begun to maximise their commercial potential, although a gap still exists for marketing products generic to the sport as a whole to enhance the corporate image. What has become apparent over the past ten years is that in the vital area of enhanced competition, standards on the field are levelling out. Again, such a contention highlights the contradictions running through the way the sport looks at itself. Many of its followers lament the fact that there is perceived to be a 'big four' that has dominated the modern era; Bradford, St Helens, Leeds and Wigan, the sides who between them have claimed all the Super League titles in its first decade. In a division of twelve clubs that is a ratio that virtually every other major sport would be proud of achieving, while if the current top-six play-off principle is applied to each of the ten campaigns – the Grand Final series not being instituted until 1998 – no less than eight other clubs (London, Warrington, Halifax, Salford, Castleford, Gateshead, Hull and Wakefield) would have been eligible to compete for the main prize. A further indication of increasing uncertainty of outcome was illustrated during the 2005 campaign when Bradford became the first side from outside the top two at the end of the weekly rounds to claim the trophy. Wigan were the first of the so-called major protagonists to miss out on the play-offs altogether and despite ending the season with a record number of points scored (1,152) and tries posted (209), Leeds finished runners-up. Moreover, of the four trophies available, each went to a different club. Leeds became World Club Champions, Bradford claimed the Super League title, the Challenge Cup went to Hull while the League Leaders' Shield was won by St Helens. Part of that levelling-up of standards has been due to the imposition of an agreed salary cap and a 20/20 rule in terms of overall squad strength for the benefit of the competition as a whole. Rugby league has never been noted for its self-worth, with the outside image it creates often placing a greater merit on its inherent values. Indeed, after the Super League had settled into its first playing season in 1996, the most frequently posed questions and debates throughout the trade press, on the terraces and in the burgeoning chat rooms were illustrative of a death-knell mentality; 'what would happen when Rupert Murdoch eventually pulled out' and the new era being 'merely the prelude for a hybrid mix of the rugby codes insisted on by the new master that would surely see league all but disappear'. It is a mindset that was instantly apparent to Richard Lewis, who came from administering tennis into the newly created post of executive chairman of the RFL at a key time in Super League's consolidation in 2002. 'The very strong impression I had was that it was a sport that lacked confidence, which amazed me because I joined rugby league really believing. Having done a lot of research from the time of hearing about the job to attending interviews, I was really surprised by that.'

Framing the continued rise of Super League with a business imperative is essential if we are to understand not just how it came about but also to produce a reliable SWOT analysis (strengths, weakness, opportunities and threats), a significant management tool applied within commerce, to fully assess the level it has reached after a momentous ten seasons. If appealing to its broadest audience is a further measure, then the acknowledged geographical spread of Sky subscribers and Radio Five Live listeners who tune in to the coverage and enter their competitions is a benchmark. So too is the continued rise of the Rugby League Conference, which, since its inception in 1998, has seen ever more amateur teams playing throughout the length and breadth of England and Wales in the summer in significant part due to the enhanced, regular coverage of Super League. Addressing the RLC delegates at their end-of-season awards ceremony in November

2005, Sky's chief summariser Mike Stephenson told them, 'What we try to do is bring people like you into our family and that is the crucial word that should never be far from your thoughts. People criticise us for the fact that our major clubs are predominantly along the M62. So what? Who cares? What a lot of people don't realise, including those in the North of England, is the amount of hard work that people like you are doing to ensure that the sport gets exposure. I know you're there because of the impact letters and e-mails we receive from nationwide are having at Sky TV. Rugby League is a national sport and you should be extremely proud of your efforts towards that end.'

The sport's relationship with television is another key tenet to be examined. A number of the most passionate fans and some noted and respected historians still maintain that the game they knew and loved effectively died when broadcasting became the pre-eminent sponsor and, by default, scheduler, with its focus almost exclusively on the elite level of competition. There can be no doubt that the initial blundering surrounding projected imposed mergers, announced at the same time that Super League was unveiled, had disastrous consequences in keeping the previously tight-knit family together as the new in-laws arrived on the scene. However, the sport, as it was structured at the time, simply could not afford to look not just a gift horse but its saviour in the mouth. As can been seen in retrospect, the decision to ally itself with what was to become the biggest and most significant player in the media was ultimately an astute one. As early as 1990, at the inception of the satellite explosion, rugby league was quick to spot the potential in the rapidly unfolding revolution and signed a contract with BSB prior to it going on air. The game's public affairs executive at the time, David Howes, commented, 'This venture is as brave as the historic decision to take the Challenge Cup final to Wembley. We have always been pioneers and satellite TV is the medium of the future. The chance of live, nationwide coverage simply could not be missed. But it was not an easy decision. The board of directors debated the issue for a considerable time, and then it was put to the full council. Only one club voted against the plan. The kick-off time (scheduled for 6.30 p.m. on a Sunday evening) is a gamble. No-one knows what the reaction might be. I appreciate it could be inconvenient for some supporters but others may like it. It will be a showcase event. We cannot stay in our own backyard for ever.'

Whatever objections the reactionaries may have, the requirement for change is undeniable. Northern Union evolved in 1895 because of the need and desire for organised sport to play a more central role in the everyday life of a rapidly industrialising society. Similarly, the global culture created by the rise of new, especially satellite, technology and the fracturing of the very bonds that had created the code in the first place meant that there was a corresponding inevitability behind the arrival of Super League. Only when such factors are examined can the success or otherwise of the response be calculated in an attempt to discover not just what has happened, and how – from as many perspectives from within the game as possible – but why.

What emerges is a picture of Super League going through four distinct phases over the past ten years; hiatus, fallout, stability and growth. There is no exact date or occasion when the game can be seen to move from one to the next although in terms of landmarks, results in the all-embracing World Club Championship of 1997, in which northern hemisphere sides were generally humiliated by their Antipodean opponents, caused a degree of re-appraisal; the financial plight after losses incurred by the 2000 World Cup crystallised the need for a change in leadership direction and style and the appointment of Richard Lewis brought the equilibrium required subsequent to a period of escalation. By taking a more detailed look at each of those phases and the implications raised both on and off the field, how Super League has tried to sell the new while confronting its traditional dilemmas, and examining some relevant case studies along the way, it is possible to get under the skin of a modern, professional, dynamic sport that has managed to virtually completely reinvent itself and not only survive but actively flourish.

'For its grace and its controlled aggression, for its sweepingly swift movements and its moments of brilliant artifice, for its palpitating climaxes where one side is pounding at the other for the couple of points that will mean victory and the adversary is defending as though the end of the world will come with defeat; for all these things and for many individual shafts of daring and courage in every match, rugby league is incomparably superior to any other game.' – Geoffrey Moorhouse, *At the George*, Sceptre, 1990

TWO

REVOLUTION OR EVOLUTION?

'Rugby League provides our cultural adrenalin. It's a physical manifestation of our rules of life, comradeship, honest endeavour, and a staunch, often ponderous allegiance to fair play.' – Screenwriter Colin Welland

One of the great truisms in sport is that it is cyclical; that on the field contentious decisions will tend to even themselves out while off it periods of boom and bust will necessitate either cashing-in strategies or crisis management. On Thursday 29 August 1895, the representatives of twenty-one of the strongest rugby clubs from across Yorkshire, Lancashire and Cheshire met at the George Hotel in Huddersfield to devise a way ahead for the breakaway competition that they had felt compelled to initiate. On Friday 7 April 1995, the chairmen, or their proxies, of the sixteen First Division clubs, plus Hull Kingston Rovers of the Second, convened at the Hilton Hotel, Huddersfield where RFL chief executive Maurice Lindsay and his chairman Sir Rodney Walker outlined News International's intention to back a new Super League. Was this a case of same place, different revolution and of history merely repeating itself, or a completely new cog in the sport's evolving wheel? The reality is probably that it was something of both. Broadly speaking, in both eras, those meetings in northern rugby's middle England were the culmination of a series of intertwined and dependent forces that ultimately demanded a radical transformation of the way the game was perceived, played and regarded. In detecting nine such factors – four of them external that shaped the boundaries and five coming from within the sport itself – what emerges is that, although the specific challenges faced were 100 years apart, traces of all of them were at the root of the respective reconstructions. Although the forces for change cannot be accorded equal weight and may have exerted a greater influence specific to a particular time, the fact that they can all be identified to some degree in both epochs lends weight to the premise that not only was the formation of Super League somewhat predictable but also that it was ultimately inevitable.

EXTERNAL FORCES

The place that rugby league occupies in society is a significant starting point for evaluating its changing face. By 1895, massive alterations to working conditions and living habits meant that a ready-made audience had been created. In late Victorian Britain, the later, advanced stages of the industrial revolution had seen the concentration of populations in larger urban towns or burgeoning cities and the fracturing of traditional smaller, principally agrarian, communities. With it, the role of sport moved from being an infrequently undertaken, disorganised, occasional pastime most usually played out on a public holiday to becoming seen as fulfilling an identifiable need and subject to the commercial forces now prevalent at work. The idea of regular competition rather than extremely parochial, narrow rivalry became the norm as did the growing realisation of the need for leisure provision. Popular recreation was becoming defined, as Neil Tranter notes in *Sport, Economy and Society in Britain 1750-1914* (Cambridge University Press, 1998): 'The numbers playing and watching increased dramatically, the social composition of participants and the spatial parameters of the sports they practised substantially widened, codification, institutionalisation, commercialism and professionalism became widespread for the first time, and the timing of sporting activity radically altered. The pace at which these developments occurred was wholly unprecedented. Sport, in its modern, organised, commercialised and extensive form, was truly an "invention" of the Victorian and Edwardian age.' Sport started to matter and, for the first time, became subject to the wiles and imperatives of business and in the North of England in particular that meant rugby, which was by far the most dominant code. By 1995 those very communities that had spawned, fostered and supported the game were in almost terminal decline under advanced capitalism. So many of them had been built around the likes of coal, steel, textiles, fishing, shipbuilding and glass, the market for which had been overrun either by international competition or because cheaper means of production had moved the manufacturing process to differing parts of the world. The rise of the out-of-town shopping centre and homogenised retail experience was gradually sucking the life out of the local, independent business community whose links and financial support had sustained sports clubs. Increasing privatisation and the promotion of self had become the norm; new technology – particularly the rise of the internet – serving increasingly to enhance links with those spread far and wide while at the same time diminishing inter-personal, local relations. Rather than bringing people together, sport, like life, had also become 'globalised', seeking to appeal to the widest market and rugby league, by virtue of its limited geographical appeal, where the club game had always held primacy, was in danger of being left behind. Undeniable business influence in sport now meant the rise of the public limited company, the pre-eminence of international competition that could tap into a broader and less regularly committed public consciousness and, at the elite level, the need for facilities comparable with others at the top of the entertainment industry. Identifying sport with a specific and particular geographical place was becoming less and less relevant; rugby league – like society – was becoming increasingly fractured.

Similarly, any analysis of the rise and subsequent repositioning of the sport in relation to society has to take the notion of class into account. Despite coming out of the public school system, rugby's phenomenal growth in the mid to late nineteenth century was due to the rise of the working class. According to Mike Huggins in his study of *Victorians and Sport* (Hambledon & London, 2004), 'By the 1880s a better-off working-class audience aided the emergence of mass national spectator sport. The rise of these commer-cialised sports forms was hugely aided by an increasingly concentrated urban market, aided to a large and growing extent by the formation of an essen-tially working-class culture, tough, resilient and adaptive with a collective self-consciousness, well able to appropriate some sports into their own cul-tural life. Sporting activities were fostered by new class subcultures, while… the suburbs developed their own sporting life.' Northern Union, as it was to become, was best able to tap into those characteristics of pride and preju-dice. A hundred years later, notions of class and its consequent identity had virtually disappeared, particularly as an economic distinction. There was no longer relevance in rugby league being seen as a predominantly working-class sport. Those who were likely to succeed in the modern environment had to have instant appeal to the most diverse market, to make itself 'sexy'; soccer famously courting the 'prawn sandwich brigade' as a result. Age was also a defining factor, Victorian society being largely young and vibrant. In 1851 half the population was under twenty and only twenty-five per cent over forty-five years old. By the mid-1990s the population was aging, the average life expectancy on a continued increase and the 'silver' generation exerting a greater influence over the leisure pound where, for them, com-fort and quality were paramount.

Societal flux creates the appropriate environment for sport but the sec-ond external force is the demand for it or, more specifically, the rise of the fan. In late Victorian Britain, more regulated hours of work from Monday to most usually Saturday lunchtime gave sport an ideal window of opportunity. Along with the rise of definable leisure time, the massed working classes had greater real disposable income, principally following reductions in the taxes on food, while a rapidly expanding public transport system enabled them to get to and from venues outside of the immediate vicinity to follow their interest. Far from the fan being paramount at the close of the twentieth century, the largesse of the corporate pound is the most eagerly sought one to bridge the expenditure gap. Sport, rather than servicing a need for recreation, is part of a highly competitive entertainment industry with allegiance at grounds because of birthplace no longer a divine right. The working week has blurred; weekends – particularly Sundays – are proving to be among the most popular days for shopping, meaning that the spectator base is splintered. There has been a growing distinction between the fan or active supporter and the spectator, someone who may be just as happy to follow a sport either on television or by occasional attendance, usually for the bigger, higher-profile clashes. Despite various government policies to promote public transport, the rise of the car has proliferated to such an extent that the need to stay closer to home for amusement and diversion has significantly lessened.

If the rise and then dissipation of the fan has been a key trend, then so too has the revised role of and need for sport between the two eras. As it came to prominence, sport provided a seasonal regimen to the year and became a distinctive emotional outlet that bound together previously disparate groups, who had principally migrated to the towns and cities searching for work. Huggins suggests, 'British cities provided space, capital, paying spectators and participants for sport while… sports grounds provided a context for recreation, an image, an identity and a haven that allowed urban residents to escape the strains and stresses of urban living. In sport, as in industry, winning and success equally mattered, and became matters of status and potential gain. By the 1880s football and rugby were becoming the games that came most to articulate civic pride in provincial towns and cities.' Equally as important was that sport became translated through the family. As it grew so did communal, generational rituals of support but again these were in danger of being ruptured come the turn of the following century as youngsters, the very lifeblood of rugby league, showed an increasing preference for staying at home in the warm, captivated by mainly solo interests such as computer games. Originally, while sport leant heavily on business principles and practice in its early years of unprecedented growth, by the time Super League came on the horizon the balance had tilted irrevocably with the commercial imperative paramount. As Tony Mason points out in his influential text *Sport in Britain* (Faber), originally published in 1988, seven years before the code's second great upheaval, 'Top-level sport has had its paying support seriously eroded since the ephemeral booms of the immediate post-war period coupled with the removal of restrictions on the earning power of players. The result has been the classic bind of falling revenues and rising costs. For survival, sport has turned to business. This would probably have been less available without the spread of television. Access to every home has prompted all forms of business to use top-level sport as a means of promoting their products. Commercial sponsors and investing businessmen want to be associated with success that seems likely to intensify the cult of the winner. Sport is over exposed. This market saturation spoils the public appetite and drains the physical and mental resources of the leading players. In professional team games such as football and rugby league, the new commercialism has created an even greater imbalance between the clubs, increasingly concentrating the best talent. Market forces push the weakest to the wall.'

Mason introduces the fourth key external determinant into the overall equation, the media. In the 1890s it was the rise and growing influence of the mass-circulation provincial and national press. Second time around it was the global requirements of the medium that knows no boundaries, satellite broadcasting, that was to the fore. Late Victorian newspapers and periodicals specifically devoted to sport were the oxygen of publicity for the newly codified, increasingly regular pastimes. From the 1880s the *Sportsman*, *Sporting Life* and the *Sporting Chronicle* were all selling 300,000 copies a day and all relied on a more structured, definable fixture list rather than the hitherto haphazard arranging of 'friendlies'. That was equally true among the new national press. Although the long-established *Times* tended to distance itself from the sports professed to be enjoyed by the masses, the *Daily Mail*, which arrived the year after the formation of the Northern Union, and *The News of the World* were quick to see the value of regular sports pages. The rapidly expanding circulation of the local evening newspaper owed much to the invention of the electric telegraph that enabled it to offer an eagerly sought results service on a Saturday evening, which was again invaluable for devotees of the Northern Union's league fixtures who were desperate to see how their rivals had fared. As the demand for sport increased so too did the almost obsessive desire to report it. With public interest inflamed, sport became an easily identifiable, almost ready-made package and the relationship between journalist and reader a self-perpetuating one. For Huggins, 'The media's importance in constructing the Victorian sporting world cannot be overestimated. Many first came across sport not by playing or watching but through media coverage, a combination of factual reportage, viewpoint and promotion, extending the audience and deepening the loyalty. The press created sporting celebrities predominantly in their regional communities; they underlined and reinforced regional rivalries and popular prejudices. Regular fixture lists began to give a firm structure to narratives and commentaries.' Similarly, it is no coincidence that the recently restored archive of stock from the studios of Mitchell & Kenyon, who came to the fore at the turn of the twentieth century, included extensive films of early Northern Union clashes with the focus as much on the watching public – who were then invited to pay to see themselves on screen in fairgrounds or specially hired halls – as on the action on the field. If the written word hastened the appeal and availability of rugby league, the arrival of accessible satellite television a century later significantly shifted the goalposts. No longer was watching a sport at home part of the background wallpaper, enhanced for many by Eddie Waring's distinctive, often parodied, commentaries. It was now a conscious economic decision. Leading sports media analysts John Horne, Alan Tomlinson and Garry Whannel in *Understanding Sport* (Spon, 1999) argue that, 'Television has exerted a transformative effect on a sport (like rugby league) helping to weaken its traditional working-class roots and foster the movement of the game away from shared collective communality towards a modernised commercialised form of individual consumption. Key to the later commercialisation of sport is the impact of technological improvements in television and a revolution in which sponsorship became a major source of revenue for the elite level of sport. In the television era, sport had become an international spectacle.' If socially driven, spectator-desired organised sport, extenuated by the interests of the media, have been the external influences on first rugby league and then Super League, how has the game itself responded to these challenges thrown at it?

INTERNAL FORCES

The first parallel that can be drawn between the early incarnation of the code and its modern doppelganger is a desire for self determination, on the back of a continued run of interest and appeal. Formed in 1871, the Rugby Football Union became increasingly wary of the support northern clubs were attracting by the end of that decade. Initially, former public school, grammar school and ex-university graduates had set up sides in Liverpool and Manchester but the sport really began to attract significant working-class appeal after the formation of clubs in places like Bradford (in 1863), Leeds (1864) and Huddersfield (1869). Most of the players were skilled workers and the successful sides quickly began to entice larger numbers of their colleagues down to watch them play with admission money starting to be charged. Sensing that control of the game was at stake, the governing body resisted initial calls, from the Yorkshire clubs in particular, to arrange their own fixtures and, crucially, make them more meaningful by cashing in on the rapidly growing industrial rivalries. What irked the leading northern clubs the most was not so much the later debate about payment of players, which was believed to be relatively widespread, if covert, throughout the country anyway, but the fact that they felt that they deserved increasing representation at the decision-making table. For Huggins, 'In the North there were complex, multi-layered beliefs about inequality of power, political influence and material opportunities compared to London. Through sport images developed about what were the perceived qualities of the North, something which was as much a state of mind as a place.' Sport, allied to rising political agitation, was giving the region a sense of place and worth and the middle-class establishment became increasingly keen to deny it a say.

Redistribution of power, this time among the clubs themselves, was also a motivation behind the move towards Super League. Throughout the early 1990s, its call was increasingly becoming part of an overt agenda. As the *Rothmans Rugby League Yearbook* of 1992/93 noted, 'The now almost annual talk of Super League was raised again following a meeting of the 'Top Sixteen' clubs. All fourteen Division One clubs, plus Division Two's Sheffield Eagles and Oldham, were invited to the meeting and a six-man committee was formed. Leigh joined the group soon after. They planned moves to give the top clubs a greater running of the game by giving them more voting power, which is currently restricted to one per club. They also sought a bigger share of television money and a reduction in the eight per cent levy Division One clubs pay to the League.'

Equally significant impetus for Super League came about due to events 12,000 miles away in Australia, where the strife was internecine but again mirrored overtones of some of the original concerns that led to the 'rebel' northern clubs wanting to break away. Over there, despite proposed expansion for 1995 that was to see their elite competition being played in Western Australia, North and South Queensland and with New Zealand set to enter a team into their neighbour's domestic league for the first time, the powerbase was still steadfastly centred on Sydney. The introduction of a commercially astute and highly successful side from Brisbane in 1988 – where four multi-millionaires owned the franchise between them – had created unpalatable waves for the governing body. The longer the Broncos and their influential backers were denied what they felt was an equal share in the future, the more likely there was to be a fracturing similar to that in the Old Dart all those years before. Again there were concerns about concentration of power and influence in the south, sport mirroring the perceived political dimension, the Queenslanders acutely aware that, in spite of their desire to reshape the competition and break the old bonds, geography would still count against them.

What is certainly true is that the principal impetus for change in both hemispheres centred on the clubs who began to feel ever-more isolated; although in the 1880s, unlike the 1990s, profit was not their primary motive. The northern clubs had grown organically as their supporter base rapidly increased and rugby quickly became the dominant winter sport. With their unexpected windfalls, the clubs became subject to commercial pressures, as rugby league archivist Dr Tony Collins relates in his seminal work *Rugby's Great Split* (Frank Cass, 1998): 'Nowhere was that more true than in Bradford where by 1885 they were forced to appoint a second paid part-time secretary due to the administrative burden now placed on the club by its success. By 1890, having paid off a capital debt of £8,000, which had been used to develop their Park Avenue ground, the club still had £7,000 available in the bank. Some of the money generated inevitably went on paying players but being irregular, they were a minor drain on resources. The greatest expenditure was on the purchase, improvement and maintenance of grounds. Necessitated by the ever-increasing numbers watching the sport, rugby clubs initiated a ground development boom from the mid-1880s.' Again the cyclical theory of sport is borne out, Bradford leading the progressive charge then just as the Bulls were to do come the switch to summer some three generations later. The difference between the two incarnations was that in the first case being part of a vibrant, growing economy drove the initial Bradford club to look at ways to service and cater for the demands of a novel, expectant sporting culture. A century later, the Bulls experience was a specifically manufactured, targeted approach to draw a new, committed and highly critical crowd back to an arena that had largely lost much of its major appeal. Whereas at Park Avenue funds generated facilitated a move towards shaping a bigger say in a confident future, the Odsal experience was deliberately designed to generate additional revenue quickly to ensure that their audacious throw of the dice was not a last one.

What the growing power of the top northern clubs desperately needed in the late Victorian era, to consolidate and enhance their new-found prominence within the communities they began to serve, was meaningful competition; the third internal influence for change. Despite the misgivings of the RFU committee, agreement for the sanctioning of a Yorkshire Challenge Cup in 1877 was to change the face and course of rugby irrevocably. Immediately, huge crowds of anything up to 14,000 were attracted to see the top, intense, derby clashes at the end of which stood the hugely coveted 't'owd tin pot'. Over the course of the next thirteen seasons the number of entrants doubled and each major town and city soon had their own local version. Seeing the undoubted success and, significantly, enhanced profile of the county cup, Lancashire clubs quickly followed suit, although the speed of their progress was partly stymied by the increasing pull of soccer in the region. That provided another incentive and stimulus to crystallise the idea of the best rugby players regularly facing each other. Even though the Lancashire RFU was initially resistant to a full-scale county cup, the evidence of crowds as high as 18,000 for the final of the Wigan Challenge Cup in the middle of the following decade was indication of a rapidly moving irresistible energy. Not only did the fans want it but so too did the businessmen, politicians and publicans who were now becoming patrons of the clubs and for whom civic prestige and accrued kudos was increasingly important. 'It was the introduction of the Yorkshire Challenge Cup in rugby that really began to create sporting loyalty. Attendances soared, local pride became linked to a crude desire for cup success. Ties that took place against bitter industrial and commercial rivals nearby, especially when teams were of similar standing, made the joy of winning far greater. Local and provincial press coverage buttressed urban identity still further.' (Huggins) It was a short step from the rarefied thrill of knockout rugby to the clamour for regular fixtures of similar intensity. According to noted sports historians Mike Latham and Tom Mather in their ground-breaking study *The Rugby League Myth* (Mike RL Publications, 1993), the instigation of league competition began following the initial success of the Lancashire Cup in 1889 when eight clubs – Aspull, Warrington, Wigan, Tyldesley, Leigh, Walkden, St Helens and Widnes – set up the West Lancashire League that, according to the *Wigan Examiner*, would see 'all the excitement spread across the whole season instead of being compressed into one month'. Although only lasting a couple of campaigns, it cast the die with the leading Yorkshire sides next to take up the gauntlet. 'At the end of the 1891/92 season twelve senior Yorkshire clubs, Batley, Bradford, Brighouse Rangers, Dewsbury, Halifax, Huddersfield, Hull, Hunslet, Leeds, Liversedge, Manningham and Wakefield Trinity formed an Alliance. They wished to form a league that they, rather than the Yorkshire County, would control and organise. The Yorkshire Union eventually set up a sub-committee, made up of one member from each of the Alliance clubs. So was the Yorkshire First Division born and with it the power of the clubs enhanced.' Not unexpectedly, the 'Yorkshire Senior Competition' was an instant success with attendances at many of the matches easily topping 10,000 and by the start of the 1893 season the majority of the county of around 150 sides was run on some kind of league lines.

The situation was mirrored in the Red Rose acres, where similar reasoning applied. 'In Lancashire the clamour for league competition was even more heartfelt. The astonishing growth in support for soccer caused not only envy among rugby clubs but also fear. Rugby, which had dominated the county, was by 1892 in danger of being overwhelmed. The failure of the county authorities to promote the game was causing it to wither on the vine. Some rugby areas had taken matters into their own hands and set up their own district or regional leagues. What was necessary, so the senior clubs thought, was an elite league. In June 1892 Swinton called a meeting in Manchester to discuss the formation of such a competition with six of the nine present – Swinton, Salford, Broughton Rangers, Oldham, Warrington and Wigan – the most senior commercially minded clubs.' (Collins) The battle lines were becoming drawn and again, as much as any other issue, the desire for the big clubs to have more of a major say in the running of the game was at the core of the drive for change, just as it was in the run up to the offering of the Murdoch millions. Plans were put in place to combine the best of the two counties, initially seeking the support of the RFU for the proposal but it was a vain hope. At the end of the 1894/95 Yorkshire Senior Competition fixtures, the senior clubs that formed it refused to sanction the promotion of junior sides Morley and Castleford from the Second Competition. Instead they preferred to unilaterally accept the retention of their bottom two sides, Hull and Wakefield Trinity. Latham and Mather indicate that that was because, 'the re-elected clubs would provide better gates than those seeking to replace them. Financial considerations outweighed the idea of promotion on merit.' The Yorkshire RFU committee's refusal to sanction the idea created a fissure between the clubs and the governing body, which eventually became central to the split. An identical dilemma has bedevilled Super League from the initial announcement of which sides – or manufactured conglomerations of them – should be eligible to compete in the first place and, equally, who should be denied a place because they could not bring sufficient financial muscle to the top table; Featherstone, Widnes, Keighley and Batley the initial 'victims'. The same economic logic was used to prevent Dewsbury and Hunslet from taking up their place after winning the Northern Ford Premiership Grand Final (for First Division clubs) in 1999 and 2000 respectively. If a desire for the most meaningful competition was a precursor to the eventual 1895 separation, then a similar rationale also applied in the mid-1990s but for a totally opposite reason. By 1995, domestic competition had all but been undermined by the continued, seemingly unstoppable, all conquering, unprecedented success of

Wigan. As broadcasting icon and feature writer Michael Parkinson – a former
director at Wakefield Trinity – so succinctly put it, 'If the definition of a great
team involves a unique blend of invincibility and glamour, a combination of
organisation and imagination, then it is difficult to imagine another outfit so
completely qualified as Wigan.' Nine titles in eleven seasons, eight consecutive Challenge Cup wins and a virtual monopoly in the John Player Trophy,
Lancashire Cup and Premiership had seen the cherry and whites become
almost unassailable, continually buying the best talent even if it meant having
an overabundance of riches. On the international front, the same could be
said of Australia. Although by the 1990s Great Britain could be almost relied
upon to win a Test in a three-match series, the Kangaroos were defending an
unbeaten Ashes and World Cup run against the Lions that stretched back to
1970. Rather than looking to the clubs to create a competition, as had been
the case a hundred years before, Super League was a desperate attempt to try
and level the title race up and with it bring back the fans, both partisan and
transient and in significant numbers, to pay the ever-increasing bills.

The fourth key internal determinant is the lot of the most underval-
ued asset in the sport, the players. The almost-meteoric rise in profile of
the code, the clubs that played it at the highest level and the new cup and
league competitions that they performed in, naturally raised the stock
of the participants in the latter part of the nineteenth century. The game
spawned its first recognised personalities – the likes of Heckmondwike's
Richard Lockwood and the imperious Jack Dyson at Huddersfield – in
the same way that modern sporting culture is built around and hinged
upon the celebrity star system with, for example, Great Britain skipper Paul
Sculthorpe currently being the marketed face of Gillette. That brought with
it further economic pressure and most specifically the calling into question
of the very core of Victorian sport, amateurism, as Tony Collins concedes.
'As the practice of payment in cash or in kind spread so too did the bargaining power of the players. Rugby had developed a sophisticated, albeit
informal, marketplace in which players sought to maximise their earning potential before the inevitable onset of old age, injury or loss of form.'
The northern club owners wanted to augment their chances of success in
the highly emotive and competitive arena their charges were now playing in and, inevitably, were prepared to pay for it. While professionalism
was becoming less of an issue to them, to the governing body it remained
sacrosanct despite the blatant hypocrisy of visiting southern sides – who
had little interest in league fixtures – having their expenses paid when touring the north. For Huggins, 'Gates provided funds for compensating players
or attracting new ones, and veiled professionalism soon appeared. In some

clubs secret monetary payments to working-class players became increasingly common, as did inducements to sign, and players demanded payment for taking time off work to train or travel to away games. By 1884 pressure from some committee members allowed "actual expenses" to be "defrayed", a phrase that allowed flexible interpretation.' In September 1893, despite travelling south with a unanimous mandate for a modification to amend the laws relating to bona fide compensation for loss of working income when playing, the Yorkshire RFU, backed by their Lancashire counterparts, were comprehensively defeated. The top clubs were then dealt the double blow of the introduction of even more stringent, almost evangelical, restrictions on player payments and accompanying witch hunts for breaches of professionalism that saw several of the clubs suspended. Just over a year later, with frustrations mounting, Twickenham similarly decisively rejected an eleven-point plan – of which broken time payments was merely one – which would have allowed the leading Lancashire and Yorkshire clubs to form themselves into a common body for the purpose of furthering the interests of the game in their respective counties. Stanley Chadwick, the sport's first unofficial biographer, records in *Claret and Gold – The Jubilee History of the Huddersfield Rugby Football League Club* (1945) 'The Yorkshire Rugby Union, when asked for its opinion, decided that the new combination was unnecessary and would not receive its support. It was therefore no surprise when in May the Rugby Union intimated to the clubs that it was unable to sanction the proposed union, which would be prejudicial to the best interests of the game and forbade its formation. When the YRU met in Leeds on 29 July 1895 it received and accepted the resignations of: Batley, Bradford, Brighouse Rangers, Dewsbury, Halifax, Huddersfield, Hull, Hunslet, Leeds, Liversedge, Manningham and Wakefield Trinity. After years of persecution and a succession of suspensions, the northern clubs at last decided to break their chains and to face the future untrammelled by laws that failed to take into account the conditions of life of their players and members.' The Lancashire clubs followed suit; the later, historic meeting at the George Hotel formally launching the new Northern Union and deciding on its fixture format.

While the early pioneers fought for their players to be professional, the modern Super League equivalents were becoming increasingly desperate to be full-time professionals in order to rein in the unique advantage Wigan had at their disposal, which was central to their continued, suffocating dominance. While there were to be later questions about to whom and in what quantities the News International funds were distributed, suddenly making a decent living out of the sport – which immediately raised its appeal among the gladiators – helped to revitalise it. Young, aspiring players could see a viable career path while the older established stars, some further induced with loyalty payments, were able to negotiate something more akin to reasonable reward. That was even more pertinent following the decision by the Rugby Football Union to finally acknowledge covert professionalism within their own ranks at around the same time. Although the amount of top-level players crossing the divide from league to union here was never more than a grossly over-emphasised, ultimately harmless trickle, without the arrival of Super League it could have been a much more damaging flood. As Peter Lush notes, 'league could have ended up isolated as a minor sport in the North of England, developing players for rugby union. At least the introduction of Super League avoided that fate.' (*Rugby's Berlin Wall* – Graham Williams, Peter Lush & David Hinchliffe, London League Publications, 2005) In both eras, the needs of the players became increasingly paramount. Tony Collins points out, 'Clubs had started to develop training techniques to enhance their players' abilities, especially for the Yorkshire Cup competition. By 1885 specialist trainers were employed to improve players' fitness along with "medicine men", there was evidence of pre-match tactical discussions and nor was diet neglected. Summer training was popular too.' Once the summer era arrived so did qualified conditioners, nutritional supplements, energy drinks, specifically designed weights programmes, rehabilitation regimes and more intensely structured warm-ups and warm downs – which included post-match swimming – as sport literally became a science.

With a burgeoning demand for more intense club-based competition involving finely honed, athletic combatants, the last internal factor for change comes into play; the need for rule amendments to ensure that the 'entertainment principle' remains paramount. Initial attraction of the committed or curious is one aspect but, to build and retain loyalty, the unfolding fare has to have sufficient drama, tension and spectacle to retain interest. Rugby League, in all its various incarnations, has never been afraid to tamper with the laws in an effort to give the best possible viewing experience and at the heart of it has been the desire to see intricate handling skills and running rugby. Like in the other eight external and internal forces at work, there is a mixture of evolution and revolution. 'By 1887, the passing game was prevalent in the North. It is clear that tactical innovation and experimentation became widespread in the mid-to-late 1880s, moving the game away from constant scrimmaging and kicking towards a 'scientific' playing style defined by the predominance of passing and running with the ball to score tries.' (Collins) Even before the split, fans in the northern counties were becoming attuned to and expectant of a sporting ethos that valued spectacle. For Huggins, what they wanted to watch and the fare on offer was an extension of what they were. 'Northerners saw themselves as supposedly and variously fair, friendly, hard-working, honest, blunt, outspoken, highly competitive and dour, and more oriented towards "t'brass" and professionalism, so more anti-amateur. The local support given to the more successful rugby and soccer sides was linked to images of aggressive working-class masculinity, valuing the 'hard' man. Northerners supposedly had a different, more aggressive style of play. Northern players were represented as highly competitive, tough, with a strong work ethic, not necessarily great stylists but very effective, while northern crowds were more fanatical.'

Once the top clubs had asserted their independence, the desire to attract a paying customer became a commercial need and, as a result, rule changes were swiftly implemented to give the Northern Union clashes greater flow and excitement. Two distinct imperatives dominated their thinking, and have done ever since; the need to see more of the ball and the establishment of an equitable scoring system that fully rewarded a try. Initially under the rugby union laws that was valued at three points, as opposed to a goal, which was variously five if converting a try (the touchdown then ceased to count), four if dropped or kicked from a fair catch in the field of play or three following the award of a penalty. Because of that system, an enterprising side that showed flair and invention to get the ball over the whitewash could be beaten by a more conservative outfit that had a good field kicker. The RFU acknowledged the imbalance in 1886 when they decided that three tries would count as the equivalent of a goal but at their second annual general meeting in 1897, the Northern Union downgraded the value of any goal to two points. That move alone, however, was not sufficient to fully encourage a more open approach to using the ball and by 1902 the Northern Union administrators were becoming increasingly concerned about the number of low-scoring matches at a time when several of the leading clubs were beginning to feel the first draught of economic reality. The 1897 AGM had also sanctioned the abolition of the lineout but a more radical move was on the horizon. In October 1895 Halifax, backed by Wakefield, attempted to reduce the number of players from fifteen to thirteen. Nine clubs voted in favour of the change while eighteen were against it. In 1903, a reduction in the number of players to twelve – deemed 'the greatest and most daring reform yet attempted' – failed to secure the requisite three-quarters majority despite the clubs voting 54-24 in its favour, but on 12 June 1906 the fundamental change was effected. Proposed by Warrington and seconded by Leigh, the amendment for thirteen men and the opening up of the field of play was accepted by 43 votes to 18. Stanley Chadwick, writing in 1945 in the *Rugby Football League's Jubilee Souvenir Brochure* concluded that, 'Early the following season it was demonstrated that the new game was more fast and open and attractive to watch.' Greater emphasis was placed on positional play with two forwards being dropped and a set half-back and three-quarter line, which contained the strike players, becoming established. That transformation was also helped by the introduction of a play-the-ball rule rather than a scrum forming after every tackle. What summer brought the sport in 1996 were the ideal top-of-the-ground conditions to play a more expansive game. The introduction of a four-tackle (1966) and then a six-tackle rule (1972) revolutionised tactics and tempo but the modern impetus for more open play had begun in late November 1992 when the offside distance at the play the ball was increased from five metres to ten. Principally that allowed the attacking side greater room to set up their plays and to protect the code's most creative midfield exponents who were becoming an extinct species having become primarily concerned with self protection rather than ball distribution. Coupled with a revised rule that outlawed holding down in the tackle, the ingredients for further speeding up the game were ready to be fully unleashed. The appointment of highly respected leading Australian official Greg McCallum as the RFL's referees coaching director two years later heralded a further raft of amendments that consolidated the move, including scrums to be packed down twenty metres in from touch to encourage blindside plays, the rewarding of the 40/20 kick with the attacking side getting the put-in to the resulting scrum, play the ball to only be backwards and without the defending marker being allowed to strike for the ball, and the move to four substitutes with twelve interchanges per side. Combined together, the effect was to infuse a non-stop, all-action Super League played by finely honed athletes with the kind of frequent point-scoring opportunities deemed vital to appeal to a contemporary sports-watching public. Nowadays one of the qualities most frequently admired by both the non-committed, irregular or first-time viewer and the participants of other top-line professional sports is the amount of time the ball is actually in play. The potential drawback, aside from alienating some of the traditional fans, was that there was a danger of the sport becoming too challenging to play. Again, though, that was a case of history seeming to repeat itself, as 'the fact they did include the spectators' interests in their deliberations was used unmercifully by their opponents to denigrate every change made as being tainted by purely commercial intentions… all the Northern Union's innovations were shunned as it was considered they would probably make the game too demanding and certainly less enjoyable for the amateurs.' (Lush)

Drawing historical comparisons and parallels serves to highlight that although each era may be generationally specific, the overall set of parameters that a sport operates in and under are clearly definable. Like any great player or visionary coach, administrators should be able to learn from the lessons of history and experience to come up with improved performance. The portents for Super League and its advancement were essentially written almost a century before it was unveiled to an initially sceptical and somewhat incredulous fan base. The commercial reality of sport had been a central tenet to the establishment of the code in 1895. 'By the early 1890s, "business-like" was becoming a vogue phrase among rugby's administrators, and one of the constant criticisms from the northern clubs of the RFU was that it was "un-businesslike" in its dealings. Although rugby clubs were not run as profit-maximising organisations and were viewed more as civic institutions, the exigencies of running a successful football side meant that the rigours of the marketplace came to bear more and more on clubs. It was the clash between the commercial reality and the practical implications of the sport's ostensibly amateur ethos that began the unravelling of the ties that bound together the RFU and most of its northern clubs.' (Collins) The Northern Union was an instant success, increasing club participation by five times in as many years while the crowd for its Challenge Cup final, which was inaugurated in 1897, had doubled to nearly 30,000 even before the end of the century. Confidence in the concept among the clubs was high, buoyed by the fact that several of them made notable profits in the first season, not least Oldham and Hull.

Once the initial honeymoon period was over though, the new competition faced some familiar problems. Although broken-time payments had been sanctioned, the six shillings daily maximum rapidly became the norm with top players refusing to play for less. Not only did that put an initial drain on the clubs, whose haphazard payments in the intervening years had not constituted a major cost, but it also priced a number of the aspiring junior clubs out of the elite market. As Neil Tranter points out, 'Except perhaps during its earliest years, the Northern Rugby Football Union made no attempt to ensure that equality of playing strength between clubs that is so essential to the achievement of profit maximisation.' By the second year of Northern Union competition, a move to go openly professional had been recommended by a specially formed sub-committee and accepted, although conditions were stipulated regarding the registration of players who had to have designated occupations and residency qualifications. That effectively heralded the birth of the transfer system and equally significantly the beginning of the wholesale recruitment of 'overseas' players, initially from Wales,   the latter still a major debating point 100 years later. Bradford even went so far as to propose the first salary cap when floating the idea of a maximum wage of £1 a week but 'this was rejected as being both impossible to police and likely to become a standard wage that few clubs could afford' (Collins). With soccer beginning to take a nationwide hold and rapidly sweeping through the Northern Union's heartlands, an even more radical venture to prevent further decline was instituted in 1901 – the formation of a 'super league'. Instigated by Halifax, ultimately fourteen of the leading inter-county clubs formed an elite division, the Northern Rugby Football League, in order that they could guarantee a greater number of viable fixtures. That had been the original 1895 plan but with twenty-two clubs at the outset, fixture congestion and the clamour to join the new body had seen the reversion to respective Yorkshire and Lancashire competitions. One of the first rugby union bye-laws to be repealed by the Northern Union within two months of the formation was that limiting membership to clubs north of the river Trent and the 1901 NRL took the unprecedented step of looking for 'franchise' applicants. As Tony Collins notes, 'Most revolutionary, they sought to expand their number to include rugby union teams from the North-East and the Midlands. South Shields Rugby Union Club joined in June, after having sounded out the NU about joining the previous year, but Leicester, which had been approached because of their notoriety for covertly paying players, declined.' Naturally, those clubs who had been founder members but now saw themselves excluded from the top strata found the move unpalatable and it caused massive division, only partly assuaged when in 1902/03, two cross-county divisions of eighteen teams was introduced.

The competition only really began to settle down two seasons later when a single, combined division was created. As all the teams did not face each other, final places were determined on a percentage basis of wins against games played, with the ultimate winners decided by a hugely prestigious top-four Championship Play-Off. Perhaps the most perceptive observation of how the Northern Union developed, in view of what was to happen 100 years later, is provided by Latham and Mather. 'No doubt many of the administrators of the Northern Union were worthy men but their horizons appeared to be narrow, their vision parochial. They failed to see that without the solid foundation provided by junior clubs their own existence was imperilled. In the first decade of the new century, eleven new clubs – including six from Wales – were at various times members of the Northern Union. None survived beyond 1913. New clubs, like Fleetwood and Blackpool, formed specifically to play the Lancashire Second Competition, struggled from the outset, with precious little support from the governing body. Some clubs, by their geographical location on the fringes of the action... saw their best players lured away and found the expenses of competing in the Northern Union simply too prohibitive. The smaller clubs were left with no real alternative but to join the Northern Union but the majority were unable to pay broken-time and, failing to swim in the big pond, failed to survive. The Northern Union was hastily thrown together and it showed. Clubs were promoted into leagues that were too strong for them in playing terms and, more importantly, placed them in situations where the costs, particularly travelling expenses, were dramatically increased. Inevitably, most clubs began to experience financial difficulties. These were exacerbated when support began to decline, mainly because of uneven contests and fixtures against opposition regarded as unattractive. Having joined the Northern Union, newcomers were left to fend for themselves with virtually no support, financial or otherwise. There was no framework in place to develop a strategy for expansion. The speed of events of the summer of 1895 pushed matters out of control and allowed no time to accommodate the junior clubs. Without a coherent plan the early years of the Northern Union were marked by a battle for survival.' In so many of those respects it would be easy to replace the 1895 with 1995, even down to the fact that the current hugely anticipated Old Trafford Grand Final that ends the season had its direct antecedents in the Championship decider. Super League has never quite come to terms with the franchising debate, which is set to take another twist if the latest proposals are instituted from 2009. However, it could be argued that it was the haphazard way clubs clamoured for inclusion in the Northern Union that laid the restrictive geographical template that has taken the sport over 100 years to reconcile. When the Northern Union was formed in 1895 it created a hiatus as the new sport came to terms with what the rarefied regular fixtures could offer for clubs. It inevitably created casualties along the way, including missing opportunities to expand and secure its future – that was the fallout. From 1905 onwards, with the formation of a settled structure, including prestigious cup competitions, there was a period of stability; and with the start of international Test matches and the invitation to clubs in Wales and the Midlands to join in the run up to the First World War, there was significant evidence of expansion. Thus it has been with Super League; what took twenty years to resolve in the early history of the game has been reflected in the first ten summer seasons.

'The game is in crisis, of course, but it always has been. It's just a question of what particular sort of crisis it is in. If my 220-mile journey across rugby league land had taught me anything… it is that the game is surprisingly well adapted to living with crisis.' – Dave Hadfield, *Up and Over*, Mainstream, 2005

THREE

HIATUS: THE ADVENT OF SUPER LEAGUE

'Being entertaining is the highest priority for professional sport. The people who pump in the money – television, sponsors and spectators – will eventually go away if it's not attractive to watch.' – Joe Lydon

Maurice Lindsay – the chief executive of the Rugby Football League when Super League was announced and who later was appointed managing director of the competition – took a look back over the opening decade in an extended interview on BBC local radio in the North at the culmination of the 2005 campaign. In it the man most often referred to, and occasionally self-proclaimed, as the architect of the new dawn, gave an insight as to how it came about. 'It was an absolute shock,' he said. 'Out of the blue I got this phone call from Sam Chisholm, who was then the boss of BSkyB, acting on behalf of News Corporation asking me would I go down and see him urgently because he wanted to put an offer to us for the creation of Super League, mirroring what was going on in Sydney. It was an absolute shock that an offer reconfiguring the game was there at all. But, of course, when the amounts became known that was an even greater shock.' In many ways, that is the popular conception of how the rugby league world was seemingly instantaneously turned upside down; somewhat ironically as, at the time, it was discussing plans of how best to celebrate and commemorate its centenary, few of which were subsequently implemented. Certainly some of the initial strategy of how to distribute the funds accruing and the accompanying splits and divisions within the ranks of club chairmen and fans that coursed throughout April and May 1995 indicated that haste and policy on the hoof rather than the time to plan was of the essence. Perhaps, more revealingly, the charismatic Lindsay went on to add, 'Yes, I

The front page of *League Express* on 1 April 1996 heralds the opening weekend of the new era.

had an inkling looking from the outside at what was going on in Australia that we would become embroiled at some stage.' What is undeniable is that his supreme negotiating skill turned an initial five-year offer of around £50 million pounds into an eventually staggering cheque for around £87 million. However, taking a more detailed look at the issues surrounding and enveloping the code from the early 1990s to the expeditious time of the announcement, it becomes apparent that what the money provided was a vital, opportune life support that ensured its very survival and existence as a mainstream sport. That fundamental change was evolving and had to happen anyway but suddenly someone else was picking up the tab. There had been some significant indications for a period of time that all was not well and something had to be done. As Lindsay acknowledged in an in-depth feature in the *Daily Telegraph* in October 1995, on the eve of the World Cup final and the Australian appeal court's decision on whether to allow Super League to take place over there, 'Sport is a very tough market-place. Until we took action rugby league was not equipped to compete. It would have withered and died on the vine.' The observations of the article's writer, Michael Calvin, in a newspaper not owned by the Murdoch dynasty are even more prescient. '[rugby league's] players are foot soldiers in a war of billionaires' egos and corporate business strategies. Its administrators are pawns in a geopolitical game of chess, dictated by the profit margins of the communications industry. Having partially succeeded in dragging his game, kicking and screaming, into the twentieth century, [Lindsay] has now to prepare league, as a viable global sport, for the twenty-first century. Lindsay, who has responsibility for overseeing expansion, is reviled by a highly vocal British minority as a traitor to his class, his community. His crime has merely been to remind an introspective sport, sliding into bankruptcy, of reality.' Super League essentially came about as the result of a three-pronged attack, the elements of which are all alluded to in Calvin's perceptive comments; the shifting nature of sport as a commodity in the advanced business environment, the fundamental need for radical change in an effort to prop up what was a floundering domestic game and the direct impact of astonishing events taking place across the world.

Although it is variously referred to as an industry, sport has a key element flowing through it that is almost antithetical to business; emotion expressed as a passion. On the basis of binding loyalty, decisions to fund and support a club have invariably eschewed standard commercial practice. Owners of hugely successful personal enterprises who – often for reasons of altruism as much as vanity – take up the reigns of their favoured club, are notorious for not employing the methodologies and practices that garnered their personal wealth in the running of their team. By the start of the 1990s, that sort of personal investment was no longer sufficient to paper over the financial cracks in virtually every rugby league club, including some of the most famous names in the code's history. Costs of staging the games including stadium management charges, paying players' market-value wages under the new contract system, which often included the additional element of agents' fees, and selling the fare to an ever more discerning public, were spiralling almost out of control. Limited sponsorship and broadcasting revenue was barely lining the coffers and new, significant outside investment was becoming increasingly difficult to come by. Rugby League followed the classic sporting business model, outlined by Beech and Chadwick, of evolutionary phases – where change is slow and incremental – followed by revolutionary ones – where transformations are rapid and characterised by high levels of uncertainty. In their representation, sport goes from 'foundation' (evolutionary) where it emerges from a folk tradition to 'codification' (revolutionary) with the formalisation of practice, usually as the result of an organisational breakaway, which was seen initially in the formation of the Northern Union. Next comes 'stratification' (evolutionary) where, as the sport grows, the body responsible for codification sets up or administers a variety of leagues, typically with an element of promotion and relegation and normally characterised by a regional dimension, especially at lower levels. In this phase, the sport remains amateur but a defined organisation has emerged. After that it enters 'professionalisation' (revolutionary) as it gains popular appeal, with spectators willing to watch and investors' support allowing the payment of the protagonists. Initially that is in terms of expenses but may extend to payment for loss of earnings. At this point the distinction between amateur and professional status may become blurred. Where full-blown professionalisation occurs, the elite players are able to play sport as a full-time occupation and clubs need to employ staff to promote their activities and administer revenues and expenditure in an effort to balance the books. During 'post-professionalisation' (evolutionary) a senior game that is professionalised typically sits alongside an amateur junior game. That is superseded by 'commercialisation' (revolutionary) as the sport develops an overtly business context and external organisations see the opportunity of using the sport for their own purposes. Typically this is by way of sponsorship to governing bodies, leagues and clubs to position and market their own brands and product endorsements involving the players.

Prior to Super League, the thirteen-a-side game was stuck in post-professionalism but aspiring and needing to be moving to commercialisation if it was to retain its standing most specifically among its traditional stronghold areas of support. The overall crowd levels were largely static, the average attendance across the divisions hovering around 3,500 spectators per game from the 1988/89 season through to 1994/95. Just over four times as many fans were watching the First Division clubs and without overall growth lay stagnation and ultimate decline. Aside from the need to find wider, mass appeal, it could no longer be assumed that, just because of the tribal nature of sport, fans would continue to simply turn up. The very nature of business forces clubs to be much more pro-active in satisfying, targeting and keeping crowds and that was a massive worry and challenge for a geographically specific sport like rugby league. In an article in the September 1994 edition of *Open Rugby*, the respected monthly trade magazine that had been an indicative barometer of the health of the sport since 1983 and a vociferous campaigner in trying to get the game to promote itself to its widest audience, Hull-based writer Kristian Barrass succinctly summed up the growing public perception of the code at that time. 'Over the years we've become so accustomed to the poor organisation and overall standards in general that we regard it as part of rugby league. As British rugby league approaches 1995 and it's centenary, it faces a major crisis. The problem lies in the fact that more and more people are starting to wake up to the realisation that, although the actual game itself has progressed immensely, the 'off the field' areas, such as packaging, marketing and standards of spectator care and comfort, more closely resemble those of 1895.

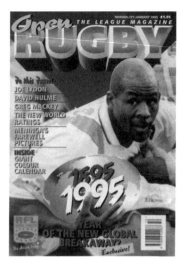

An article in the January 1995 edition of *Open Rugby* gives the first real indication of how a world-wide Super League could work, three months before it is formally announced.

Not only will the League face increasing difficulty in trying to hang on to existing fans, it faces an even tougher task attempting to attract new support, and therefore prospects for expansion look bleak. I don't think that league as a whole appreciates the fact that we are living in the 1990s and not the 1890s. By that, I mean that I don't think it sees itself as part of the ever expanding hi-tech, multi-national, multi-billion pounds entertainment and leisure industry, having to compete in the highly competitive marketplace for the attention of the consumer… to make itself a viable and attractive proposition to the ever increasingly sophisticated public. By sophisticated I refer to the fact that as the 1990s become ever more commercialised, the population as a whole has come to expect much higher standards of customer care, comfort, entertainment, packaging and value for money. One of my main criticisms is the way in which league is packaged and marketed. Too much emphasis is placed on the shoulders of the individual clubs.'

If the rapidly shifting commercial environment was in danger of leaving the code cast adrift on sport's ever-decreasing margins, the game itself was undergoing severe introspection regarding the quality and sustainability of its competition. In 1991, the RFL elected its thirty-sixth professional club, Scarborough Pirates, which enabled a restructure into three divisions. That they only lasted a season on the East Coast gave a strong hint that the game was becoming unsustainable but the sport was also struggling to find the right balance with its product. The First Division was palpably failing to produce enough players of lasting quality or to attract sufficient junior talent. The top performers were being asked to play too many matches, particularly against clubs caught in the promotion/relegation trap between the divisions who were struggling to provide creditable opposition. In turn, that tended to drop the standard to the lowest common denominator. Promoted clubs were finding it almost impossible to adjust to the demands and pace of the top flight, especially those coming up who had finished second and third, and the structure was seemingly suiting no-one. The radical blueprint proposed by the top clubs in April 1992 was effectively overruled by the unwieldy policy-making Rugby League Council where, under the traditional system of one club, one vote, the tail continued to wag the dog. Nevertheless, there was a groundswell building for independent, unified governance and more high-quality, better promoted shop-window games. There was also a growing realisation that all clubs would need to face standards-driven assessment in the areas of playing strength, available resources, sponsorship prospects, crowd catchment area, commercial organisation and ground facilities. The unexpected collapse, at around the same time, of the British Aerospace owned Sportscast satellite channel, which relayed live and recorded Division Two and Three matches predominantly to pubs, cost the lower clubs half a million pounds in outstanding rights revenues and further exacerbated the distinction between the have-littles and the have-nothings.

The growing trends, realisations and potential responses were concentrated into a new all-encompassing report that came out seven months before the announcement of Super League, in August 1994, and was regarded as one of the widest-ranging discussion documents the game had produced in the modern era. 'Framing the Future' advocated the formation of a Premier League similar to soccer's and brought up the idea of mergers. It devised criteria for inclusion in the elite division that went over and above merely winning promotion to it by virtue of playing record and looked at full-time staffing requirements clubs would need to run effectively and meet the current demands of professional sport. They included key areas such as administration, finance, commercial and media together with a football secretary and chief executive. The hope was that, with each of these crucial areas covered, clubs would be better administered, successfully promoted and in a much healthier position to exploit commercial opportunities. Commissioned by the RFL from sports marketing firm GSM, the findings of the 'crisis document' were the result of a twelve-month survey that encompassed all stratas of the sport and revealed that no more than four of the game's members could be said to be profitable.

On the back of the threat of a proposed breakaway by the top sides, the Rugby League Council phased in agreement for a sixteen-team Premier League, a gradual reduction in the eight per cent levy that the top sides paid to help fund the lower ones and a change to the voting rights that would see Premier sides having three votes, Second Division teams two and Conference outfits one. It introduced an overseas transfer ban, a reduction in the import quota from three to two players and the imposition of a salary cap that would see no club allowed to spend more than fifty per cent of its income on players' wages, subsequently reducing to forty-five per cent, then forty. Movement on the levy was deemed as an important concession. It had long been regarded as a millstone holding back the bigger and more ambitious clubs who brought in the most revenue, while the wisdom of artificially propping up some very weak clubs had begun to be questioned by many within the game.

There is a strong case for saying that, although the pace of change was substantially altered by the News International cash injection, the sport had already recognised and taken steps to put its house in order and address the issue of a need for a Super League. Just prior to the start of the first summer season in 1996, the RFL Board of Directors issued a revised fifty-one-page 'Framing the Future II', which was designed to contain the criteria by which the initial News disbursements would be issued to Super League members.

The last Ashes Test series before the announcement of Super League in both hemispheres and the consequent subjugation of international competition was a further eye-opener for the British game in late autumn 1994. Against the odds, the Lions pulled off a sensational narrow victory at Wembley with the winning try memorably coming from a tremendous arcing run by Jonathan Davies to seal an 8-4 success. The lead up to the game, though, was filled with stories of doom and gloom as the debate over the 'Framing the Future' proposals and underpinning economic problems gave the usual detractors all the ammunition they needed to predict impending demise at a time when the national press were dispensing with bespoke league correspondents. The message was reinforced by the attendance, which was an extremely disappointing 57,000; it appeared that even the faithful were starting to lose their belief. In the following two Tests matters were put into even starker relief, the Kangaroos not only cruelly exposing the skill levels and shortcomings of the British players with comprehensive victories but again demonstrating the lack of quality depth at the highest

levels, leaving the game with the need to further reappraise its entire structure in an effort to match the visitors' seemingly effortless dominance.

League folk had never needed an excuse to deride their own efforts
but, with the action fought out in front of the BBC's cameras, the point
of no return, relating to what place the code would have in the nation's
sporting consciousness, was rapidly arriving. There was even less cheer in
the domestic competition, the first round of the Regal Trophy providing
ample illustration that a revamp could not come soon enough. There was
no rejoicing when Huddersfield broke the record score in totally humiliat-
ing Blackpool 142-4 and lowly Barrow followed suit against Nottingham,
winning 138-0. Everyone associated with the code shuddered with embar-
rassment at the ensuing publicity and discredit. Perhaps of most concern
was the fact that both clubs on the receiving end were ex-professional clubs
in the outposts, where the game should have been progressing if it was
to succeed. At the turn of 1994, news that a 'Super League' competition
was being debated in Australia and former rugby union supremo Jacques
Fouroux was planning a similar shake-up to revolutionise the league game
in France was largely welcomed, the phrase quickly becoming an accepted
part of the sport's vocabulary. Publisher and managing editor of *Open Rugby*
Harry Edgar wrote in his January 1995 editorial, 'Survival is the name of the
game right now in England, not celebration, and that's the ultimate tragedy
when you consider the superb quality of football being provided week in
week out and also when you consider that six or seven years ago we were
all so optimistic about developing and expanding the game to new areas.
Now we have famous clubs in the traditional heartlands hanging on by
their fingernails. British rugby league's problems lie in the middle ground,
those professional clubs who aren't at the very top and able to attract the
same players, finance and public support as Leeds, Wigan, St Helens etc. A
quick glance at the First Division table would suggest only seven clubs in
our 'Super League' category as we enter 1995. The way ahead has to be the
creation of a 'Super League'. A concentration of promotional and stadium
development resources on ten, definitely no more than twelve, clubs – and
the creation of a secondary level of competition for the other current pro
clubs, with a lessening emphasis on professionalism among them. Big events
are what the public and the media want and will support. If the clubs won't
change things voluntarily for the overall betterment of the game, which
effectively would mean their own survival, then change will have to be
forced on them by a breakaway. A breakaway to form a new governing body
that will promote the game in a manner demanded by the social conditions
of the times… will take brave men, with vision, drive and the welfare of the

game as a whole at heart. Too revolutionary for rugby league in the North of England? But wasn't that just what people were saying 100 years ago?'

   While the game in Britain was reaching a nadir, with First Division Doncaster appearing to be going to the wall and Halifax desperately looking for the salvation of a merger, quite the opposite was true in the antipodes. There, a media war was set to break out with the arrival of satellite television and, more specifically, pay-TV rights as the information superhighway began to take hold. The battle was on to win subscribers and with two of world's biggest hitters in opposite corners – Rupert Murdoch and Kerry Packer – any such confrontation was likely to be fierce, bloody and costly, not just in terms of finance but also by way of long-established friendships and allegiances. Both of the moguls were acutely aware of the quickest way to win a new audience, it was a tried and tested strategy that had worked throughout their newspaper and subsequent broadcast empires. Quite simply, sport sells and in Australia's major states, New South Wales and Queensland, that meant rugby league. What the Australian Rugby League gave them was the canvas on which to flex their corporate muscles, Murdoch's News Corporation buying into the Brisbane Broncos' perception of a global future, of whom they were major sponsors, while Packer's Optus Vision fought to maintain the rights it already owned but had not yet chosen to fully exercise in an existing deal with the ARL. What made the sport so tempting was that by the middle of the decade it was in such rude health. The code had made itself almost irresistible to the general public partly as a result of one of the finest marketing campaigns ever undertaken, which showed Tina Turner training on a beach with the current icons of the game, backed by a title track that was becoming synonymous with the sport there, *Simply the Best*. Unlike in Britain, the Australian game had embraced commercialisation and was striding forward with attendances on the increase, a plethora of outstanding young players coming through at the majority of clubs, a 'State of Origin' competition that was on the verge of overtaking Test rugby as the pinnacle of the sport for standard and intensity and a domestic competition that new franchise areas were increasingly desperate to be a part of. The decentralisation away from the game's traditional Sydney stronghold was already creating tensions, Brisbane winning back-to-back Premierships in the early 1990s with a club that had only been formed five years previously but was totally focused and committed to a proven, overt business plan. Perhaps the three-year interregnum that nearly decimated the game could have been avoided if the Murdoch organisation's original plan, to take over sponsorship of the domestic league through their Traveland and Ansett Airline subsidiaries, had been accepted by the governing body in 1993. The ARL had to sign up a new partner because previous naming rights holders, cigarette manufacturers Winfield, were unable to renew owing to new government regulations banning tobacco sponsorship. They held out for their seemingly preferred option of a deal with Coca-Cola – who subsequently withdrew – and ultimately became the victims of their own success. As Mike Colman points out in his enlightening study, *Super League – The Inside Story* (Ironbark, 1996), 'How did things go off track so badly? The game's popularity was at a peak, the league was talking expansion and a glorious future. But even the ARL's greatest supporters would concede that complacency had set in. No-one thought to look for danger looming from behind or, even more unthinkable, from within. Yet if a financial whiz with no knowledge of rugby league was to look at the history of the game, the reaction would not be "How was this organisation hijacked?" but rather, "Why did it take so long?"'

The seeds of its own destruction were best illustrated in the traditional governing body's relationship with one of its newest, and quickly highest-profile, members from north of the state border, the Brisbane Broncos. The competition they graced was administered by a body called the New South Wales Rugby League, so the incoming upstarts knew where they stood when joining, but from the very early days tensions were instantly apparent. As Colman makes clear, 'they brought a new rogue element into rugby league. No more was it just about football and trophies and tradition at club level. It was about profits and percentage points and market share… despite being shouted down by the ARL whenever they came on with their "sport is business" line too loudly, they spoke about how much more could be done. They attracted like-minded people into the game. People whose financial resources could buy and sell the game – if they had a mind to.' The Broncos' position was summed up by their chief executive John Ribot, the mastermind behind the original global Super League concept: 'It was like they (the ARL) had no idea of running a business or making a sound commercial decision. From day one we would try to do what we felt made good business sense and they would stop us for political reasons.' That had included an audacious but financially sound plan submitted in 1992 to take the 1995 Grand Final to the Queensland capital, which, despite offering greater profits for the game as a whole, was summarily rejected. Ribot called the decision 'commercial suicide'. However, according to NSWRL general manager John Quayle, like Ribot a former wearer of the green and gold, 'Their charter was always different from the other fifteen clubs. With them it came down to profit. We had to make decisions based on how they would impact on all the members of the League.' While the British game was struggling to find the wherewithal to pay the wages of the RFL staff, their Australian counterparts, led by ARL chairman Ken Arthurson, could afford to be choosy about their investors. He was equally wary and at times scathing of what became known as the 'Broncos mentality' and was unintentionally prophetic when stating, 'If they don't want to play by our rules they can go and start their own competition.'

One thing the British game did have was Wigan. Although, for many, their continued pre-eminence at home was unhealthy and undermining the domestic competition, on 1 June 1994 they produced arguably the best club performance ever by a British side. Having just completed an arduous forty-five-match programme – which had seen them claim the title, Challenge Cup and Premiership as well as providing the backbone for the Great Britain side that whitewashed the touring Kiwis for the first time in forty-two years – the Riversiders travelled to Brisbane for the World Club Challenge, the first and so far only time the match has officially been played in the southern hemisphere. Despite facing a hostile, almost capacity crowd of over 54,000 and being without their first-choice props, internationals Kelvin Skerrett and Andy Platt, and facing a side of which eleven of the starting thirteen were Test players, the cherry and whites stunned the baying hordes with a momentous 20-14 success. The sensational backs-to-the-wall victory helped to reinforce Ribot's plan for the future of the sport, confirming his belief that there was a genuine international dimension to it at club level that would appeal principally to global broadcasters but also to the fans if sold to them in a progressive manner. His other major concern was the players, who he wanted to include as an integral part of the process and who would receive a stake and a say in any new competition. What he eventually outlined to them and the club bosses was a wide-ranging and far-reaching scheme. The concept consisted of fewer teams, higher average player quality, better pre-game entertainment and ground facilities, broader national and international coverage and more vigorous promotion. That was expected to bring bigger crowds, greater fan loyalty to the sport and, as a consequence, higher television viewing figures and – most importantly for the broadcaster who wanted to maximise advertising revenues as a result – even better ratings. His plan had everyone winning; more revenue through the gate, TV rights, sponsorship, merchandising and endorsements for the game and the clubs while the players would become full-time athletes, receive a percentage of merchandising sales and, crucially it was felt, be trained for a career after football. Initially, discussions centred on the ARL administering the new Super League but when they decided against it and, with News Corporation on board and ready to significantly invest, civil war broke out.

In the lead-up to the final formulation of the Super League plan senior News executive David Smith, the logistical supremo behind how the project would be implemented, visited Britain towards the end of 1994 to outline its general aims to the RFL. At that stage, according to Ribot, it was not a priority to sign them up, 'it was stage two, probably a few months down the track' but events cascaded when the Super League organisation began signing up Australian players and, indeed, whole clubs commencing on 31 March 1995. Ribot's comment illustrates that although the timing may have surprised those at the helm of the British game, the idea and possibilities it offered did not and it seemed to be tapping into a way of thinking that sport was already seeking to adopt. What hastened the need for the RFL to take sides, although the amount of money being offered meant that the formal decision to throw in their lot with Super League was scarcely a difficult decision, was the initial Packer-backed ARL fightback, spearheaded by Australian coach Bobby Fulton and influential coach, mentor and selector Phil Gould. Their initial pitch to dissuade the players from signing up with a rebel organisation was that it would prevent them from representing their country. That forced the Super League's hand and the decision was taken to isolate the ARL by signing up the other major playing nations, principally Great Britain and New Zealand. Maurice Lindsay remembers, 'It became clear to them that if they had a schism in Australia, international football would then become extremely important. They moved very quickly to try and embrace us and they could only do that by funding our league structure.' It was an area that the renegade Australians knew a significant amount about because, for the start of the 1994/95 season, the Brisbane Broncos had bought into the London Crusaders, who were then desperately seeking to find a way of staying afloat in the mid-reaches of the Second Division but with seemingly limitless potential in a huge but untapped market. As Colman relates, 'Dominated by big-spending Wigan and a poor cousin to the national winter sport of soccer, it was ripe for the plucking by anyone with a good business plan and a suitcase full of money. And David Smith had both. The deal Smith put to Maurice Lindsay when they met on the Wednesday morning (5 April) was like a gift from the football gods. The traditional British Cup competitions, with the famous Wembley Challenge Cup final, would still be played as before, but the winner of the Euro League would also play the winner of the Australasian Super League to determine the world champion. Test matches against Australia would be played as they had for the best part of ninety years.' Back in Australia it took another thousand days, two huge court rulings – one reversing the other – millions of wasted dollars, the rise, death and amalgamation of clubs and for a season in

1997 an immensely damaging and polarising split competition that threatened to disastrously fracture the support base, before compromise could be found. What they went through had distinct overtones of the original Northern Union breakaway with the added element of high finance. As Brad Fittler, the skipper of the ARL-selected 1995 World Cup-winning side revealed in his autobiography *Freddy* (Brad Fittler & Richard Sleeman, Harper Sports 2005), 'It was a funny thing with the players – we never had a cross word. I'm aware that officials who'd been mates all their lives fell out over the footy wars. I know journalists and the TV people took sides and, on occasions, came to blows. On talk-back radio and in the letters pages of newspapers the war of words was bitter and angry and full of bile. It consumed people's lives. You were either a traditionalist who loved the game or a believer in the vision for the future.' The ultimate irony is that what effectively ended the war there was pragmatic commercial reality, not sentiment. Once the appeal decision that allowed Super League to come into being had been delivered, Kerry Packer's Channel Nine network that had so assiduously backed the old order (the exact opposite to what it had done with World Series Cricket in the 1970s) immediately negotiated for and won rights to show Super League games.

For the British game, which had stood on the threshold of implosion, there was now the genuine prospect of deliverance but the reaction was similar to that across the world as news leaked out. Maurice Lindsay called the deal both agony and ecstasy because although the five-year sum on offer seemed to give the code capital prosperity, the restructuring meant that some would miss out. What should have been dancing in the streets became demonstrations at grounds as the dreaded words 'merger' and 'fast-tracking' dominated debate. What News Corporation wanted for their rapidly expanding Sky Sports TV schedules was a tight, highly competitive league for 1996 that had prospects for expansion, which would run parallel to the Australian competition, rolling throughout the summer, and would help sell satellite dishes and subscriptions. The initial problem facing the RFL was to how to create enough sides of similar high standard when Wigan were so far ahead of the others. Six weeks after the announcement of Super League, they completed arguably the finest season in their history, becoming the first side of the modern era to do the Grand Slam of Division One title, Premiership, Challenge Cup and Regal Trophy. Their powers showed little signs of waning, the concluding match being a record-breaking 69-12 hammering of second-placed Leeds in the Premiership decider in front of 30,000 fans at Old Trafford. Wigan loose forward Phil Clarke, who later became one of Sky's principal summarisers, said at the time, 'It's pretty scary when we can do that to the second-best club in the country.' The only way that those at the helm of the game could see to match them was to amalgamate the best of what they had in the hope that the sum of the other parts would create a viable whole. In a sport built around – and indeed founded on – fierce local pride and loyalties, that was always going to be an extremely risky approach that needed delicate negotiation, skilful and detailed planning and a cogent and believable public relations strategy to sell the largely unpalatable idea. In the event it had none of them, the unseemly haste with which the announcements and recants were made immediately played into the hands of the detractors both within the game and outside it, right up to government level in the House of Commons. The club chairmen were really in a no-win situation. They had to accept the unexpected windfall to secure their future but the other side of that coin was the idea of going back to their fan base with the news that they were set to lose their history and identity and worse, move in with their fiercest rivals. Within two days of the initial announcement on 8 April that there would be a fourteen-team Super League comprising of Bradford, Halifax, Leeds, St Helens and Wigan and newly created sides Calder (Castleford, Wakefield, Featherstone), Cheshire (Warrington, Widnes), Cumbria (Barrow, Carlisle, Whitehaven, Workington), Humberside (Hull, Hull Kingston Rovers), Manchester (Oldham, Salford), South Yorkshire (Doncaster, Sheffield), London, Paris and Toulouse, Leeds chief executive Alf Davies accused the League of 'holding a gun to the heads of the clubs. It was either vote in favour or you are out.' At the time of that first unveiling, appropriately at Wigan's home Central Park, Maurice Lindsay said, 'It is not a highjack or a takeover. It is a glorious opportunity, which we have decided to accept.' Ten years later he recalled, 'I don't think anyone was comfortable with mergers. People who were representing those clubs actually agreed they would do that. They went back to their clubs and found themselves unable to deliver once their own spectators said "no". There were great divisions in the media, great divisions on the terraces, great divisions in the boardrooms, but at the end of the day everyone realised that rugby league needed to step forward and enter the new century with a firm financial footing, and Super League was the only way to go. This was a chance for us to raise our standards. You've got to think in global terms, and if not in global terms, in European terms. We've got to be a bigger game. It takes a long time to create a rugby league culture.'

As he found out, though, it did not take any time at all to be seen to be destroying one and, by 30 April, after endless manoeuvring, public rancour and widespread bitterness, the revised twelve-team elite division comprised of the top-ten finishers in the old First Division at the end of the 1994/95 season plus the upgrading of London and the rushed inclusion of Paris. With the competition not due to kick off for another year, only those who were intimately involved in the decision making at News Corporation and the RFL will know how urgent it was to announce the exact structure so quickly, rather than that the code was to receive substantial new backing and would take representations on the implications that would have for the game. Instead, the whole package was presented as a *fait accompli*. The conspiracy theorists claimed that what was in operation was a standard business practice of announcing the unacceptable, mergers, which would be revised, so that the real critical issue, the move to summer, would go through virtually undebated and unopposed. As Maurice Lindsay said of the scrapped merger plans, 'The revisions take account of the concern raised over the past three weeks. I believe that we have now been able to allay the fans' fears over club mergers and the loss of the game's traditions.' Promotion and relegation was also left on the table, signalling the end of the franchise debate, although the rethink brought the final £10 million of the deal into the clubs' collective coffers, with an increased share for the First and Second Division sides to enable them to clear historic debt. There were, however, lingering frustrations about the way the whole episode had been handled as Harry Edgar relayed in his *Open Rugby* editorial of May 1995. 'The Murdoch money was a lifeline to a lot of drowning men. The turmoil that followed 8 April was a poor reflection on the planning and understanding of where the game needs to go. The RFL left themselves open to all the anger and criticism that followed by their failure to portray themselves as people sure of what they were trying to do. So, instead of being the massively positive event the Murdoch deal could and should have been, it turned into a public relations nightmare. There was no sign of any standard criteria of what was deemed suitable for Super League membership. More importantly, there were no positive guidelines about what was to happen to the game outside Super League, about the need to preserve community clubs and the grassroots.' With the distributions available, perhaps there was an alternative that would achieve both. Rather than merging clubs, new ones could have been created that sat above the existing sides, who would then effectively have become feeders to the region's showcase outfit but maintained their individual identity and history in the lower division while still playing lucrative derby fixtures. The absolute need would then have been to make the regional feeder leagues meaningful in their own right so that those clubs that were tied into smaller, local communities would have an attainable prize worth winning and wanting to retain. At the same time they would also be producing a conveyor belt of talent that would remain in the area playing for a new Super League 'franchise' team in which the existing clubs would have an equal share. Cumbria, for instance, is a prime example of an area that produces copious junior talent, the best of which has invariably been sought to ply their trade elsewhere. All of the four clubs that were earmarked in the initial merger to form the county side have vital community links but, despite incessant hard work, are unlikely to ever have the facilities or individual catchment areas to challenge the big city boys. A new stadium, based perhaps around the Copeland Athletic Arena, which was receiving substantial lottery funding, could have hosted a Cumbria Crusaders in Super League while Workington, Whitehaven, Barrow and possibly even Carlisle – who were eventually and bizarrely from a geographical point of view to throw their lot in with Barrow – could have remained as First or Second Division outfits. Of course, that assumes that the Cumbrian public would have taken to the new amalgam as well as their own traditional allegiance but that again is about having real confidence in the worth of the product. If the franchised club played at a different time over a weekend and competed against the other top sides, the attraction of watching the likes of Wigan, St Helens, Warrington et al every other week would have been an enticing one if sold and marketed correctly. More than that, the existing clubs could have had a better chance of flourishing at a sustainable level, cutting their cloth according to their actual means. Once the Premiership was cast in soccer, a whole raft of lower division clubs with great history, tradition and a precious place in their towns were forced to cap their ambition but survived at a sustainable level. It is unlikely, for example, that Bury – who won the FA Cup in 1900 and 1903 – now seriously aspire to be on a par with Manchester United; nor, under current economic conditions within that sport, should they. Rather, if they could sell their illustrious neighbours an up-and-coming player to keep themselves out of debt and possibly win a lower division title, a feat they achieved in 1961 and 1997, that would keep their passionate band of fans backing their efforts. What happened in Cumbria was that Workington tried valiantly to go it alone but failed, getting relegated from Super League I while averaging less than 2,500 fans, and have subsequently slipped down into the bottom tier of the semi-professional ranks. Whitehaven are strenuously building a model community-focused club and increasing their attendances to above a self-sustainable level. They are encouraging and fostering strong links with their local amateur clubs, which is maintaining a flow of young, eager talent, and have appeared in and graced the last two National League Grand Finals, the last stepping stone to Super League. In 2005, amid scenes of delirium within the town, they won the first trophy in their history when finishing top of National League One. Should they eventually make their way into Super League, there is every reason to think that despite their best efforts they would struggle to compete, being extremely unlikely to take advantage of the £1.8 million salary cap maximum that the bigger clubs can generate. Being in the very top tier could unravel all the outstanding work that they have so meticulously achieved and yet Super League is poorer without some sort of Cumbrian representative presence. That is the dilemma that the game failed to solve in 1995 and has struggled to come to terms with ever since.

TOP 10 MATCHES

1996 PARIS ST GERMAIN 30-24 SHEFFIELD EAGLES
Charlety Stadium, 29 March
Joy and surprise in equal measure signalled the dawning of a new era, marked by Sky TV's Mike 'Stevo' Stephenson introducing the players to the crowd while dodging the fireworks. A perfect opening night outcome.

1997 LONDON BRONCOS 38-18 CANBERRA RAIDERS
The Stoop, 21 July
Given that the Broncos had lost 66-20 against the same opponents on their trip Down Under, this was an amazing turnaround and announced the club as a serious, credible force.

1998 LEEDS RHINOS 4-10 WIGAN WARRIORS
Old Trafford, 24 October
Over 43,000 turned out on a grim October night to see the inaugural Grand Final, making the concept an instant success that has provided a superb climax to each subsequent season.

1999 WIGAN WARRIORS 28-20 ST HELENS
Central Park, 5 September
A symbolic rugby league moment, as one of the sport's most historic stadiums staged its final match, though it was to be Saints' Tommy Martyn who posted the final try on the ground, ninety-seven years after the first.

2000 ST HELENS 16-11 BRADFORD BULLS
Knowsley Road, 22 September
This play-off match will be forever remembered for Chris Joynt's last-gasp winning try, which was desperate, audacious and yet brilliant all in the same breath. News Corporation could never have dared to dream that Super League would provide reality television as dramatic as this.

2001 HULL FC 20-24 ST HELENS
The Boulevard, 28 September
A memorable encounter in the penultimate season at Hull FC's old stadium. Nip and tuck all the way, with a Paul Sculthorpe-inspired Saints leading 10-6 at the break and Tommy Martyn's try sealing it four minutes from time.

2002 BRADFORD BULLS 18-19 ST HELENS
Old Trafford, 19 October
The most dramatic and controversial Grand Final of Super League's first decade. Bradford threw everything at St Helens, but Ian Millward's team maintained their big-game hoodoo over the Bulls with Sean Long's late drop goal and some controversial tactics from Chris Joynt on how to best use his time in possession.

2003 LEEDS RHINOS 22-23 WIGAN WARRIORS
Headingley, 10 October
The most captivating of four magnificent matches between the clubs that year, with a memorable brace of tries from winger Brian Carney and a late Danny Tickle one-pointer edging Wigan through to the Grand Final.

2004 CASTLEFORD TIGERS 7-6 WIDNES VIKINGS
Wheldon Road, 11 September
Skills and free-scoring were put on the back-burner as both clubs scrapped for their Super League lives. Spectators and players alike were almost sick with nerves as the teams battled with themselves and each other in a gripping encounter. The Tigers prevailed, but only delayed the drop by seven days.

2005 WARRINGTON WOLVES 33-16 LEEDS RHINOS
Halliwell Jones Stadium, 10 September
The world's finest, Andrew Johns, made an inspirational Super League debut as the Wolves marched towards their first play-off place, with a comprehensive defeat of the champions in front of their biggest attendance of the season.

FOUR

FALLOUT: SELLING THE NEW

'Every time you step on the field you market some aspect of the game. What we are producing out there is superb quality entertainment.' – Oldham Bears' commercial manager and ex-Lancashire county cricket star David Hughes

A strange thing happened on 11 February 1996, six weeks before Super League came into being. After a staggering and record-breaking 43 consecutive victories, Wigan lost a Challenge Cup tie, surprisingly going down 26-16 at unfashionable Salford, who were coached by former Central Park hero Andy Gregory. Even before the sport had moved to summer it appeared that the old guard just might be changing. If that was an omen, the events at Charlety Stadium, Paris on the opening night of the brave new world surprised virtually everybody; hopeful television executives, nervous administrators, sceptical supporters, fervent detractors and evangelical expansionists alike. Almost 18,000 people were attracted to the functional, modern stadium in the suburbs of the French capital to watch the hastily put-together team who carried the branding of the famous local soccer side face Sheffield Eagles, an up-and-coming, progressive side from a city that, although still within the confines of the traditional heartlands, represented an outpost. The eighty minutes could not have been better scripted and at the heart of it was French international Freddie Banquet. After all the pre-match glitz and glamour that was to become such an integral feature of defining the new game-day experience, it was he who set the competition in motion, had the first try ruled out by a video referee whose adjudication could be witnessed by all at the ground on Sky's big screen, and then posted the inaugural try in the tenth minute – celebrated with a musical soundtrack that got the stadium rocking. Amid all the gathering furore, flag waving and drum beating, PSG then did the unimaginable; they won the match 30-24 having attracted the largest turnout of the opening round of matches across the two hemispheres.

Like so many times in its history – not least when in 1929 the bold but much-derided decision to take the Challenge Cup final to Wembley drew the then second-highest crowd in the competition's history to see Wigan defeat Dewsbury – innovative rugby league had risen to the occasion. It was an auspicious opening weekend for Super League, completed when the other 'promoted' outpost side, London Broncos, unexpectedly triumphed 24-22 at Halifax. That seemed to be a fitting end to a week of unprecedented build-up that gave the new concept the ideal kick-start. The press carried a plethora of in-depth analyses, profiles and predictions in the lead up, the majority of them complimentary, supportive and anticipatory. They were backed up by a series of eye-catching full-page adverts, for the code as much as for the Sky dish that was needed to watch it on. Significantly, even the southern editions caught the bug, with the mass circulation *News of the World* and *Evening Standard* almost liberal in their coverage. The mood at Sky was naturally upbeat; the nightly 'Sports Centre' featured the preparations of a different side in each bulletin and frequently ran the promotional videos previewing the season ahead. Radio probably got into the spirit more than any other medium. Locally, commercial stations carried frequent details of forthcoming matches and ticket information while specialist discussion and debate abounded on all wavelengths. More stations seemed to be devoting a greater amount of time to their coverage, be it live match action or studio conjecture. The biggest early impact came from national BBC Radio Five Live. Daily inserts into the popular early evening show leading up to the Paris jamboree highlighted a different aspect of the competition. The addition of touchline comment and insight from guest pundits such as Andy Gregory, plus a brief musical interlude – Jimi Hendrix's *Crosstown Traffic* – after a try was scored, added to the fervently generated atmosphere once match commentary started. Their revised schedule indicated a new commitment, *Super League Saturday* even eating into the network's most popular programme, the soccer phone-in *606*, which would have been unheard of under usual circumstances. The trailers advising of their coverage, which had extensive airplay across that first day, featured a backing track of *Roll with It* by Oasis. Suddenly rugby league seemed contemporary, raunchy and in your face. On the BBC's *Clear the Air* programme, London listener David Thomas posed the question, 'Could the powers that be please explain why Five Live is going rugby league mad; do audience figures justify this?' prompting producer David Oates to respond, 'The increased coverage is mainly due to the fact that rugby league matches no longer clash with football but are played at complimentary times. Five Live had the option of whether to carry on with its traditional coverage of brief match reports or to go the whole hog.

As no sport previously pushed by Sky has failed, Five Live decided that if they weren't there now the audiences would soon build.' A seven-page introduction to Super League on Teletext was another indication of the new higher profile, while the Murdoch-owned *Times* – unlike 100 years before – became one of the competition's subsidiary sponsors. The early promise, vibrancy and momentum of increased attendances throughout all the divisions were given a further impetus when St Helens beat Wigan at Knowsley Road in thrilling fashion, 41-26 in the traditional Good Friday derby. By then, it had become clear that Saints would be realistic challengers for the silverware, previously so monopolised by their neighbours, and the win – and the expansive manner by which it was achieved – boosted Super League's credibility about claiming to level-up standards. Big names from other sports were starting to add their seal of approval to the new venture, Manchester United's England defender Paul Parker one of the first to profess his admiration and allegiance along with golfer Lee Westwood. The game at the elite level was becoming well-respected and highly regarded and was making no apologies for its shift in emphasis. Referees' controller Greg McCallum was particularly upbeat. 'We have designed a high-speed, high-power game, the aim of which is to score tries and as many points as possible. Nowhere in the rule book does it say that the team making the most tackles will win.' Not everyone was in agreement though, Halifax skipper and former GB Test prop Karl Harrison – echoing the sentiments of traditionalist, winter watchers – bemoaning, 'The speeding up of the game has gone to the extreme. I'm all for improving the game but I think there has to be a limit or we are in danger of losing so many skills that the game will be barely recognisable. Specialist positions are really under threat and I fear us big fellas are next.'

Throughout May 1996 the code received another huge boost, albeit from the most unlikely of sources. Around the same time that Super League was formulated, rugby union finally came clean and went openly professional, leading to continued speculation, after it had also done a deal with News Corporation for coverage, that a merged code to rival soccer would be high on the Murdoch agenda. That was never a realistic possibility. What the Sky bosses were buying was programme content for their increasingly voracious schedules. By moving to summer, Super League not only gave them a year-round oval-ball option – which wherever possible their forthcoming event trailers linked together, assuming it was appealing to the same generic audience – but suddenly the traditional rivals were no longer in direct competition, except for the 'Save and Prosper' Cross-Code Challenges and the Middlesex Sevens. In two television-manufactured and much hyped

and debated clashes seventeen days apart the respective reigning champions played off, each experiencing the demands and delights of the other's
province; Wigan taking on Bath firstly under league rules at Maine Road,
Manchester and then subject to union's laws at Twickenham. Although
money was the primary motivation for bringing the two sides together,
both benefiting substantially at a time when player contracts in particular
were spiralling, the effect of Wigan's performances on an inquisitive audience that under normal circumstances would not have given 'the northern
game' a second glance cannot be underestimated. Their combination of
pace, balance, power, athleticism and particularly instinctive understanding
and support play when moving the ball in cavalier fashion won massive
admiration and, to many of union's players, coaches and spectators was eye-
opening. In the league encounter they posted sixteen tries, Martin Offiah
claiming six of them, in a dazzling performance that saw Wigan 52-0 ahead
at the break before easing off and putting on some of their young up-
and-coming stars to canter home 82-6. In the return, Bath played to their
strengths of retaining possession and using their superior scrum, lineout and
maul techniques to build a 25-0 interval advantage. In the second period,
Wigan gave up trying to match them and reverted to type, using the ball in
mesmeric fashion to post 3 outstanding tries that had the 42,000 crowd on
their feet in acclamation, before eventually going down 44-19.

In between the two games, the Twickenham set had already seen
the Wigan machine in all its majesty as they claimed the Russell Cargill
Memorial Trophy at the prestigious Middlesex Sevens in front of a record
61,000 fans and millions more watching on the BBC. Running in 25 tries
in all to account for Richmond, Harlequins, Leicester and emphatically
Wasps in the final, their exhibition handling and interplay was irresistible
and unstoppable. The reaction to their performances accorded the cherry
and whites awe and respect and Super League massive kudos. Bath's Man of
the Match in the full union encounter, Andy Robinson, was so impressed
by what he saw that on becoming England supremo in 2004 he hastened
closer coaching links between the sports. He was not alone. *The Times* feature writer Simon Barnes was first to join the appreciation society: 'Rugby
League has for years been the best-kept secret in the national sporting life, a
game for fitter, faster, stronger men, harder in the tackle and more elusive on
the run. Now the rules favour inspiration over perspiration.' Bath's try-scorer
in the league clash, Jon Callard, could not hide his veneration. 'Wigan were
awesome. I had a huge amount of respect for them before the game but now
they are bordering on god-like figures. It was a real pleasure to be part of
something very special. I would like Bath to do one rugby league training

session a week. If we did that we would be a far better side.' Recently retired England union international Paul Ackford was equally effusive. 'Bath were buried, completely overwhelmed by Wigan's sheer footballing ability and this is where union begins to eat buckets of humble pie. Wigan were not better because they were fitter, Wigan were better because they are better rugby players. Full stop.' The leader in *The Independent* exclaimed, 'Wigan's players are fitter, more flexible, more skilful, better disciplined and cleverer than their union counterparts. They think harder and more analytically about each ingredient of their game to work out how to win. As a result, they produce thrilling, entertaining, running rugby. Wigan's win was not just the victory of a team, but the triumph of an approach to sport.' The other lingering feeling that endured was that, far from moving the codes closer together, the clashes served to emphasise their considerable, unique differences. Phil Bennett and Alex Murphy were two legends on opposite sides of the fence that were of the opinion that peaceful co-existence was now the likely outcome. Outside the confines of the professional sporting environment, the effect was even more significant. Suddenly, rugby league was no longer a pariah, a number of union converts such as Scott Gibbs, Jonathan Davies, Scott Quinnell and Va'aiga Tuigamala returning to their earlier parish. Rather than the wholesale exodus of league players to the fifteen-man game some predicted, the perceived higher skill levels saw the switch of coaching gurus including the likes of Phil Larder, Clive Griffiths, Joe Lydon, Ellery Hanley, Shaun Edwards and most recently Denis Betts and Daryl Powell. It was a compliment that has not always been recognised on both sides of the so-called divide. In concert with Sky's Friday night coverage, junior union clubs throughout the country, suffering from being cut adrift in the professional era, became predisposed to the formation of amateur league sides in the summer, seeing the prospect of all-year-round bar takings at the very least. Part of the driving force for them to do so came from their players, a number of whom were desperate to have a go at the intense, handling game they had now witnessed first hand. Wigan through Super League helped to open a 100-year-old gate, the impact of both of them being key factors in the formation and continued rise of the nationwide Rugby League Conference; started in 1998 with fourteen clubs and now the largest playing league in the sport.

Initially impressive on-field momentum alone was not going to be enough to convince the traditional rugby league public in particular that Super League was going to be the salvation of the stumbling game. At the same time, a whole raft of marketing initiatives were introduced, some of which worked while others – like the perennial debate about franchises – floundered. There was obvious controversy attached to a few of them, not least the addition of marketable suffixes to traditional team names, a process actually begun by the ill-conceived Huddersfield Barracudas in the early 1980s and revitalised by the enterprising Keighley Cougars in 1991. Some, like the Bulls at Bradford, backed by a concerted commercially-minded staff, worked instantly. One or two such as Leeds Rhinos had to overcome initial scepticism and scorn but now have become an integral part of the club's and the competition's identity. Others, most specifically Halifax Blue Sox, missed the mark completely or, like Hull Sharks, were thought to connote the wrong image and were subsequently dropped. Although the introduction of squad numbering raised some hackles, the commercial spin-offs were obvious and have proved to be more than justified. Replica shirt sales, carrying the name and number of the wearer's favourite, have soared and continue to do so with a significant proportion of the public in most Super League towns and cities acting as walking billboards for their team. Following the introduction of the salary cap and more specifically the 20/20 rule – where only the top twenty players in each squad are allowed to earn over £20,000 per year – the numbers also had some relevance for aspiring junior players who could chart their progress or otherwise by how they moved up or down the list when it was announced at the start of each season. The only irony was that when Warrington signed Aussie superstar scrum half Andrew Johns for his cameo stint at the end of the 2005 season, they were not allowed to register him as number 77 under the highly astute proposed slogan 'so good they numbered him twice'. Mascots proved generally to be a massive hit with the younger fans enticed to grounds on summer evenings, although the ferocious head of the initial Huddersfield Giant had to be toned down after being deemed too scary. Again, with originality there came reward; the decision by Headingley operations director Stephen Ball to put Ronnie the Rhino up as a parliamentary candidate in the Leeds North-West ward, which included the ground, for the historic 1997 General Election, had a touch of genius. It was a masterstroke that not only won massive virtually free publicity for the Leeds club but cemented the name and the image among their more sceptical fans. Pre-match entertainment eventually became honed to a more comfortable mix of themed parades and stuntmen; live tribute bands or, somewhat incongruously, opera singers; better choreographed cheerleaders and dance troupes; lottery draws and fans' competitions and, importantly, junior touch and pass matches featuring local schools or clubs at half-time.

More professional on-field 'hosts' and P.A. announcers and a more enlightened attitude towards concessionary pricing helped to erase the memory of some of the first year's more excruciating efforts at most venues. The ritual of teams warming up in the midst of it all added to the feeling of anticipation and general atmosphere. Many are the singers who thought he or she was receiving rapturous applause while belting out the final note only to find that behind them the real stars of the show were out and beginning their callisthenic routines. The status of the Grand Final, which now attracts the likes of Lesley Garrett and Madness to perform, shows how far the production values have come. For the 2006 season, Huddersfield will break more new ground by having their 'match-day experience' sponsored by the nearby hugely popular interactive children's museum Eureka!

Sponsorship profiles generally began to change, as they had to, from the traditional beer and cigarettes image. In came the likes of Compaq, Hewlett Packard, Sainsbury's and, perhaps most significantly, Virgin, when Richard Branson was convinced of the sport's potential and took a controlling interest in London Broncos. For the launch of Super League II in London, he was joined by fellow multi-millionaires Paul Thompson and Dave Whelan while, in a new spirit of enterprise, H. & C. Saatchi were appointed to help market the competition. When British Gas agreed to endorse the Great Britain side in 1997, their marketing director Simon Waugh commented, 'Rugby League has transformed itself and we can identify with that. They have re-engineered the way the game is played to make it more entertaining and to give it more appeal for spectators.' Sponsorship even extended to the stadiums with Castleford's Wheldon Road becoming the Jungle, renamed after an internet company, and in 2006 Headingley adding the word Carnegie in an historic link up with the city's metropolitan university, who provided finance to help rebuild the famous old ground complete with the provision of lecture rooms. New stadiums came on stream to replace two of the most character-laden, intimidating venues; Wilderspool, with its distinctive 'zoo', in Warrington and The Boulevard, and its notorious 'threepenny stand', at Hull. Far from their gleaming new Halliwell Jones and Kingston Communications edifices lacking the same vitality and advantage, their state-of-the-art facilities and unrestricted views have attracted almost double the average amount of fans and far more families and supporters of visiting clubs. Several clubs extended their commercial operations to include branded town centre shops; St Helens reported 'excellent trading figures' over the Christmas period in 2005 that, like a number of their rivals, included significantly increased season ticket sales.

Academy curtain raisers, initially televised by Sky, have further enhanced the pre-match ritual and countered inevitable admission price increases, although a common season ticket for juniors where their home purchase allows free admission at away grounds has shown a great awareness of the importance attached to attracting the next generation. Similarly, text voting for the Man of the Match, growing e-commerce opportunities and highly professional official internet sites have increased direct fan involvement and added value to the relationship.

Not everything has worked; the ill-fated *Supermag*, which attempted to produce and distribute a common, generic match programme, was discontinued after barely two months. The 'new' game even became identified by distinctive terminology and, although irksome to some, suddenly offence, hard yards, hit ups, marker tackles, big hits and off-loads were becoming the norm when the outcome was debated post match by the coaches and later, in the playgrounds, when the weekend's action was reviewed through adolescent eyes. To capitalise on the greater need for a marketing strategy – the initial slogan of 'same game, different attitude' should have been 'stronger game, better attitude' – the Super League clubs set up their own company in September 1996, Rugby League (Europe) Ltd, to exclusively run the competition's affairs, although the Rugby Football League was given a stake in it. In an effort to address the traditionally thorny question of capricious, staid and often stereotypical media coverage, which to a degree had returned after the initial love-in waned, RLE's first appointment as chief executive was former *Daily Mirror* and then *Sunday Mirror* editor Colin Myler. He was part of the famous dynasty that had contributed so much to the on and off-field success at Widnes over the years and was based in London. He was bullish about his aims and objectives. 'I'm here to take the game forward. I'm afraid nostalgia won't save it. The Super League clubs felt that the new league hadn't been marketed strongly enough. Super League was not a brand that could be immediately associated with its product. I'm here to make it a corporate image and to bring new income into the game. Sky has given the game a nationwide platform that allows us to sell it from London. If you knock on the door of a multinational corporation looking for backing they are likely to say "rugby league is not our market." Now we can begin to convince them that it is. The game can and will fit their profile. League needed a younger profile. Now the game is a fast, open spectacle, attractive to spectators and sponsors alike. I want to move away from selling individual clubs and start selling Super League as a single entity of which the clubs are constituent parts. I think any prejudice that exists (in the national media) is with a small 'p'. I don't believe sports editors spike all rugby league stories, but I do believe we need to push them and sell them more positively.'

He, like so many of those who followed into the marketing role, failed to stay long enough to make that impact but the major problem in the early years centred on the word 'Europe' in the organisation's title. With under-resourced and isolated Paris struggling by the middle of the second season

– RFL senior executive Harry Jepson, who was sent across to help them, recalled that it was only ever a side not a club – the global dimension had an increasingly hollow ring to it. From the start brash claims of expansion had been espoused, and halfway through the opening campaign Maurice Lindsay had said, 'The board of directors are not going to weaken their resolve to restructure the game. We should be aiming at Cardiff and Dublin for next year. Eventually I can see us going to sixteen teams but I'd like to reserve that final place for a very special application such as Barcelona or Milan.' Newcastle, under Sir John Hall's idea of creating an all-embracing sporting club for the North-East, were on their way in for 1997 but also never quite arrived. Towards the end of Super League II, franchises were again on the agenda with concern simmering that with the competition looking essentially like a slimmed-down version of the old First Division, Rupert Murdoch's benevolence, patience and interest would lessen. Despite increasing viewing figures, the fear began to grow that if the game could not increase its sphere of influence, and by implication Sky its satellite dish coverage, it would be terminally cast adrift. A leaked letter from retiring News Corporation head Ken Cowley to Maurice Lindsay in September 1997 just before a full council meeting, purportedly said, 'The only way we will get a return on our investment is if Super League develops into a better product and delivers a new viewing audience to television. An elite national league that is attractive to a television audience is vital to your future. Your plans must include new areas.' Thus yet another plan was adopted for franchising to be introduced in time for the 1999 season, with a new independent commission evaluating and overseeing bids from both existing and potential new clubs that had to be lodged by 1 May 1998. Glasgow (and subsequently Hibs in Edinburgh), Dublin, Birmingham, the North-East and South-West, including Wales, where interest had been declared in Cardiff and Swansea, were all said to have been targeted areas with new-monied consortia showing interest. Conversely, the likes of Castleford, Oldham, Halifax and even Warrington were supposedly put on notice that their facilities and size did not fit the overall profile or blueprint. Even outside the elite, those clubs who had been excluded were revisiting ideas that had seemed so unpalatable. Dewsbury president Jack Addy noted, 'If we want to go forward we're going to have to merge whether we like it or not. The alternative is to remain in the First or Second Division forever. Sometimes tradition does get in the way,' while vociferous Super League opponents Keighley looked at becoming the Pennine Cougars and switching their operation to Burnley.

If finding the right structure was proving to be a major stumbling block, the greatest missed marketing opportunity was the chance to change the name of the sport. Say the word 'rugby' and invariably the uninitiated or casually interested assume that talk is of rugby union. Over the last century, the establishment code almost exclusively annexed the sport's mythical birthplace as its own, further marginalising the standing and impact of the thirteen-a-side version. Very little irritates a staunch league devotee more than news items or features, particularly in broadcasting, that just refer to 'rugby' when they are talking about union. With 'Super' and 'League' the opportunity presented itself for the reinvention to be made complete. The two words convey and define exactly what the sport is and if the word 'rugby' had been permanently dropped, then a definite rebranding would have been made so much easier. Enormous effort over the past ten years has gone into making Super League unique and distinctive. With a bit more foresight and imagination, the top level could have been the 'Super League Premiership' and the lower leagues 'Super League National One' and so on through the pyramid structure. Again, history is a guide. In 1922 the council's members voted to change the name of the sport from Northern Union to rugby league in an effort to establish uniqueness. It would have meant some pride being swallowed by those outside the elite in the early days, when resistance to being excluded was at its highest, but by now the benefits for all would have been substantial.

The key early battleground to be won, though, was the contentious switch to summer. There was a steady increase in average crowds but, crucially, the demographic appeared to be changing. From being a sport for men, Super League was becoming a family sport as more women and face-painted and bedecked children were seen and less hostility felt on the terraces. Inevitably, some traditional, predominantly older male support was lost but, with grounds easier to get to in the light and better weather, more people were seemingly prepared to make the effort and a cultural transformation was starting to take place. One of the primary movers behind the seasonal exchange – although with a playing campaign currently running from February to November it is hardly accurate to call it a summer sport – was Gary Hetherington. There is barely a role in the game that the former Wakefield, York, Wigan, Leeds, Huddersfield, Hunslet and Kent Invicta goal-kicking hooker has not undertaken. This one-time chairman of the Professional Players Association, when struggling to be given an opportunity in the coaching ranks set about successfully forming his own club, Sheffield Eagles. At the Don Valley Stadium he did everything; player, coach, administrator, salesman before becoming chief executive at Leeds Rhinos in 1997. An assistant Great Britain coach under Ellery Hanley in 1994, he has also been president of the RFL and a leading light on most of the committees and boards that have run the game in the current era. 'The move to summer was inevitable. Initially there were a few lone voices for it, including myself, the traditionalists were not really looking for solutions; they just dismissed it out of hand, saying that the grounds would be too hard and threw up a multitude of other reasons. We had to systematically look at each one in a scientific way to disprove them all. But because of the need for change there was a growing feeling that summer rugby may provide an option so the hardened attitude against it was softening. The RFL set up a working party to look at the move to summer made up of myself, Jim Quinn from Oldham and Bradford's Chris Caisley. We were all for it anyway so it was a recommendation that was going to happen, News money just brought everything forward by a year.'

Always a lateral thinker, during the hardships of the mid-1990s he had variously proposed a three-division format, the scrapping of the Challenge Cup to be replaced by an Australian-type Grand Final and play-offs, and a mid-season winter break. 'There was a real concern in the game because it wasn't moving forward; attendances weren't healthy and club finances were one of the major driving forces towards change because they were horrendous. Roy Waudby had done a survey on them and concluded they were in a perilous state – some clubs were spending 110 per cent of their income on players' wages, for example – so there was a need for a salary cap and financial management because a number of the clubs were perilously close to folding. There needed to be change; the concept of three divisions was to better prepare sides who were coming up to the top flight and in that respect it worked extremely well. Hitherto we had such a wide variety of standards. Those getting relegated from the first tier were coming up against some exceptionally weak clubs that gave them no form of preparation to go back into the Championship and ultimately survival. Wigan's dominance was equally a factor but how could you break it? Leeds and Widnes had both tried to chase them but had ended up virtually bankrupt and that was a major concern. We had a background of fundamental issues prevent-ing the game from going forward and there was a real worry that, unless there was radical change, we could end up becoming a real minority sport, which was always going to be there but in a very, very small, limited way.'

Not surprisingly, he was a staunch supporter of the Super League con-cept from the start. 'It was a godsend for the game, although ultimately it got managed in a really poor way from both the top at the RFL and the clubs them-selves, who squandered a lot of money, but there is no doubt that it presented the game with a once-in-a-lifetime golden opportunity for radical change for the better. The figures were so huge compared to what we were used to and for some clubs it created more problems than it solved. Full-time professionalism was one of the immediate results that brought its own problems because clubs and players didn't really know what being full time was all about. Prior to that only Wigan had been, which meant they had all the best players, which gave them their dominance, and so were Leeds but only in the sense that their players didn't have any other job but they weren't training as full-time athletes as such. Other clubs were then a mixture of both. They had some players who were paid well enough to consider rugby as their primary source of income and others in the squad who could only train in the evenings. Super League wasn't a breakaway, it was all done very constitutionally but it was emotive; Maurice Lindsay pulled together the chairmen of the clubs who were to form the elite Super League but it was also going through the RFL Council and all the clubs voted on the proposals. I remember the council meeting where the proposal was put and everyone put up their hands and said that the first thing that the game had to do was accept the offer and then decide how to apportion it. That was a difficult one because News Corporation wasn't giving the money to the game; they were saying "this is for twelve teams to form a Super League". Their interest wasn't the social game or the grassroots game, it was solely for an elite division. What the sport had to wrestle with was how do you look after the whole but also create that top strata in itself? Inevitably there was self interest but it was a professional clubs' decision.'

Despite his Sheffield operation being initially paired with local rivals Doncaster, Hetherington could be a somewhat dispassionate observer of the initial merger proposals. 'The feeling was that if you weren't going to be in this new Super League then you had virtually disappeared because promotion and relegation was coming off the agenda. We were looking at the creation of super clubs and if you were not in it at the outset then you were never going to be, so there was a scramble for places. The way it was sold to us, and now I would question its validity, was News said it had to be twelve teams and to include ones from France and London. I'm not so sure that was a condition on their part because I don't believe that they put many conditions on at all. I think they were just saying to the game you sort us out a Super League and Maurice, who was the driving force, probably had the best intentions in the world when he said there needed to be the European capitals dimension. That in itself created its own difficulties because you are elevating two unprepared sides into a competition where you are already reducing the number of places for heartland clubs to ten from a previous base of sixteen in the old First Division. That's where all the debate started about what should constitute membership of the Super League; surely it can't be a club playing in poor facilities in front of 800 people and officials started to think that the only way they could survive was to merge with their next-door neighbour, but nobody had a real stomach for merger because there is no such thing, in truth. In hindsight, the opportunity we missed was that we didn't have any clear thinking about a strategy of how to utilise this money effectively, it was all given to the clubs without conditions put on it, which was a mistake in itself. Ultimately it was an expedient decision to put the ten highest-placed clubs at the end of the previous campaign into Super League. That was a convenient cut off that did preserve the so-called bigger clubs. Sheffield weren't a big club but was seen as one who could become one because of its city status, which fitted the mould. It wasn't ideal; looking back we should have worked towards creating the competition a year later, to buy ourselves more time because it was hurriedly done and rushed into. There were so many unknowns and uncertainties and we were ill-prepared as a game and as clubs and we suffered initially because of that, there is no doubt about that. We were too preoccupied with our own problems to worry about the split going on in Australia and if we were seen as a pawn in that, so what? There were eighty-seven million good reasons to be. We were saddened to see how the events unfolded there but they were beyond our control anyway. You'd have to question how well or badly the loyalty payments scenario was managed. Inevitably the game was under the possible threat of losing a lot of its best players to the ARL and while that was an inevitable consequence of the split over there it just meant that money was flowing straight out of the game. It was done in a manner that again hinted at vested interest; the Wigan players got looked after but the St Helens and Leeds ones claimed that they didn't.'

Once the initial maelstrom had subsided, he found that News Corporation were quick to offer backing and support to the new competition. 'They were impressive in terms of their perceived enthusiasm for the game; they felt that they could elevate it into becoming an extremely popular, more of a global, sport. They talked a good game and being such a major company in the world you would expect them to be able to deliver and, to be fair to them, they supported the World Club Championship, a very inventive, creative concept that was ahead of its time, unfortunately, but they backed it to the hilt. They also recognised the need to invest in personnel. They took all the chief executives to Los Angeles – flying business class and putting us up at the Ritz Carlton Hotel in Marina Del Ray – to meet our Australian counterparts. That was a unique experience and, credit to them, they were putting an investment in over and above simply giving money. The meeting had two purposes; to bring together all the clubs from both hemispheres and to make them feel part of a new global brand. It showed how there was a role for all of us to expand Super League into new territories and how they could help us facilitate that and that we had the future of the game in our hands. It was also an attempt to invest in our ability to be able to promote and market a new brand, a new game, and what better people to look at than the Americans? It was a really valuable initiative. We looked at the major US sports from a number of levels; promotion and marketing the game, facility development, the legal side, we had a presentation from Michael Jordan's agent who cost a fortune to hire, we flew up to Candlestick Stadium to watch an NFL game and went to Anaheim to study the Mighty Ducks' operation. There were a number of impressive speakers including Jerry Jones, billionaire owner, president and general manager of the Dallas Cowboys, who outlined the professional sports business and industry and keynote addresses from the likes of the Chicago Bulls, baseball's Cleveland Indians and Orlando Magic's basketball team. It was important because we had not really been a fully-fledged professional sport and we were going into the great unknown in many ways. We were talking to the likes of Nike about the potential for worldwide merchandising of replica shirts for the first time, for example, but equally we were trying to integrate our own ideas in what we could learn from the Australians and vice versa.'

Come the opening match of Super League, he was uniquely placed to assess the impact made watching his Eagles side play the supporting role on an unforgettable occasion in Paris. 'It's a night that will stay with me forever, although when the first draft fixtures came out it was to be Paris *v.* Oldham, and that didn't quite ring true to launch a new global era being beamed around the world. The thought was that maybe a bigger impact could be created with a more recognisable name and probably a team that Paris had a chance of beating. We'd had a good year and achieved our highest-ever finish in the league the previous season and, although Super League meant a big turnaround for us moving full time, we still had a pretty competitive team. There was great excitement going over to the French capital. We took about 2,000 people, which were more than the number of fans we actually had, but it was a terrific expedition and adventure. Nobody knew what the crowd was going to be; 5,000 were expected then revisions took the figure up to 8,000 and on the night it was just terrific to see people flooding into the stadium and they created a tremendous atmosphere. As the coach you just want to concentrate on winning and we started pretty well, created and bombed a lot of chances and even though we were leading, after about fifteen minutes I looked at my assistant coach Steve Ferres and I told him there was no way we could win. As a coach you just get a feeling if things are going to go your way or not. I'm a big believer in fate and destiny and it was just their night even though we were the better side, it was almost inevitable that they were going to triumph. Although that was disappointing for us, it was a great thrill for the competition. I remember when I was interviewed in the aftermath commenting that it couldn't have got off to a better start and was terrific for rugby league in France. It was an historic, significant, thrilling night for the game but unfortunately they weren't able to maintain it for a whole variety of reasons. It was a bold decision to include Paris but as we all know in business and sport, you have to have firm foundations and that had none at all. It was wrought with internal politics. Paris weren't supported by the French Federation or the clubs over there who didn't want a team in the capital but down in the south, but that had not been gone into. We'd not looked at the cultural aspects and simply creating an Australian-based team in a corner of Paris led by English administrators coming into a competitive environment was always going to be a recipe for failure, unfortunately, and that remains a missed opportunity for the game purely through haste and lack of planning. Winning matches might have got them through some of those troubles but it was doomed.'

Another side struggling to make an initial impact was fallen giants Leeds, whose reticence over the switch to summer had seemed to infuse the whole club. 'People don't realise how close to closure the business was. I'd been speaking to the board there with a view to taking on the franchise of Leeds Rugby League. I'd got to a stage at Sheffield where, for the first time, I felt that the club needed a new direction and was capable of managing itself without me and that I needed a new challenge. Super League presented the Eagles with a great opportunity and now there were people interested in taking ownership. I didn't have the means to take on the historic debt and other problems at Leeds where they were losing money every year. The idea was that I would take all the rugby business; the players, coaches and so on, and set up a new company for that, remain at Headingley and pay the Leeds CFA a rent to play there while they retained control of the bars, catering, advertising revenue etc but they wouldn't have to worry about funding and maintaining the team. At the same time they were talking to Paul Caddick about possibly taking over the site. Their ultimate solution was to sell the whole operation; the rugby league team to Leeds United to play at Elland Road, but the rugby union team wouldn't have had any-where to go. Yorkshire cricket had already decided to move to Durkar anyway and to realise the value of the site for £6 million to pay off the debt. There was a reaction from the fans and as a result Alf Davies put Paul and myself together. We talked about the potential, the problems and everything else and all Paul's advisers were saying "don't do it." I knew we could turn the side around and that there was a market for rugby league in the city.

Yorkshire cricket were tied by their existing lease and the union offered potential for a winter business, but it was a desperately disjointed operation. The cost of servicing the debt was a massive millstone and there was low morale, an unsuccessful team that had just avoided relegation and a dwindling support base because of that and a lack of belief about where the club was going. They hadn't embraced the idea of summer rugby enthusiastically and made quite a lot of mistakes, and that attitude pervaded through to the fans. The club was in a pretty desolate state, I remember going to watch the last home game of the 1996 campaign and I knew I would be taking over but was due to go on tour first with Great Britain and didn't want anybody to know. Leeds were playing Workington – who were destined to finish bottom – and the attendance was just over 4,900. The gate receipts would have been miniscule and I walked round every facility and part of the ground just to get a feel of it all. The tables had been set up because sponsors had paid a year's membership but it was almost like a ghost town, there was nobody there and there was real sense of going nowhere with those left just coming out of habit. In many ways though, that made it a real challenge – in some ways you are better coming from the basement. I could see from the due diligence I'd done when auditing the players' contracts that they were managing their assets really badly and that the players were on ridiculous amounts of money and that the staff numbers were too high. While I knew that it would take time, respecting existing contract arrangements, I was sure we could turn that part of the business around but, in terms of marketing, it was all about trying to give people a sense of belief. I reassured anyone who was speculating that their jobs would go, including the coaching staff, that it was a fresh start, and for the first couple of months I did nothing at all other than look and listen. Eventually I put three lists together of those things I felt were being done well, those that weren't being done well and those that weren't being done at all and should be and that was by far and away the biggest list. There were so many responsibilities that nobody was carrying. For example, I called together a meeting to look at the sale of season tickets and asked who was in charge of the marketing plan and strategy and Mike Hodgson – who ran the ticket office and is a lovely man, a really good operator – came up with the classic response, "we don't sell season tickets, people come and buy them." I could see then that there was a bit of work to be done and there was a need for reassurance, support and direction. From a marketing point of view the key thing to run the business properly was to say that we didn't have a magic wand to create overnight success but it would be a building process, that's my whole ethos. The significant element was the rebranding as the Rhinos, which we did at a very early stage and very thoroughly – it almost went to another name but that's one of the very few times when Paul came in and actually had a big influence – and we had a marketing company working down the line. The Ronnie mascot followed and although there was a fair amount of opposition at the time it was a bold move that repositioned the club and gave it a different, recognisable identity. The other key factor was to immediately put in place a community programme. It was obvious that the only way the public in and around the city could access Headingley was to pay to watch a sporting event and the club were doing very little to go out into the community and we needed to completely reverse that. We invested in getting the message out that we did care about the game in the city, particularly the junior clubs and in the schools. We eventually convinced Leeds City Council to join us in appointing a rugby league development officer, all as part of a big community outreach programme. That didn't have an immediate impact in terms of a recognisable return but it did show people that we cared. On top of that we made some significant signings, the first of which was Paul Sterling from Hull, but I remember getting about thirty-odd letters about that. Most of them were really well constructed and argued but they all basically said "is this the standard of player we can expect to come to Leeds, someone who is thirty-two years old?" We swapped him for Matt Schultz and got £15,000 as well, it was one of the best deals I have ever done. That may not have got us off to the best start in the eyes of the public but then we followed it up with the captures of Kiwi international Richie Blackmore, Ryan Sheridan and Anthony Farrell from Sheffield and overseas players with a great work ethic like Martin Masella and Wayne Collins, which immediately gave the place a different feel. They replaced ones who had been here too long, were coming to the end of their careers and needed to go. We then signed Iestyn Harris for a club-record fee, which was a major statement.'

Hetherington was conscious that the initial recruitment not only had to instil the right dressing room culture but it also had to be prudent with the salary cap coming in for Super League III in 1998. 'The salary cap has been a very significant factor. When you consider that Wigan's wage bill at their peak of dominance was £3.1 million how on earth could you have a competitive competition? It has taken some time but it is only now that clubs generally are realising that the cap imposes a real management skill, it's not just a case of restricting how much they can spend. It creates a discipline within clubs and means that you can't simply focus on the players. There have to be other aspects of the club you need to address. It has added a competitive edge to the League and closed the gap between clubs, it has been vital to building a sustainable competition and viable clubs. I've been a supporter of the 20/20 rule, it's done an exceptionally good job, although I think it's less relevant now that the Super League has settled down and levelled out a little bit, but nevertheless it has created more of a spread of talent and restricted the clubs who can afford strength in depth of senior players and it forces you into putting aspiring young players in positions twenty-one to twenty-five in your squad. In a club environment it gives something for people to strive for; we've got forty youngsters fighting to get those spots but they know they've only got a limited life span to make the top twenty and if they don't they'll have to move on because they'll be replaced by somebody else. It's created a real conveyor belt system for clubs who really do produce young players.'

The opening three seasons of Super League had seen the sport turn a corner but there were still significant problems relating to the fallout. A snapshot of where the game had reached can be seen when examining the evidence given to the House of Commons Culture, Media and Sport Committee looking at the future of professional rugby, which met at Wigan Investment Centre on 28 June 1999. All sectors of the game were represented, providing written memorandums before answering questions from the assembled MPs. For the Players' Association, despite the top performers now being able to make a living out of the code, there were still some obvious concerns. 'Historical debts and the inability of clubs to separate ambition and reality mean that the constant threat of financial insecurity is prevalent. Many of the clubs have struggled to create a steady stream of income capable of sustaining the salaries needed to fund full-time professionalism. Bright lights for the future are Leeds Rhinos, closely followed by Bradford Bulls, with various income streams backed by sound community investment working in harmony with corporate development. Modern facilities will assist the long-term financial future of the game, as cultivating the corporate sponsor is essential for the game's future.' Their chairman, former GB athlete and future Bradford chief executive Abi Ekoku, added, 'On the field, the product is thriving. Professionalism has allowed the players and coaches to produce an exhilarating product, which I believe is second to none in terms of sheer entertainment. The players have always made it sellable – that has been the greatest asset of the game, the product.'

Administratively, the game was fractured, each level having its own management arm but Super League Europe's (the name had been changed to reflect that it was only concerned with the elite level) chairman Chris Caisley was adamant that his organisation was necessary. 'There is a need to focus on the elite side of the sport, both in terms of income-generating opportunity, in terms of managing its day-to-day affairs in a more cohesive manner and in terms of perhaps distancing itself from negative aspects that sometimes come about from the media in relation to other sides of the sport, the politics if you like. We want to get away from all that. We have done that successfully. We are able to focus very much on Super League issues for the benefit of the shareholders, i.e. the member clubs.' He was supported by new RFL chief executive Neil Tunnicliffe, 'The truth is that were Super League, the competition, to have remained under the auspices of the Rugby Football League then there would still have been dedicated staff committed to the marketing and commercial exploitation of the competition. Within the Rugby Football League we have an unincorporated members' association, which is a more or less perfect radical democracy. The will of the member clubs is the one that will reign. I think since then (the formation of SLE) you can point to the very real successes of Super League. They have negotiated a very substantial sponsorship for the competition through JJB Sports. They have expanded their broadcast portfolio quite considerably both within this country, with the new domestic broadcast agreements and abroad, taking the game to Australasia and to Europe to raise awareness of it. In terms of our own operations within the Rugby Football League it has enabled us to concentrate perhaps more effectively on other areas of the game that need greater exposure.'

In truth it was an uneasy alliance that was holding back concerted progress, which could only be achieved by a unified administration. The catalyst that brought that to a head were the large, unexpected losses made by the badly mismanaged World Cup in 2000, which sought to focus minds, not least that of Gary Hetherington. 'There had been a coup to remove Maurice Lindsay from the RFL and overnight he did his own deal with Chris Caisley and came over to Super League. I was on the board of Super League at the time and supported Chris as chairman because he wanted that to happen. That was a remarkable sequence of events and with the RFL being weakly managed by its board and management and SLE developing and enhancing their structures, the two bodies started moving in opposite directions. There was no synergy or support. The RFL was getting deeper into debt and what the World Cup did was to showcase how perilous their situation was. On the Super League board at the time, myself, Nigel Wood and Tim Adams were becoming increasingly worried. Others were rejoicing in it but we were then joined by Shane Richardson, who was another who was particularly concerned about what was best for the game as a whole. Looking at what had happened in Australia, we couldn't afford for such a scenario to continue and, of course, we still had a huge vested interest in the RFL anyway as members of it and taking part in the Challenge Cup and providing the players for the international game. A real power struggle began to emerge as to which direction we should go in but we made representations to Sir Rodney Walker, then chairman of the RFL, about the need to pull the administration together into a single, unified governing body. The only way of making it happen was to constitutionally bring the RFL to a crisis point, which initially meant Sir Rodney coming clean about the problems faced and the need to create a working party to identify them and produce recommendations about how to solve them. We then needed an implementation group to bring those changes about and offer him a feathered landing. We laid out all the strategy and Sir Rodney managed the process really well, chairing a group that was criticising the organisation he was responsible for but he had such weak people in there that they could only fall over. The initial strategic review board meetings were some of the most clear-thinking I have ever been involved in. We brought representatives in from every section of the game; Ray French from the BBC sat on it, Richard Evans of Featherstone and other representatives from the NFP clubs had a say and we all took our individual club hats off to look at the wider picture in terms of divisional structures, funding allocation and so on. Super League wasn't part of that process, it was a new, independent little group and out of that came the strategic implementation committee and that's where Maurice came back in, which was good because it was better to have him on board and helping drive the proposal through than it was to have him resisting it on the outside. Again that was a really good body; Sir Rodney was nominally chairman but rarely came to the meetings, myself, Maurice, Tim Adams, Nigel Wood, Malcolm White from Swinton who was the RFL president at the time and was really constructive. We effectively took over control of the RFL. We looked at everything including the management structures and set about giving it some stability, which also meant stopping it haemorrhaging money. It was about at the stage where they had to go to the clubs to survive in terms of them either sanctioning an overdraft that they would all be party to or writing individual cheques out. Inevitability there were some redundancies but there had been a lot of squandering of resources, which we managed to bring to a head and slowly the strategy took shape that brought about an independent board. The sport has to be seen to be independent; people will never be convinced that decisions are made in the best interests of the game otherwise. Also, while there are fairly powerful figures running individual clubs, there has to be a sovereign element outside of that. We set about the search for a new executive chairman, which was a crucial appointment. We used head hunters and interviewed some very high-profile people (including Graham Kelly who had recently left the Football Association) but, to be honest, were never really comfortable with the candidates put before us. Then Richard Lewis came up on the rails at the last minute. There was a sort of a quiet confidence that he would be able to deal with the game's problems and structures in a fair-minded way without looking to hog the limelight. The other significant person in that is Nigel Wood who, unlike Richard, does have a feel for and understanding of the sport's background and culture, which makes him an exceptionally good number two and the combination complimentary to each other.'

The changes Gary Hetherington has helped bring about at Leeds are an indication of how well the game has managed to adapt and sell the Super League concept to an ever more willing audience made up of traditional fans and new converts. 'We are now looking to do a lot more market research to give a better picture of who our customers are, their likes and dislikes and where they come from. Our last survey indicated that around seventeen per cent of our crowd travel more than twenty miles to a game and if you'd undertaken that count ten years ago it would have given a very different figure. We are now reaching out to a much broader market and we hope we are developing fan loyalty. We are a very open organisation and there is now far less rumour and innuendo about the place; part of our mission statement is to make a profit, we unashamedly set out to do that because we stated where and how we want to invest it. The East Stand – the first new construction at the ground for over seventy years – and now the proposed North Stand could not have been considered if we were not making money. We try to promote from within and encourage and develop a local pride, not only with the players coming through but with staffing and I think we do genuinely try and engage the supporters with regular newsletters, opportunities through the website and the setting up of things like the veterans club to give them a sense of belonging because, at the end of the day, it is really their club. Paul and myself are merely guardians. As I remind our staff constantly, all our customers don't have to come and we have to continually make them feel that this is their club and not just a form of entertainment. It is more than that, there is a spiritual bond. There is a demand for modern facilities and that is not just seating but also things like quality toilets and food. It's the whole ambiance of the place, and that's something we've tried very hard to do. Headingley will never be the biggest stadium in the country, we don't want it to be or need it be, but we can strive to make it the most vibrant and atmospheric on a consistent basis. We want it to be a place where people enjoy being a part of and coming to and can feel it's got a friendly and hospitable ambiance.'

Sometimes it needs an unfettered eye to evaluate how successful the whole process has been. As part of the commemoration of the Rhinos being World Club Champions in 2005, world-famous composer Carl Davis was commissioned, in partnership with the city council, to compose a new piece of music for the team to run out to for the 2006 campaign. To gather inspiration he attended his first ever match, at Headingley on a balmy mid-July evening, with Salford as the visitors. For the majority of those present the outcome was a perfunctory 54–14 win by Leeds but the chief guest was absolutely enthralled. 'It was amazing, very different to what I expected. I had an impression it was going to be rough, muddy and very violent but it was a beautiful night and a beautiful game. I was particularly impressed by the way the sides kept pulling back into formation, the constant movement of the vertical lines. I had a wonderful view of the action from the centre of the grandstand and it looked extraordinary, the speed and the tension combined with the teamwork, co-operation and interplay between the players was magical. I thought the participation, colour and atmosphere from the public was fantastic; it was incredibly serious, exciting and thrilling. I needed to know more in order to get a real feel for the piece and I realised that any march would only be a triumphal one after the game is over, before that it is constant action for an hour and a half. It worked on a number of levels; I was introduced to some old fans who have been supporting the club since 1926 and they spoke with such obvious pride that I realised the depth that went into their experience, which I had not previously understood. It was very personal, varied and human and the whole ground had a very homely feel to it helped by the fact that, I'm told, most of the players are locals, which is very important. I don't think I will need to make a demarcation between the sizes of the players and certain instruments; it is not intended to be as literal as that. When you're at such a dramatic, emotional event that can only be beneficial to creating a form of music; the two feed off each other. Any interpretation I may put on it will not be as good as the game itself for the fans but hopefully it will convey the spirit and teamwork.'

TOP 10 INNOVATIONS
(ranked in no particular order)

1 THE VIDEO REFEREE
Even he doesn't always get it spot on, but there is no doubt that the use of video technology has been a great asset to the sport and generally a thrilling addition at grounds. Roll on blanket coverage.

2 40/20 RULE
Rugby League has never been afraid to tinker with its rules for the benefit of the spectacle and this reward for precision kicking skill is the best of its modern measures.

3 GRAND FINAL

The tired old Premiership format was ditched in favour of this concept in 1998. Some said that the Challenge Cup final provided sufficient drama for one season, but three full houses at the end of Super League's first decade would suggest otherwise.

4 TRI-NATIONS SERIES

Although not strictly Super League, a concept that stuttered in its infancy – before the Millennium – has quickly become established as a success in showcasing international rugby league, with New Zealand's unexpected, emphatic win in 2005 giving the highest level of the game the shake-up it required.

5 SUBSTITUTIONS: THE 'TWELVE FROM FOUR' RULE

Props who no longer play throughout might not agree but another successful tinkering with the rules has enabled spectators see league at full throttle for eighty minutes.

6 RESCHEDULING OF THE CHALLENGE CUP FINAL

Having travelled successfully around Britain in recent years, the game's most historic event was switched from its traditional spring date to finally fall into line towards the climax of the summer season. An August Bank Holiday slot appears to be perfect timing for an old, dear friend.

7 SALARY CAP

A subject that still courts controversy among Super League's member clubs, but one that has undoubtedly helped to encourage both fiscal prudence in a game that was almost bankrupt and also showcase youth development.

8 TECHNOLOGY FOR OFFICIALS

The stakes in professional sport are so high that, as with the video referee, any assistance given to the man in the middle can only be a positive. The 'miking-up' of the referee for TV, plus the links between him, his touch judges and the fourth official has been a boon and valuable insight.

9 TRANS-WORLD INTERNATIONAL

The Rugby Football League were keen to maximise the commercial value of the sport when renegotiating its TV contract in 2004, and their use of TWI as an agent in the process was a smart move that achieved the desired result.

10 JOHN INNES

Well, not strictly John Innes – though no-one ever thought they'd hear _Nessun Dorma_ being sung with such gusto by the South Stand regulars at Headingley – but pre-match entertainment. Love it or loathe it, it is here to stay and if it helps to attract or retain paying spectators, then it has to be considered a successful addition.

FIVE

STABILITY, ON THE FIELD

'Rugby League's simplicity is its essence. At one level, a battle for territory; at another level a battle for scores and, at its most fundamental and compelling level, a battle of wills.' – The Sunday Times feature writer David Walsh

While the ministrations and machinations of administrators have variously moved forward or held back the game; the skill, honesty and commitment of the players has never been in question, in any era. When Neil Tunnicliffe took over the reins of the Rugby Football League in 1998 he commented, 'We need to get away from the situation where the outside world knows who the chief executive of the RFL is but not the Great Britain captain.' As Super League began to come to terms with the upheaval created in its wake and the new mechanisms needed to make its presence felt, one factor remained constant right from day one; the effort put into the product. Stability was eventually brought about because of adaptations on a number of fronts but the discernible annual rise in standards between the combatants was its underlying bedrock. Without a viable competition, virtually everything else would have paled into insignificance. Tracing how the sport evolved out in the middle is vital to any understanding of how the last decade can be seen as one of definable progress.

A JOURNEY THROUGH TEN SEASONS

1996 – SUPER LEAGUE I: THE SUNSHINE SPORT!

A sensational, confounding start; Paris's opening-night victory was the perfect, dramatic fillip that would lay the foundation for a thrilling new season. The following Thursday more history was made when London hosted the French, the first time two capital cities in the northern hemisphere had played each other in the sport. Those 1990s yuppies would probably have said 'It's Super

League, take it on board if you wish' and, while teams such as St Helens and Bradford did just that, Wigan's domination of the game was (only just) ended, while Leeds found the going particularly tough. Not only did that final pre-Rhinos season open a few eyes at Headingley, it also had club directors generally predicting financial trouble in future years with the playing of only eleven home games in the regular season. With coaches constantly crying out for that in the twenty-first century, it is worth remembering that Super League I did at least try to live by the decree of quality, rather than quantity.

With the reinvention of the game came the rebirth of Bradford, who at the end of the winter era were averaging crowds of around 5,000 at Odsal, but with the addition of the suffix 'Bulls', and the chance to play at a time of year when the fans could actually see the players without risk of losing them in the habitual mists, spectators turned up in double those numbers to see them play Leeds, St Helens and Halifax, while a thirty-five-year high was registered when Wigan went home on the end of a 20-12 reverse. By the time Super League kicked off Bradford were already on their way to Wembley for the first time in over twenty years and, although they were to lose the big one, they were only beaten on three more occasions to finish third in the final table. Having already seen the Challenge Cup slip from their grasp after a remarkable eight-year hold on it, pre-Warriors Wigan ended 1996 with only the old Premiership trophy, losing out by one point for the first ever Super League title to arch-rivals St Helens. Though for most clubs this would still have been an excellent season, Wigan's high standards meant that the beginning of a new era signalled the end of theirs, something that they have not since recaptured. Perennial gladiators of those great Central Park sides, such as Shaun Edwards and Martin Offiah, began to look for pastures new, and only two five-figure attendances at Central Park suggested that some of the fans had the same idea too. Nevertheless, Jason Robinson, Henry Paul and Kris Radlinski had superb seasons for the cherry-and-whites, the latter earning himself a call-up on the ill-fated 1996 tour of New Zealand, Fiji and Papua New Guinea.

Like the sport, Leeds went through a transitional period in 1996, though the club had much less immediate success than the game. With legends Ellery Hanley and Garry Schofield now departed, the firepower was blunted. Dean Bell's appointment as head coach did not get off to the best of starts, with the club's first four league matches ending in defeat, and the Loiners won only six games all season. While Headingley had its troubles, things could not have been better at Knowsley Road, with St Helens finally emerging from the huge shadow that had been cast by the successes of their arch-rivals Wigan, to land the Super League-Challenge Cup double. In Shaun McRae, Saints seemed to have found almost the perfect coach. Building upon a typical Australian bedrock of defence, McRae encouraged his players to continue with the flair that has become a prerequisite at the club. In addition, the former Canberra, Australia and New Zealand conditioner had a positive effect on those around him, his gregarious personality winning over fans and the media alike. Saints boasted a pack led by Chris Joynt and a young Keiron Cunningham, and with Bobbie Goulding and Karle Hammond calling the shots at half-back, and backs including Alan Hunte, Anthony Sullivan, Steve Prescott and Paul Newlove – who crossed for 28 tries from centre to top that particular chart – the points piled up. A record of 20 wins and only 2 defeats in Super League saw St Helens narrowly take the crown, and a remarkable 40-32 Challenge Cup final defeat of Bradford, after being 26-12 down with just twenty-three minutes remaining, marked Saints out as the team that had adapted the quickest to the summer era. Meanwhile, propping up the table were Workington – whose one season in the top flight remains the only Cumbrian club involvement in Super League – and who frankly did not stand a chance, given the list of personnel they had available. Coach Ross O'Reilly was praised for his efforts in trying to galvanise a team that included Welshman Rowland Phillips and current Leeds Rhinos coach Tony Smith, but lacked star quality. However, just two desperately tight wins against Oldham and Paris, plus a draw at home to Halifax meant they had only five points to show for their efforts, and their tenure, as far as the heartlands of the sport were concerned, was all too brief. As a footnote to all that, not only did Town slip back into Division One, but the financial ravages of trying and failing to stay in Super League meant that their slide continued, with the drop from the top flight to Division Two occurring in back-to-back seasons.

1997 – SUPER LEAGUE II: BULLDOZED!

If St Helens had been first out of the blocks in the summer era, then Bradford were only a stride behind, and the Bulls' charge gathered momentum as Super League II kicked off in March 1997. Matthew Elliott had taken over the coaching reins in August 1996 after Brian Smith had returned Down Under, and he already had his team well on the way to a second successive Challenge Cup final appearance by the time they thrashed Warrington 58-20 at Odsal to open their championship campaign. It was unlucky for Bradford that their unbeaten league and cup run came to an end in match thirteen of their season, when Saints again denied them the Challenge Cup, this time running out 32-22 winners at Wembley. After that it was business as usual for a Graeme Bradley-inspired Bulls, who passed off a dismal World Club Championship in which they lost all of their matches by continuing to pick up two Super League points at every opportunity, and the odds on them going unbeaten for the entire season were very short by the time Wigan arrived at Odsal for Bradford's final home match. Although not the force they once were, the Warriors were not about to let the newly-crowned champions have it all their own way and pulled off a 33-18 win to take a little of the shine off the homecoming party. A reverse at London a week later meant that Bradford had dropped just those four points in a magnificent season for the club, with hooker James Lowes an appropriate winner of the Man of Steel Award. Attendances at Odsal soared, with 18,387 turning up to watch them exact immediate revenge on St Helens, winning 38-18 just a week after Wembley, while all their home gates exceeded 10,000, something that would have been unthinkable two years earlier.

Chasing the Bulls home, albeit 4 wins adrift at the finish, were the London Broncos, whose finest Super League finish came in this season. With former Australian Test winger Tony Currie doing the coaching, plus a predominance of his countrymen in the playing ranks, London had a major impact in finishing runners-up with a squad that had not looked particularly strong to British observers. Terry Matterson, Peter Gill and Tony Mestrov worked the Broncos' engine room, while Scott Roskell ended the season with 19 tries, and he was ably supported by the potency of Shaun Edwards and Martin Offiah, who had headed to the capital as the sun began to set on their glittering careers, while Robbie Beazley looked a star of the future. Super League new boys Salford City Reds surpassed all expectations – posing their intent early on with a run to the Challenge Cup semi-final – and eventually finished in sixth place. Centres Scott Naylor and Nathan McAvoy impressed, while Andy Platt and Aussie Test star John Cartwright proved astute signings up front, and a young, dynamic hooker Malcolm Alker made his first-team debut. The season's improvers turned out to be Leeds, whose rise from tenth to fifth in the ranks coincided with the arrival at Headingley of Iestyn Harris, hooker Wayne Collins and winger Paul Sterling, who proved to be a revelation, scoring 20 tries. Despite losing to arch-rivals Bradford in the Challenge Cup semi-final for a second time in succession, the Rhinos showed signs of resurgence, seemingly booked for third place until defeat to St Helens and Wigan in their last two matches. Despite the improvement, coach Dean Bell – who had an uncomfortable couple of seasons in the hot seat – took a sideways move to look after youth development at the club, allowing former Fiji and Hunter Mariners coach Graham Murray to step in at the head of affairs.

1997 was also the year when Super League said goodbye to two of its clubs, with Oldham Bears and Paris both folding after finishing bottom and second bottom respectively, with Castleford just avoiding the drop on points difference. It was a disastrous campaign for Oldham who, aside from an amazing

20-16 World Club Championship success at home against North Queensland Cowboys, managed just 4 Super League wins and averaged only 3,453 through the turnstiles, to leave the competition's detractors once again asking whether the British game really did have enough talent to sustain a twelve-team league. With Paris also struggling for a second successive season and the Tigers making heavy weather of retaining their Super League status, the penultimate round of the competition proved to be both dramatic and decisive. Castleford's trip to Warrington proved to be a fruitless one, meaning that they had to wait twenty-four hours and watch as Andy Goodway's Paris St Germain hosted Oldham in the relegation decider. Despite a gallant effort the Bears simply could not raise their game sufficiently, and Goodway sent his former club tumbling out of the top flight following a 23-12 success, ensuring Castleford's safety into the bargain. Relegation confirmed the game's worst fears, as Oldham were forced to liquidate, reforming for the start of the 1998 season in Division Two. Despite missing the drop, the Paris St Germain experiment ended, with Super League chiefs deciding not to re-admit the club for Super League III, with the promise of reconsideration for a return after a twelve-month sabbatical. History records that return never materialised.

1998 – SUPER LEAGUE III: GRAND FINAL FEVER!

1998 was the year when Huddersfield (for whom Garry Schofield became the only coaching casualty of the campaign) and Hull made their entrances into Super League, and Gateshead Thunder were awarded a place and had to move quickly to get everything in situ for the following season. The competition was also allotted a three-week mid-season break, originally intended for international competition, but once the logistics of that proved too difficult as the Australian competition reunified, the Super League management decided to use the time to take the game 'on the road' as a promotional vehicle. Gateshead International Stadium, Cardiff Arms Park, Sixfields Stadium, Northampton, and Tynecastle Park, Edinburgh, staged Super League matches for the first time, as each club played the extra round at a neutral venue, their opponents being decided by final placings in the Super League II table. In another ultimately revolutionary announcement, it was agreed that the Super League crown would now be decided by a Grand Final at Old Trafford, rather than the team who accumulated the most points during the course of the season.

An intensely gripping new climax to the season was born at the 'Theatre of Dreams' on 24 October 1998, when Wigan – with John Monie back at the helm – returned to the top of the tree by defeating Leeds 10-4, on a sodden evening in front of 43,553 enthralled spectators; uniquely in British sport, the winning players picked up specially commissioned solid gold championship rings. The Warriors had begun the season in tremendous style, conceding only 18 points in 4 matches to make it to their first Challenge Cup final for three years, and warmed up for Wembley by winning their opening four Super League starts to head the table as they set off for the capital. A crowd of 60,669 was in attendance at the home of English sport as Sheffield Eagles confounded all pre-match predictions by pulling off arguably the greatest upset in cup history. Their 17-8 victory over Wigan was the stuff of dreams, with Mark Aston lifting the Lance Todd Trophy, and the passage of time has taken nothing from the brilliance of the young club's achievement, with John Kear making his mark as their coach. The Warriors would have taken little comfort from a 36-6 Super League win over their Wembley opponents just seven days later, except that it meant they remained top of the table. Monie's marauders, led by Andy Farrell, ended the campaign with six men in double figures in the Super League try charts, showing that they still retained plenty of that old attacking flair and ambition that had served them so well in the late 1980s and early 1990s. Not only that, but their defensive record was far superior to every other club, conceding just 222 points in their twenty-three league matches, of which they lost just two, both to their Grand Final opponents Leeds.

The system for the end-of-season play-offs was based on what had been happening in Australia since 1930, and involved the top five clubs in the final standings. Those who finished higher earned an advantage over those below them, and the initial reaction was a very positive one. After slipping down to fifth in the league ladder, champions Bradford had the toughest possible route to the Grand Final, needing to win three away matches to qualify for a one-off defence of their title. As it turned out, their challenge petered out at the first attempt when St Helens defeated them 46-24 in Britain's first-ever Elimination Play-Off. Second-placed Leeds opened their play-off campaign with a dogged 13-6 home defeat of Halifax, leaving the Blue Sox to back up at The Shay against Saints. St Helens duly obliged by 37-30, knocking Halifax out of the competition. Enter Wigan, who had sat out the first round of matches, courtesy of their top ranking, and who overturned earlier season form to see off the Rhinos 17-4 at Central Park to become the first team to reach a Grand Final. Leeds would not slip up twice though, and Shaun McRae's last match in charge of St Helens before he went to Gateshead saw them comprehensively outgunned in a 44-16 defeat at Headingley, ensuring that the Rhinos would appear at Old Trafford a week later. Graham Murray's powerful and uncompromising team took the game to Wigan, and it looked like Richie Blackmore's opening try would be enough for Leeds to hold the half-time advantage, until the brilliant Jason Robinson popped up three minutes before the break to score what turned out to be the game breaker. Andy Farrell's conversion and two further second-half penalties were enough to ensure that Super League silverware would grace the Central Park trophy cabinet for the one and only time in the first decade.

1999 – SUPER LEAGUE IV: HANLEY INSPIRES SAINTS

The addition of two further clubs, making a total of fourteen in Super League IV, did nothing to halt the return to form of St Helens, who found the winning habit again under Ellery Hanley. The former Great Britain skipper returned to British rugby league after a spell playing in the now-defunct ARL competition, and walked straight into one of the game's top jobs at Saints. Nothing if not controversial, Hanley fell out with the club's board and was suspended, before being reinstated and having the last laugh as the players did his talking on the pitch. However, whereas Ellery took the end-of-season plaudits, a number of Super League coaches found keeping their jobs the biggest challenge, with eight of them moving on for a variety of reasons by the end of the season. The 1998 Coach of the Year John Pendlebury ended his tenure at Halifax after the club suffered a mid-season financial crisis – the award turning out to be something of a poisoned chalice, Andy Gregory (Salford), Dan Stains (London) and his replacement Les Kiss all quit their posts, while John Monie was given the elbow at Wigan, and Malcolm Reilly parted company with Huddersfield, who merged with Sheffield to become Huddersfield-Sheffield Giants after the season had concluded. Huddersfield and Hull – who came perilously close to extinction – struggled both on and off the field, while promoted Wakefield attained a respectable finish, and fellow new boys Gateshead enjoyed a great time of it, finishing just two points outside the play-offs and promising a bright future for the game in the North-East. However, all that potential was wasted as the code's latest attempt at expansion was again to prove short-lived. The original Thunder – who boasted in Captain Thunder the most iconic, galvanising mascot – lasted just one Super League season before merging with and being forced into a move to Hull, their newly-created fans left high and dry.

On-the-road fixtures were also ditched, as rugby league again withdrew largely into its heartlands. 1999 was also the year when London Broncos finally hit the big stage, seeing off Castleford in a memorable Challenge Cup semi-final at Headingley to earn a crack at Leeds in the last decider at the old Wembley Stadium. Chairman Richard Branson tried to relax his team by leading them out across the hallowed turf in a pair of jeans but, despite a tremendous start when they led 10-0, they succumbed to the Rhinos 52-16, with winger Leroy Rivett proving unstoppable in a record-breaking four-try romp. In Super League, defending champions Wigan suffered an immediate setback, being knocked out of the Challenge Cup at Leeds on Valentine's Day and suffering a trio of defeats to St Helens, Halifax and Castleford in their opening 7 matches to leave them with plenty to do. Despite another fine season for both Jason Robinson (19 tries) and Kris Radlinski (17), the Warriors rarely rose above their ultimate resting place of fourth in the league. Central Park was waved an emotional goodbye on 5 September, when St Helens were beaten 28-20, but although the play-off system offered Wigan the opportunity to cling on to the title, Castleford put paid to that by spoiling the opener at the new JJB Stadium, knocking out the champions 14-10.

The Tigers, whose Wheldon Road ground had become the more menacing-sounding Jungle, had made good progress since narrowly avoiding relegation two seasons earlier and, under the tutelage of Stuart Raper – son of the legendary Kangaroo loose forward Johnny – they were making an impression on the play-offs for the first time. With Dean Sampson, Aaron Raper and Man of Steel Adrian Vowles in the pack, and half-backs Danny Orr and Brad Davis causing plenty of problems for their opponents, the Tigers were a match for anyone on their day, as Leeds found out in the Elimination Semi-Final. Graham Murray had earned his place in Headingley folklore by taking the Rhinos to Wembley earlier in the season, where they won the Challenge Cup for the first time since 1978 but, having announced that he would be departing for Australia at the season's end, he could not work any further magic in his final home game. Castleford must have fancied their chances of making it all the way to Old Trafford from fifth place, after an Aaron Raper-inspired performance saw them run out 23-16 winners at the old enemy, but backing up a week later at Knowsley Road proved beyond them, St Helens ending their Grand Final dream. That came after Saints were themselves thrashed 40-4 by Bradford at Odsal in the Qualifying Semi-Final, prompting suggestions that the table-topping Bulls merely had to turn up in Manchester to win their first Grand Final. However, a compelling match proved anything but a cakewalk for Matthew Elliott's men. Towards the end of a tense opening quarter, Harry Sunderland Trophy winner Henry Paul stepped his way into the clear to sprint sixty metres for a brilliant individual try, though his conversion proved to be the end of the Bulls' scoring for the match. Under the rain-soaked Old Trafford skies, Saints weathered everything else that Bradford could throw at them, at times showing unswerving desperation in defence, while on attack they had just a Sean Long penalty to show for their first-half efforts. Aided by video referee David Campbell, who ruled out 'scores' from both Leon Pryce and James Lowes, St Helens stayed in the game after the break until Kiwi centre Kevin Iro finally found a way over fifteen minutes from time; Long's towering touchline conversion edging them in front at the business end of the game to lift the title for the second time.

2000 – SUPER LEAGUE V: GIANTS SHUDDER

The merging of Hull Sharks and Gateshead Thunder as Hull FC, and the joining of Sheffield Eagles and Huddersfield Giants as Huddersfield-Sheffield Giants – added to the fact that Northern Ford Premiership winners Dewsbury did not satisfy the entry criteria of the independent franchise panel – meant that Super League was again reduced to twelve clubs as it moved into the fifth summer season. However, less clubs did not mean much of a reduction in terms of matches, as pressure from club chairmen meant that teams now played 28 games, including home and away fixtures against all the other eleven clubs, and six additional rounds against those who had finished in their half of the table the previous season. The new millennium saw little in the way of changes at the top end of the Super League table, as the previous season's top five remained the same, simply swapping the order in which they finished. Wigan rang the changes before the season began, sacking former player and ex-Great Britain coach Andy Goodway the previous November, and appointing his New Zealand counterpart Frank Endacott to take charge at the JJB Stadium. Former Super League (Europe) chief executive Maurice Lindsay was also back as club chairman, while Dean Bell returned west of the Pennines from Leeds as head of youth development. The changes ushered in some stability at the club and that was reflected on the field, with the Warriors never out of the top three during the weekly rounds and finishing as the league leaders, having won 24 of their 28 matches, piling on the points in a 10-match winning run-in to the play-offs. Bitter rivals St Helens emerged from an early-season wobble when they lost to Leeds in the Challenge Cup and Bradford in the opening Super League match a week later – Ellery Hanley's last game in charge before being sacked – to eclipse the Warriors with a run of 11 successive victories to briefly lead the table on a couple of occasions, before finally settling in second spot.

Earlier, Saints had taken their Super League title belt to the JJB Stadium and put it on the line in the World Club Challenge, against Aussie premiers Melbourne. Kangaroo Test half-back Brett Kimmorley was outstanding for the Storm, who cruised home 44-6 to provoke unwarranted alarm at the state of the British game. A new-look Leeds Rhinos enjoyed contrasting fortunes as the season opened. Former Canberra forward Dean Lance replaced Graham Murray as coach, guiding the team through to the first Challenge Cup final to be held outside England, at Murrayfield. At the same time the players were unable to get any Super League points on the board until their 20–10 round six home defeat of Huddersfield-Sheffield Giants a week before their trip north of the border. The 24-18 defeat to a Michael Withers-inspired Bradford Bulls, after an Edinburgh flood had threatened the staging of the match, was probably about as good as they could have expected given their inconsistency. Then, after a couple more wobbles, they went on Super League's longest winning run of the campaign, picking up the two points on thirteen consecutive occasions to climb from the foot of the table to a more respectable fourth overall. The Bulls strengthened their already formidable pack with the addition of Aussie former Test star Brad Mackay and set the early season pace, going on a fifteen-match unbeaten Super League and Challenge Cup run. In addition to lifting the silverware at Murrayfield, Bradford routed all their early season Super League opponents, posting their intent with a 32-10 win at Knowsley Road, to become hot favourites to do the 'double'. But Matthew Elliott's team could not maintain their momentum in the second half of the campaign and slipped to third place. It would prove difficult from there. Castleford Tigers had no such lofty winning streaks to boast of, never stringing more than three wins together, but while a defeat for Stuart Raper's team was never far away, Darren Rogers (20 tries), Jon Wells (13) and Michael Eagar (12) ensured that they scored enough points to earn fifth place, just missing out on fourth to Leeds on points difference. With Warrington, Hull, Halifax and Salford battling it out in their own breakaway group in mid-division, it was left to Wakefield, London and the merged Giants to scrap over who – if anyone – would be relegated. Broncos coach John Monie paid the price for his club's worst ever Super League finish, while the combined club finished bottom (for the third time in the case of Huddersfield), coach John Kear departing before the season was out. With two games in the season still to play, the directors at the McAlpine Stadium announced that they would return to the name Huddersfield Giants under new coach Tony Smith for Super League VI.

Meanwhile, back on the field, the play-offs kicked off with what is probably still the most remarkable finish to any match in the Super League era. The opening night saw the Qualifying Play-Off between 1999 finalists St Helens and Bradford at a packed Knowsley Road. In a tense affair, the Bulls led 4-0 at the break, and 11-10 as the game ticked into its final seconds. But on the very last play of the match, Saints broke Bradford's hearts with a truly amazing try, passing through numerous pairs of hands, one boot and the length of the field before being finished by club captain Chris Joynt. Bulls coach Matthew Elliott famously and theatrically fell off his chair with the shock of it all, while his Saints counterpart Ian Millward – in his first season after being snapped up from Leigh – was quickly earning his own legendary status at the club. Leeds exacted revenge on local rivals

Castleford, coming from behind to win 22-14 at Headingley, though their dreams of a first title since 1972 were dashed seven days later as Bradford pummelled them into submission with a 46-12 success at Odsal to move into the Final Eliminator. They were joined there by Wigan, whose two-week rest had counted for little against a Saints side with momentum, their neighbours posting nine tries in storming to a 54-16 win at the JJB Stadium to book their place at Old Trafford. Bradford then backed up the theory that it looked particularly difficult to qualify for the Grand Final from third place. They were never in the Final Eliminator, being thrashed 40-12, a Brett Dallas hat-trick ensuring that Wigan would not slip-up in successive home matches. But Saints would not be denied, and confirmed that they were the team of the early Super League era with their third championship win under as many coaches, becoming the only side in the decade to retain the title. Jason Robinson said goodbye to the sport he had served with both brilliance and great dignity, finishing without a try as, despite a second-half fight back, the Warriors went down 29-16 in another nerve-jangler.

2001 – SUPER LEAGUE VI: BULLS RETURN TO THE SUMMIT

After their disappointing end to Super League V, Bradford Bulls came back a more determined side in 2001, making Valley Parade a fortress. All 16 league and cup matches at the home of Bradford City AFC – which the Bulls were to use while Odsal was being redeveloped – resulted in wins for the home side. Although their form away from Bradford was not as consistent, the Bulls did enough to finish top of the table on points difference from Wigan. After having gone down 13-6 to St Helens in a dour Challenge Cup final at Twickenham, Brian Noble – who had replaced the departed Matthew Elliott as coach – was doubly determined not to let his players lose their way again in the play-offs. 2001 also saw a Hull FC resurgence under Shaun McRae. The Airlie Birds emerged as genuine title contenders, benefiting from strengthening the team with the likes of Lee Jackson, Steve Prescott and the unrelated Smith trio of Chris, Jason and Tony and a lop-sided set of repeat fixtures to claim a top-three finish and knock Castleford out of the play-offs. However, the black-and-whites' first taste of post-season rugby proved to be a damp squib, losing successive matches to Wigan and St Helens to limp out of the competition. The Warriors enjoyed a fine though ultimately fruitless season, with full-back Kris Radlinski posting 30 tries in the regular season to top the try charts, while his captain Andy Farrell was again leading points scorer as the club's new half-back combination of Adrian Lam and Matthew Johns created plenty of opportunities. Despite 6 wins, 1 draw and 3 defeats from the first 10 rounds of Super League – a record that most clubs would settle for – 'Happy' Frank Endacott was shown the door after a 31-30 defeat by Salford at The Willows, and was replaced forty-eight hours later by Stuart Raper, who had done as much as he could at Castleford. Raper settled in quickly and his Warriors were soon back up to second in the table, routing Salford 70-4 in the return fixture at the JJB Stadium, and losing only two more matches in the regular season. Over at Knowsley Road, St Helens were involved in an off-field scrap with Halifax for the signature of Leigh's promising young hooker Micky Higham before the season began and audaciously gave him his debut in a friendly against Wigan despite the RFL not having sanctioned the transfer. A sensational 20-18 defeat of Brisbane Broncos in the World Club Challenge coupled with their Challenge Cup success over the Bulls meant that Ian Millward's men held all three trophies at the same time; though their record 74-16 defeat to Leeds at Headingley a week after the Twickenham final was a reality check. Even so, Man of Steel Paul Sculthorpe (24 tries) and hooker Keiron Cunningham (20) were outstanding as the Saints attempted to make yet another final, this time from fourth place, until Wigan denied them at the last hurdle. Leeds, who had opened their Challenge Cup campaign with a resounding, club record 106-10 thrashing of Swinton Lions, enjoyed a good start in Super League, winning their first two matches, but their Challenge Cup semi-final failure against St Helens, sandwiched in between three league defeats, spelt the end for coach Dean Lance, who was replaced by Daryl Powell. Nevertheless, despite having the likes of New Zealand centre Tonie Carroll, Iestyn Harris and the talented Robbie Mears in the ranks, the former Great Britain star could not produce an upturn in fortunes for his team, who finished fifth before crashing out 38-30 in the Elimination Play-Off at St Helens.

With London, Warrington and Castleford mixing it just outside the top five, there was a real dogfight at the foot of the table, where Halifax, Salford and Wakefield – the latter in spite of a deduction of two points for a breach of the salary cap – just did enough to ensure that Huddersfield finished bottom yet again. This time the Giants could no longer cling on to their Super League status, as Widnes Vikings' NFP Grand Final defeat of Oldham meant that the Merseyside club had earned their return to compete with the game's elite. With Leeds and Hull FC departing the play-offs at their earliest respective opportunities, it was left to minor premiers Bradford to take route one to Old Trafford, with Henry Paul inspiring his team, for whom brother Robbie scored two tries, to a 24-18 success at Valley Parade over Wigan. That left the Warriors to take on St Helens at the JJB Stadium in the Final Eliminator, and a third successive play-off match took its toll on the visitors, who were swamped 44-10 after an Adrian Lam masterclass took Wigan to their third Grand Final. However, Stuart Raper's first decider as coach ended in defeat as Bradford stunned the 60,164 Old Trafford crowd with an awesome display. Tries from Jimmy Lowes and a hat-trick from Michael Withers shot the Bulls into a 26-0 half-time lead and, despite brief respite with a Lam try of their own, two further Bradford scores and a Henry Paul drop goal left Wigan on the wrong end of a 37-6 hammering. Brian Noble's team had narrowly missed out on the double for a second time in the Super League era, but his players had quashed the media's suggestions that the Bulls were chokers with a consummate display that remains the best in a Grand Final to date.

2002 – SUPER LEAGUE VII: TRIO ON TOP

If Bradford had designs on holding all three trophies concurrently then they certainly set about 2002 in the right manner. A bitterly cold February night drew a crowd of 21,113 to the then McAlpine Stadium to see the Bulls defeat Aussie premiers Newcastle Knights – Andrew Johns et al – to become World Club Champions for the first time in their history. However, success brings its own pressures. Brian Noble's team was now there to be shot at and it was Leeds whose aim was clinical at the first attempt. Just eight days after that heady night in Huddersfield, the Rhinos were creating history of their own, being the first club to win at Valley Parade in over a season, as their 17-4 victory dumped the Bulls out of the Challenge Cup and ended their treble hopes. The champions recovered well, winning a tricky opening Super League fixture away at Wigan and, with the arrival of both Brandon Costin and Kiwi Test winger Lesley Vainikolo, they appeared to have even greater firepower than ever before. Michael Withers (20 tries), Tevita Vaikona (19) and Robbie Paul (16) hit a rich vein of form to take the Bulls back to the top of the table for most of the season. As it was, Wigan were to be the next team to lift silverware, when the Challenge Cup went to the JJB Stadium for the first time since the club left Central Park.

Their early-season league form had been patchy and included a 19-0 defeat at Knowsley Road, prompting the bookies to make Saints strong favourites but, buoyed by an inspirational effort from Kris Radlinski, Wigan upset the applecart with a 21-12 triumph to lift the cup for the first time since 1995. The success helped the Warriors to improve their Super League form and gave them a glimmer of hope of snatching pole position for the play-offs, but defeat at Bradford and then at home to Leeds meant they had to settle for third place, seven points behind both the Bulls and Saints, with the latter finishing league leaders on points difference. Knowsley Road was introduced to a trio of Aussie recruits as the season commenced, with speedster Darren Albert and uncompromising forwards Barry Ward and Darren Britt all persuaded to join the Ian Millward success story. After scraping home 15-14 in their opener at Widnes, courtesy of a Tommy

Martyn field goal, Saints made the early running until an uncharacteristic thrashing in the capital. Success against arch-rivals Wigan and then back-to-back wins against Leeds, firstly in Super League and latterly in the Challenge Cup semi-final, had the club in confident mood. However, a controversial 54-22 defeat at Valley Parade just a week before the final – after which they were fined £25,000 for fielding a weakened team – plus the Murrayfield disappointment, meant that St Helens had not been full of joy during the spring. That all changed, however, as Millward got his team to regroup and win 15 of their remaining 17 regular season fixtures to claim top spot and a home play-off tie with old rivals Bradford.

With the play-offs now having been expanded to six teams, Leeds (fourth place), Hull FC (fifth) and Castleford Tigers (sixth) were all eyeing the chance for glory, despite having been fighting it out in their own mini-league along with Widnes for much of the campaign. But only Leeds kept their hopes alive beyond week one, as Great Britain centre Keith Senior crossed for three tries in his team's 36-22 home defeat of Hull FC, while skipper Andy Farrell led from the front as the Warriors were too good for Castleford at the JJB Stadium. With Wigan far too strong for Leeds in the Elimination Semi-Final and Bradford squeezing past Saints in a 28-26 thriller to reach another Old Trafford Grand Final, the fierce red-rose rivals had to meet again to decide who would take on the Bulls. St Helens were determined not to squander their last chance of making the big one and they ensured the local winter bragging rights by seeing off injury-hit Wigan 24-8 in the Final Eliminator, giving themselves a chance to break Bradford hearts once more.

There are few teams who have fazed the Bulls in either league or cup since the dawn of the summer era, but if Bradford fans had to name one club that has given them sleepless nights over that period then it would surely be the men from Knowsley Road. Three Challenge Cup final defeats, the Chris Joynt try and a Grand Final loss in those first five years suggested that Saints had a hex on the West Yorkshiremen when it came to the big games. 2002 saw Saints reopen those old wounds and shovel in the salt as they came out on top in a taught, tense finale that included another huge bout of controversy. Bradford began confidently but ended up trailing 12-8 at half-time. Scott Naylor had crossed as early as the third minute, with Paul Deacon adding the conversion, and it was the young scrum half who thought he had put the Bulls 12-0 up when he raced between the posts soon after, only for the video referee to incorrectly rule that Jamie Peacock had knocked-on in the build-up and deny the score. Having lost full-back Paul Wellens early with a fractured cheekbone, Saints clung on in defence and then hit back through Mike Bennett and Sean Long, his two conversions putting them ahead. Robbie Paul and Michael Withers tries put the Bulls back in front in the early part of the second half, but Saints just would not submit. Martin Gleeson's try brought them to within two points, and though Long missed the conversion he was on target with a penalty to level the scores with sixteen minutes remaining, ensuring another tense finale. Both tried desperately for the decisive scoring blow, St Helens failing with two attempts at a one-pointer, before Tony Stewart's run gave them one final chance of some field position and Sean Long's angled twenty-metre pot shot sailed between the posts to edge them in front with just seconds remaining. It was 19-18 to Saints and only one last-ditch hope remained for Bradford, to take a short kick-off and try to win the ball back for a final tilt at their opponents' line. But St Helens came up with possession and skipper Chris Joynt, along with referee Russell Smith, became embroiled in one of the biggest controversies in the summer era, after Joynt appeared to take a voluntary tackle on the very last play of the game and Smith chose not to penalise him. It was a gripping conclusion to an enthralling season that was perhaps the best of the first decade of the competition.

Elsewhere, Warrington failed to capitalise on their progress in 2001 by being too closely involved for comfort in the fight to avoid the drop, alongside Halifax, Wakefield and Salford. The appointment of former Australia assistant coach Steve Anderson saw the Wolves lose 6 of their first 8 league and cup matches, and so former Castleford winger David Plange was handed the responsibility of arresting the slump. However, only 4 wins from 16 matches in charge meant that Plange was also shown the door, paving the way for the return from Whitehaven of club stalwart Paul Cullen before August was out.

Wakefield were also going through changes, with coach John Harbin leaving in the off season, eventually ending up at soccer side Crystal Palace, allowing former Halifax and Keighley boss Peter Roe to move into the Belle Vue hot seat, under the watchful eye of long-serving legend Peter Fox. But with the club propping up the table, Roe was ditched in July in favour of Queenslander Shane McNally, who managed to secure the few points needed to survive. However, Salford's decision to sack coach Steve McCormack after 2 wins from 11 starts and appoint Karl Harrison did not pay immediate dividends, as their last-day defeat at home to Castleford, coupled with Wakefield's win against the Wolves, meant that they were relegated and replaced in Super League by unbeaten NFP champions Huddersfield.

2003 – SUPER LEAGUE VIII: BULLS AT THE DOUBLE

They say that great champions need great challengers in order to push back the boundaries of excellence, and if St Helens can claim to have been the team of Super League's first decade, then Bradford have been counterpunching all the way, and judges might even make a split decision. Having lost their grip on any silverware in 2002, the Bulls produced a magnificent response to land the Super League-Challenge Cup double, and were to go on and hold all three trophies at the same time before the advent of Super League IX, with a convincing 22-4 win against Newcastle Knights at the then McAlpine Stadium the following February. Technically in bottom spot in the table on points difference after their 46-22 defeat at Knowsley Road on the opening day of the Super League season, Bradford were not beaten again until June. Even then, it took a remarkable effort from London Broncos' Dennis Moran, who scored his second hat-trick in a week, having flown home to Australia and back in the interim, to see his team pull off a memorable 22-12 Odsal win. The Bulls were consistent throughout the first half of the season and became the first club to lift the Challenge Cup in three countries, when they beat Leeds Rhinos 22-20 in a desperately tense final at the Millennium Stadium, Cardiff. With Jamie Peacock epitomising the very essence of a Man of Steel Award winner, James Lowes postponing his retirement for one last, glorious campaign, and Lesley Vainikolo in tremendous try scoring form, even 6 defeats in the regular season – perhaps indicating a levelling out of the competition – could not keep the Bulls from entering the play-offs in pole position.

Their closest pursuers in the title race were the men from just ten miles away at Headingley. The Rhinos spent all season jostling for position at the head of the table, holding sway for sizeable portions of it, but the one team they could not beat in five attempts during the campaign were their bitterest rivals. Ultimately it was down to that, plus 3 drawn Super League matches for Leeds, that left Daryl Powell's men second-best going into the play-offs. Wigan's slow start to the season, including 4 defeats in their opening 7 matches and a Challenge Cup semi-final exit against Bradford, put coach Stuart Raper under plenty of pressure. Ironically, the Aussie had turned things around – with just 2 defeats in his next 10 matches to guide the Warriors back up to third in the table – before he was relieved of his duties in favour of his assistant Mike Gregory. The former Great Britain star steered the JJB ship home in third place and faced up to the prospect of knock-out football in the play-offs.

Meanwhile, things weren't going quite according to plan at Knowsley Road. A 38-0 humiliation by Sydney Roosters in the World Club Challenge, three early season Super League defeats to Leeds, Wigan and, more surprisingly, Huddersfield, plus a Challenge Cup exit after a classic semi-final against the Rhinos, left them with much to salvage. There seemed to be no respite for Ian Millward's injury-hit squad. Before May was out, they – along with Hull FC and Halifax – had two points deducted after being found in breach of the 2002 salary cap. A run of 4 further defeats and a draw from

6 matches in mid-season left them with a mountain to climb from eighth until a nine-match winning run saw them wind up in fourth place.

Under coach Tony Rea, things continued to take shape in the capital. London Broncos appointed Jim Dymock to take over the captaincy from the injured Jason Hetherington, while the signing of Bill Peden from Newcastle Knights, and the outstanding form of Dennis Moran – who finished as Super League's top try scorer for the second year in succession – all contributed to the Broncos' climb to fifth in the table.

Warrington's rise was even more rapid and could not have been better-timed with the club saying goodbye to their Wilderspool home of 108 years with a 52-12 demolition of Wakefield Trinity Wildcats in September. Prior to that, coach Paul Cullen had seen his team go out of the Challenge Cup to Bradford at the first attempt, but then produce some much better form – if still inconsistent – to come home in sixth place and turn the previous season's turmoil into a play-off spot.

One man's success is another team's disappointment, and that was the case with Hull FC, who were amid the early pacesetters and included St Helens and Wigan among their KC Stadium scalps, until a disastrous August and September saw them lose 7 of their last 9 matches to drop out of the play-offs.

Elsewhere, both Castleford and Widnes had begun to show signs of the decline in fortunes on the field that would ultimately mean relegation into the National Leagues, while Wakefield were somewhat fortunate that Halifax were around. Financial difficulties at The Shay meant that nine backroom staff were made redundant and Gavin Clinch, Brett Goldspink and Robbie Beckett all left the club before the season had kicked off. The Blue Sox tag was also dropped and the club was bound for the abyss.

Making their first step towards oblivion, Halifax went out of the Challenge Cup at Hull FC, but then produced a shock 26-22 win at London in the Super League opener a fortnight later to suggest that things might work out after all. However, a decimated squad was soon bottom of the table, losing all its remaining twenty-seven league games. Having had Martin Moana banned for a month for traces of ephedrine in his urine and their only two points deducted for breach of the salary cap, Halifax contrived to set a record Super League low that can never be broken. Despite the new names in the play-offs the 'big four' clubs still held sway. The opening Elimination Play-Offs saw Wigan make home advantage count with a hard-fought 25-12 win against play-off virgins Warrington, while twenty-four hours earlier the Broncos had succumbed to St Helens 24-6, with Sean Long becoming only the third Saints player to score 100 tries and 100 goals in the club's history. A week later the Elimination Semi-Final saw Wigan's outstanding end-of-season form continue with their fourth win from as many starts against

St Helens in 2003. Andy Farrell battled through the eighty minutes with a knee injury to inspire his team to a 40-24 success, after a whirlwind opening had them 34-6 up at the break, though a significant casualty was half-back Adrian Lam, also to a knee injury.

After a two-week break, table-toppers – and thereby inaugural League Leaders Shield winners – Bradford turned an 8-4 half-time deficit into a 30-14 win against Leeds at Odsal, to complete the nap hand over their closest rivals. It was a tight contest throughout, until Leon Pryce turned things in the Bulls' favour with a sensational solo effort. The confidence-sapped Rhinos now had to back-up at home a week later against Wigan, the team who had all the momentum with them, and it was that belief that they could be the first club from outside the top two to reach Old Trafford that would prove decisive. For the fourth time in the season, Leeds and Wigan put on a show fit for a final. It was nip and tuck all the way, as first the Warriors led through Brian Carney before Leeds went ahead with tries from Danny McGuire and Rob Burrow. Sean O'Loughlin then replied to make it 14-10 in favour of the Rhinos at the break. Burrow's second try increased the home side's advantage early in the second-half, before O'Loughlin, and then Carney – with a spellbinding solo effort – completed braces to level the scores. That left the teams to play out a nerve-wracking final quarter, and it was Danny Tickle who emerged the Wigan hero, slotting over a left-footed drop goal with just three minutes remaining, to edge the Warriors into the Grand Final after an incredible match finished 23-22. Coach Mike Gregory and his assistant Denis Betts celebrated by signing two-year contracts to maintain their partnership at the JJB Stadium, but while their team were going to Old Trafford with 11 successive wins to their name, they were now to receive the ultimate test of their will and endurance against the Challenge Cup winners Bradford, who were hunting the double. Bulls coach Brian Noble had problems to contend with after Michael Withers and Robbie Paul had missed much of the season through injury and, although skipper Paul was back for the Grand Final, youngster Stuart Reardon had grabbed his chance well at full-back and his try-scoring display at Old Trafford would earn him the Harry Sunderland Trophy as man of the match. A sell-out 65,537 crowd saw Danny Tickle's opening try, converted by Andy Farrell, put the Warriors ahead where, despite two Paul Deacon penalties, they would stay until half-time. A third Deacon two-pointer levelled the scores after the break, but tries from Reardon and centre Shontayne Hape in an eight-minute spell midway through the second half turned the game Bradford's way. Deacon's perfect night with the boot meant maximum points from both efforts, and his twenty-metre field goal made it 19-6 to the Bulls with just ten minutes remaining. Right on cue

Wigan launched a fightback through Kris Radlinski, who got on the end of a wonderful Martin Aspinwall break to score, Farrell converting to reduce the deficit to seven points. But when Tickle knocked on the restart the game was up for the Warriors, and it was just left to James Lowes to round off his brilliant career with a trademark dummy-half try to give Bradford a deserved 25-12 success and their own place in the sport's history, as the first team to win both the Challenge Cup and Grand Final in the same year.

2004 – SUPER LEAGUE IX: 'LEEDING' THE WAY… AT LAST!

On the face of it Gary Connolly and David Furner would not appear to have too much in common, apart from being exceptional exponents of their respective arts. But aside from a spell playing together at Wigan and squaring up for their respective countries at Test level, they shared the dubious honour of being the only two members of the Leeds squad who had been born when the club last won a championship, in 1972. To say the Rhinos had waited a long time for the ultimate prize in domestic rugby league would be an understatement even by the standards of their phlegmatic coach Tony Smith. The former Huddersfield supremo had been brought in for a defined two-year period while Daryl Powell took a sideways move with the club, and where coaches of the quality of Syd Hynes, Peter Fox, Maurice Bamford, Malcolm Reilly, David Ward and Graham Murray had failed, the studious Smith hit the jackpot at the very first attempt. Remarkably, with only one signing – Papua New Guinea international Marcus Bai – the new coach was able to elicit a marked improvement from his team. With unprecedented consistency in the Super League era, Leeds became the only club to date to have led the table from start to finish, drawing twice and losing only away at Wigan and St Helens to finish nine points clear of defending champions Bradford. The Rhinos had gone out of the Challenge Cup in round five, at eventual winners St Helens and so could channel all their energies into getting that King Kong-sized monkey off their back. Their early momentum – 8 successive wins – was halted once again by Saints, who upset them with a 56-10 hammering at Knowsley Road. Wigan's 26-22 success at the JJB Stadium six weeks later was another slight mishap for Leeds, but a 70-0 home romp repaid St Helens with interest, and Smith's players charged on once more to record a total of 24 regular season wins.

Meanwhile over at Odsal, the World Club Challenge trophy stood proudly in the Bradford cabinet after their comprehensive 22-4 success against Penrith Panthers at the McAlpine Stadium. However, the Bulls' title defence didn't go according to plan. An early exit from the Challenge Cup, inevitably at the hands of St Helens, meant that Brian Noble's men had relinquished one piece of silverware and, after Leeds and Hull had beaten them in Super League before April was out, it meant that they were always chasing the Rhinos' tail. The Bradford left-hand side was awesome, with centre Shontayne Hape and his winger Lesley Vainikolo posting 62 tries between them to give opposing defences sleepless nights. Jamie Peacock and Stuart Fielden again led the way up front but, despite the high-profile signing of former Rhino Iestyn Harris, the Bulls were always playing second fiddle to their neighbours. In fact, Leeds reversed the previous season's form by winning all three regular season Super League matches against the old enemy.

Hull, who also had the beating of the champions on two out of three occasions, equalled their best ever finish in the league table, coming home just one point behind Bradford in third. This, however, probably merited more than their 2001 campaign, given that the extra six regular fixtures were now no longer decided by which half of the table teams had finished the year before, but instead by a fairer system of matches against teams who had finished in either odd or even positions on the previous season's ladder. 2004 was also a sad one for Hull and the British game in general, as ambassador Shaun McRae announced that he would be leaving the club at the end of the season to take up a post with NRL outfit South Sydney Rabbitohs.

Wigan's season started badly, with defeats in 3 of their opening 4 matches, and wingman Brian Carney out with a broken ankle. Despite reaching another Challenge Cup final, the 32-16 defeat by St Helens – preceded by the desperate news that coach Mike Gregory was suffering from serious illness and would require treatment in America – meant that the prospects for the remainder of the campaign were none too bright. If that was the case, no-one told Andy Farrell. The Great Britain and Warriors skipper – who had announced he would be leaving the game for the fifteen-a-side code at the season's end – was a colossus. Despite the strong claims of Leeds star Danny McGuire, it was Farrell who picked up his second Man of Steel Award, and he was to top that by receiving the Golden Boot as the world's number one player a month later. However, the Warriors' slow start to the season meant that they had to come from well off the pace, and fourth place was probably as good as they could have hoped for at the halfway mark. If a barren season and a Challenge Cup final defeat to St Helens was hard for a Wiganer to take, the club at least had the satisfaction of outdoing their rivals in Super League.

Ian Millward's magic formula did not extend to the treatment table or to the common sense of either Sean Long or Martin Gleeson – and his team produced their worst finish for some time. No stranger to taking an understrength team to Bradford, Millward was forced into a repeat by injuries, the double Easter weekend programme and a Challenge Cup semi-final a week later.

Anti-clockwise from top:

1   Australian legend Mal Meninga and RFL chief executive Maurice Lindsay toast the birth of the concept at Headingley.

2   The Grand Final is now synonymous with top-class entertainment. Madness entertain the Old Trafford crowd before the 2005 clash.

3   Rugby rebranded: cheerleaders became an integral part of the pre-match fare in the summer era.

4   The perfect ingredients for a Super League game: a modern stadium, firework entrance of the gladiators and the big screen.

5   *Above left:* Mascots became an integral part of the marketing vision and a key element for attracting young fans. Captain Thunder at Gateshead was something of an icon.

6   *Above right:* 1996 – Wigan and Bath enter the arena at Twickenham for the return cross-code challenge encounter; matches that made the sporting world sit up and take notice of the merits of Super League.

7 *Below:* One of the code's most famous stadiums and the only dual Test arena in the world but, in the initial hiatus, Headingley was almost sold off and lost.

Clockwise from top:

8 Stability – off the field – principally arrived with the appointment of former Davis Cup tennis player and coach Richard Lewis to the newly created post of executive chairman of the Rugby Football League.

9 The view from the box: Sky Sports summariser and former Great Britain skipper Mike 'Stevo' Stephenson rapidly became the game's primary television analyst at the dawn of the satellite revolution.

10 Former top whistler and now referees controller Stuart Cummins demonstrates the technology that links the man in the middle with his touch judges and support staff.

11 Selling the new: top-level, innovative administrator Gary Hetherington has played a key role in shaping the governance of the sport in the modern era.

Summary

- Super League to expand to 14 clubs
- Super League Membership criteria strengthened / promotion method amended
- Player workload / season calendar assessed
- Positive emphasis on developing club businesses
- Ongoing support for Junior Player Production and Coach Education Programmes
- 'Employed' Match Officials

12 *Above:* The view from the pitch: uncompromising Bradford enforcer Brian McDermott characteristically charges at the Wigan defence. He is currently an assistant coach at Leeds.

13 *Left:* The merger between Huddersfield and Sheffield was never destined to last. Pictured are respective skippers Danny Russell and Darren Turner at the McAlpine Stadium.

14, 15 & 16 *Above, from left to right:* Former Kiwi international Dean Bell has been responsible for numerous top-class juniors making the grade in the Super League era. Gregarious Aussie Shaun McRae led St Helens to the double in 1996 before moving to Gateshead and then improving the fortunes of Hull; he is one of the most media-friendly coaches in the business. Ian Millward – Never short of an outspoken opinion or quotable line, few could have carried off being forced to leave St Helens and subsequently re-emerging at their greatest rivals Wigan.

17   *Far left:* Great Britain and Bradford supremo Brian Noble served his apprenticeship under Matthew Elliott and has since taken the Bulls to five consecutive Grand Final appearances.

18   *Left:* Aussie Tony Smith brought respectability to Huddersfield before delivering Leeds their holy grail; a first title for thirty-two years in 2004, followed by the mantle of World Champions.

19   Coming to London as a player in 1994, Tony Rea has steered the men from the capital through various troubled waters as chief executive and head coach, and is still in charge as they enter the Harlequins era in 2006.

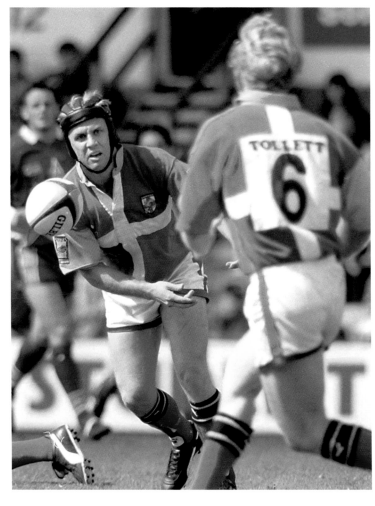

20   *Left:* Stalwart prop Terry O'Connor made over 200 Super League appearances for Wigan before moving on to home town Widnes, cherishing each of his eleven tries.

21   *Right:* Classy back-rower Steve McNamara breaks through the Halifax ranks. Playing spells for Bradford, Wakefield and Huddersfield in Super League have been followed by a growing reputation among the coaching ranks.

Clockwise from above left:

22　Two of St Helens' finest, Tommy Martyn and Apollo Perelini celebrate Saints' convincing victory in the 2000 Grand Final against arch-enemies Wigan.

23　One of the greatest finishers in the sport's history, Martin Offiah ended his career as Super League started with cameo spells at London (pictured alongside current media star Tulsen Tollett) and then Salford.

24　The player opposing fans loved to hate, Bradford's Graeme 'Penguin' Bradley, a key factor in the Bulls' run to the 1997 title.

Clockwise from above left:

25 1999 'Man of Steel' Adrian Vowles – named 'Mr Indestructible' by his coach Stuart Raper – produced a series of sterling performances as outsiders Castleford came within forty minutes of Old Trafford.

26 One of London Broncos' greatest servants, making over 180 appearances in seven seasons, Steele Retchless still holds the competition record for an astonishing 66 tackles in a match.

27 The only player to have started every Super League season wearing the same squad number, Saints' outstanding hooker Keiron Cunningham.

28   *Above:* One of the heroes of Super League. Wigan's Andy Farrell still holds the competition records for points in a season (388), goals in a career (979) and points in a career (2,228).

29   *Left:* Jason Smith's arrival from Parramatta in 2001 signalled a return to the big time for Hull. Supremely gifted as a ball player, his creative know-how instilled direction and belief into the side.

30 *Left:* Bradford's Michael 'The Ghost' Withers celebrates a try in the 2001 hammering of Wigan at Old Trafford, a match for which he was named Harry Sunderland Trophy winner after a typically commanding performance in a big game.

31 *Below:* Saints' effervescent scrum half Sean Long adds a touchline conversion to his own try in the 2002 Grand Final. His late field goal was to break Bradford hearts.

32   *Above:* A fairy-tale ending for an outstanding champion as James Lowes calls time on a wonderful playing career at Bradford with the final try in the 2003 Grand Final. He was arguably the greatest exponent of the dummy half art in the modern game.

33   *Right:* Simply unstoppable when on the charge, Kiwi winger Lesley 'Volcano' Vainikolo in distinctive rampaging style. He was Super League's top regular-season try scorer in 2004 and 2005.

34   *Above:* Leeds Rhinos' sensational young talent Danny McGuire dives over for the clinching score in the 2004 Grand Final to send the hordes of blue and amber fans into ecstasy as they become champions for the first time since 1972.

35   *Left:* The archetypal modern day forward, Jamie Peacock stampedes through the tackle of Salford's Cliff Beverley in his final campaign for Bradford before leaving for home town Leeds.

36   *Above:* A typical piece of dexterity from multi-talented Leeds Rhinos skipper Kevin Sinfield, one of a number of players who came through the Headingley Academy system to shine in Super League.

37   *Right:* Although only here for three games in a cameo role at the end of 2005, the world's best player Andrew Johns made an enormous impression on the public of Warrington and guaranteed Super League greater column inches.

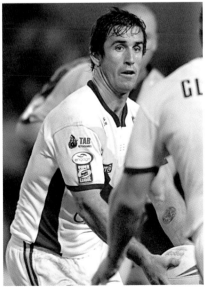

38   *Above:* One of the biggest derby fixtures on the Super League calendar, Wigan's Neil Cowie takes the ball into the heart of the St Helens defence. In March 2005 the clash between the two old rivals drew a Super League regular-season record crowd of 25,004.

39   *Right:* Warrington regroup after conceding a try in the 1997 World Club Championship, an all-too-familiar occurrence for the British teams who were generally comprehensively outgunned in the bold but unbalanced competition.

Clockwise from above left:

40   Club representatives line up for the formal launch of Super League VIII, unveiling that season's new look.

41   Leeds' diminutive scrum half Rob Burrow is congratulated by his teammates after getting on the end of a magnificent flowing move as the Rhinos defeat Canterbury in the 2005 World Club Challenge.

42   Bradford become World Club Champions for the third time in five years, Stuart Fielden – the night's stand-out performer – tormenting the Wests Tigers' defence.

43   *Above:* The final hooter goes and Bradford Bulls celebrate Grand Final revenge victory over neighbours Leeds at a packed Old Trafford in October 2005.

44   *Right:* The end of the first decade of Super League as Bradford lift the trophy to equal St Helens' record of four title wins in the summer era.

45   The newcomers for the start of the second decade as Super League returns to France in the shape of Les Catalans Dragons, who sensationally beat Wigan 38-30 in Perpignan in round one.

With Jon Wilkin sent off and subsequently banned for four matches for a high tackle, a 54-8 defeat and derision from the press, the St Helens coach was once again the centre of attention. However, any pressure on Ian Millward was forgotten about when two days later the *Daily Mail* revealed that Long and Gleeson had backed Saints to lose the match. An RFL investigation two months later found them guilty and 'Odsalgate' earned the pair lengthy bans. Although they coped admirably on the field for a time, the depleted Saints squad lost 7 of their last 10 matches to enter the play-offs knowing only knock-out success would be good enough with no second chances.

The top six was completed by Wakefield, whose coach Shane McNally was rewarded for improving his team by five places and fifteen league points by being presented with the dreaded Coach of the Year Award. Half-back Ben Jeffries, forward David Solomona and centre Sid Domic all had fine seasons as McNally's men showed that they could compete with anyone, and their 41-22 home thrashing of St Helens was a portent for play-off success to come.

At the foot of the table, Castleford – one of the game's great community clubs – propped up the table from round five until round twenty-eight, and suffered their first relegation since the reintroduction of two divisions in 1973/74. Along the way the Tigers parted company with coach and former star player Graham Steadman, appointed Gary Mercer in a caretaker role, and even lured Ellery Hanley back into the game for what turned out to be a brief spell as coaching consultant. However, injuries to key players such as Ryan Sheridan and Paul Newlove – who was forced into retirement – contributed to some dismal form. Despite giving themselves a chance of survival with a gutsy 7-6 win against fellow strugglers Widnes on the penultimate weekend, the West Yorkshire club could not seize the moment in round twenty-eight, and it was left to local rivals Wakefield to press the Super League ejector button by virtue of their 32-28 win at The Jungle. As most of their relegated predecessors had done, the Tigers vowed to remain full-time in National League One in order to give themselves the best chance of an immediate return to the top flight.

It was a case of 'there but for the grace of God go I' for the likes of Widnes, London and Salford, who all finished within four points of Castleford and the panic to avoid the drop certainly affected the Vikings. After just 4 wins from the first 17 rounds, Widnes sacked coach Neil Kelly in July and appointed Stuart Spruce as caretaker, bringing in Frank Endacott in a similar consulting role to that which Hanley had flirted with at The Jungle. Huddersfield showed improvement to finish a place outside the top six, while Warrington were plagued by inconsistency again and this time around they had to miss out, but not so Wakefield. The Wildcats won their last 5 league matches to hit the play-offs with momentum, and shocked many by producing a storming Ben Jeffries-inspired second-half fight back to knock Hull FC out of the competition 28-18 at the KC Stadium. The following night once more pitted old adversaries Wigan against St Helens at the JJB Stadium and, as on the previous eight occasions when the two sides had met there, the home side was just too strong. Sean O'Loughlin was outstanding for the Warriors, who emerged 18-12 winners in front of over 20,000 people, to dump their cup conquerors out and earn a visit from the Wildcats.

Seventeen minutes into the following week's Elimination Semi-Final Wakefield must have been pinching themselves. The Wildcats led 14-0 at the JJB Stadium and ran Wigan ragged with tries from Colum Halpenny, Duncan MacGillivray and David Solomona. The Warriors hit back before the break with Kris Radlinski and Kevin Brown crossing to reduce the deficit to four points, and the second half was as tense as it gets. There was no further score until Andy Farrell – unusually nervy with the boot – kicked a successful penalty for Wigan fourteen minutes from time and he was on the mark again with a conversion to Adrian Lam's match winner, before the home side had to give everything in defence to hold the determined but ultimately fruitless challenge of McNally's men.

Enter the champions Bradford and the pretenders to their throne from Headingley for the Qualifying Semi-Final. Despite pre-match favouritism borne out of their dominance of the Bulls in the weekly rounds, Leeds lost their composure and nerve with a final close enough to touch. Shontayne Hape gave Bradford a dream start with an early brace of tries to which Danny McGuire's reply made it 8-6 in favour of the Bulls at the break. Then an outstanding second-half effort from the visitors saw Robbie Paul and Rob Parker put them out of sight, before Lesley Vainikolo iced the cake in the dying moments to send them to defend their title with a 26-12 win. Rhinos' dominance of the weekly rounds earned them the right to a second home chance in the play-offs and this time they ran riot, racking up a 22-0 lead over a shell-shocked Wigan after thirty-three minutes including a stunning touchdown from Danny McGuire, before winger Marcus Bai completed a hat-trick to restore his team's confidence in a 40-12 success.

The first all-Yorkshire Grand Final took place in front of another sell-out crowd across the Pennines. In contrast to the 'total rugby' approach that had seen off Wigan, Rhinos coach Tony Smith opted for a much tighter tactical game, and his team dominated the field for extensive periods as a result. Battering the Bulls with a brilliantly executed kicking game backed up by aggressive defence, Leeds ensured that their opponents would have to take the longest route to their try line. It was Bradford who did just that when who else but Lesley Vainikolo – who had been enjoying a private battle with Danny McGuire at the head of the try-scoring charts all season – crossed to post the opening try after just seven minutes. An earlier Kevin Sinfield penalty had given Leeds the game's first points, and when he converted Man of the Match Matt Diskin's fifteenth-minute touchdown and added a further penalty, the Rhinos held a 10-4 advantage at the break. Kiwi Test star Shontayne Hape brought the champions back to within two points immediately after half-time but Paul Deacon's missed conversion left the league leaders with a two-point lead. Leeds poured on the pressure, forcing Bradford to drop-out twice, but they just could not put the game to bed in the face of some typically stoic Bulls defending. Eventually, the sheer volume of tackling left its mark on Bradford and, after a tired unforced error from Robbie Paul in his own '20', McGuire crowned an imperious season with the deciding touchdown just five minutes from time to ensure that Kevin Sinfield would bridge a thirty-two-year gap by lifting a first championship for the club since Alan Hardisty had done just up the road at Swinton all those years earlier.

2005 – SUPER LEAGUE X: INCREDI-BULL!

Each of the first nine Super League seasons had witnessed notable feats and special performances but, since the introduction of the play-offs in 1998, no team had come from outside the top two at the end of the regular season to lift the trophy at Old Trafford. In addition to that, no club from outside the so-called 'big four' had lifted the Challenge Cup since John Kear had inspired Sheffield Eagles to do so in 1998. Kear would again have a major role to play as those statistics were rewritten in a remarkable 2005 campaign. Having suffered at the hands of their old adversaries Leeds Rhinos in the final match of 2004, and then looked on as Tony Smith's team kicked off the campaign by defeating Canterbury Bulldogs 39-32 to become World Club Champions, Bradford needed to produce a response. However, after the sacking of Ryan Hudson – who was found guilty of using the banned steroid Stanozolol – and the loss of centre Shontayne Hape until later in the season due to a knee reconstruction, Brian Noble's team struggled to find their usual consistency, languishing in seventh place in the table after 5 defeats in their opening 9 fixtures. The loss of Lesley Vainikolo and Paul Johnson through injury and a three-match suspension for Leon Pryce did not help matters either, but the Bradford board backed their under-pressure coach Brian Noble by extending his contract at Odsal for a further two seasons. In fifth, and well off the pace by mid-July, the return of Kiwi stars

Hape and Vainikolo was the catalyst for a revival in fortunes, and how! A 58-12 defeat of rubbing rags Leigh may not have surprised too many people, but further wins by 74-24 at home to Widnes and 58-12 again, this time at home to Salford, launched the Bulls on a meteoric rise up the table and into the play-offs in third place on the back of 8 successive wins.

Defending champions Leeds had become hot favourites to retain their title, despite the loss of GB hooker Matt Diskin for the early part of the campaign due to a knee injury. New boy Gareth Ellis settled in well and, after that defeat of Canterbury, in front of another sell-out crowd, this time 37,028 at Elland Road, Rhinos were not beaten until round eight of their defence, when Wakefield took them by surprise. Wingers Mark Calderwood and Marcus Bai both announced their departures from Headingley for Wigan and Bradford respectively, but played out the full season, scoring 35 and 19 tries respectively, and with seven scores of 60 points or more during the campaign, Leeds could lay claim to the most potent arsenal of attacking weapons in the competition. That flair and determination to reach the try line would be tested to its limits in the play-offs and, despite finishing top of the league table, they went into the knockout stages in shuddering form. The Challenge Cup campaign had seen them reach the final but it would again be an unhappy trip to Cardiff for them after Hull FC came out on top by the odd point in a remarkable match, and the side-effects from that agonising defeat were palpable as the Rhinos went on to win just 2 of their remaining 5 matches in the season.

Changes were afoot at Knowsley Road, where the signings of Jamie Lyon and Vinnie Anderson did much to give St Helens a good start on the field, though differences off it saw Ian Millward lose his job. The colourful coach had been the longest-serving in Super League until he received his marching orders in May, after the club charged him with three counts of swearing and abuse. Millward was replaced immediately by former New Zealand boss Daniel Anderson and subsequently pursued and then dropped legal action against Saints, but not before he had signed up with Wigan, of all people, within a fortnight of his Knowsley Road departure. St Helens became Leeds' closest pursuers throughout the majority of the season, losing only at Headingley, Wigan and Hull during the regular rounds, plus their sole home defeat – in the twenty-eighth and final round at the hands of the Bulls. The Rhinos' late dip in form meant that St Helens' consistency was enough to ensure they carried off the League Leaders Shield as top dogs, which gave them the best chance of making another final.

Elsewhere, Warrington blew off some early cobwebs, after losing 5 of their first 8 league matches and exiting the Challenge Cup at Leeds, by staging a tremendous revival in fortunes to claim their best ever Super League finish of fourth place. Paul Cullen's continued role as coach was the subject of much media speculation, with many predicting the club stalwart to become the first casualty of the season. But the former on-field hard man showed that same steel off it to pull through and steer his team to 10 wins in their next 11 matches, taking them as high as third place in July. The stunning signing of Great Britain centre Martin Gleeson from St Helens, the brilliant form of full-back Brent Grose and the attacking potency of Kiwi former Test winger Henry Fa'afili (23 tries) on the wing were major reasons behind the Wolves' resurgence. Not satisfied with that, they splashed out the cash to make a short-term signing of Andrew Johns, widely regarded as the world's number one player, creating huge publicity for the club as he helped them to achieve its first crack at the play-offs. Hull FC ran third in the competition for the majority of the season. Although they struggled to beat teams from the 'big four', notable exceptions being the games at home to St Helens and away at Wigan, John Kear's team were in the main very consistent against clubs from outside that cartel, until 3 defeats in the last 4 rounds left them resting in fifth place and facing knockout football in the play-offs. Not that the unique demands of sudden-death rugby league would have caused the Airlie Birds to lose too much sleep. They had, after all, enjoyed wins against Wakefield, Bradford, Leigh and – in the semi-final – St Helens, on the way to their first Challenge Cup final since their shock defeat by Featherstone in 1983. Targeting the cup throughout, Kear had his team believing that they could move mountains when they arrived at the Millennium Stadium for the decider and, after the eleventh-hour loss of full-back Shaun Briscoe due to illness, he inspired them to a late comeback to pip Leeds 25-24 in an epic contest, with Paul Cooke's try, converted by youngster Danny Brough – who had earlier potted a vital field goal – proving to be the decisive scores.

2005 was a year to forget at the JJB Stadium, as the Warriors became the first club that had won a Super League title to finish outside the play-offs, again fuelling the theory that the competition is becoming more and more unpredictable. Dennis Moran moved north from London to boost the Wigan squad, but long-term injuries early in the campaign to new signing Luke Davico – who was released – Gareth Hock, Sean O'Loughlin and Brian Carney, meant that coach Denis Betts had a tough task, and he ultimately had to step aside for the incoming Ian Millward. The arrival of the former Saints supremo had little short-term impact though, with a 70-0 drubbing at Leeds followed by the ultimate humiliation, a 75-0 humbling at St Helens in the Challenge Cup quarter-final shortly afterwards. Despite 4 wins from their last 5 matches, they were just edged out of the play-offs by London Broncos. Coach Tony Rea, a stabilising figure at Griffin Park, after the club made eight new signings to completely revamp their squad, was rightly proud of his players who improved by four places on their 2004 finish of tenth. One of those recruits, Luke Dorn, proved to be a huge influence on the team, scoring 24 tries in 31 appearances, and creating any number of others, while centre Paul Sykes was an ever-present. A stuttering first half of the campaign found the Broncos – who it was later announced would be playing under that guise for the final season – being involved once more in the fight to avoid the drop. However, 4 successive wins in mid-season, notably including one at the JJB Stadium, saw them breach the play-off barrier where, despite an inconsistent end to the regular rounds, they would remain. Huddersfield managed to repeat their record of 12 wins and 16 defeats from 2004 to notch up 24 points, dropping a place to eighth, while Karl Harrison led Salford to three more wins during the season and, though they did not climb the league ladder, they finished only two points adrift of the Giants along with the disappointing Wakefield Trinity Wildcats – who sacked coach Shane McNally in favour of Tony 'Casper' Smith – and were ultimately well clear of the drop zone.

For the first time since its inauguration, there was the prospect of Super League losing two clubs by right through relegation and that was a fate that would befall both Widnes and Leigh. The introduction of Les Catalans Dragons for 2006, which had been announced on 26 May 2004 was the reason and, from long before a ball was kicked-off, promoted Leigh were odds-on favourites to return from whence they had striven so hard to come. Battling with a shoestring budget and few players of Super League quality still available by the time they had won the National League One Grand Final, Centurions coach Darren Abram had a thankless task. Although they made it to the last eight of the Challenge Cup, just 2 wins and a draw in the league meant that after years of trying Leigh would only enjoy one season in the top flight, the coach losing his job in August when there was no way back. Widnes used a total of 35 players as their Super League tenure came to an end. Even coach Frank Endacott struggled to display his renowned smile as his players, who on paper had the ability to maintain their place among the elite, failed to deliver where it mattered – on the field. The Kiwi announced his departure from the club in the week leading up to a 68-10 away hammering by London, which concluded the Vikings' miserable campaign. Three weeks later, Castleford's National League One success ensured that Widnes would be taking the slide down a division after a four-year Super League stay.

Back at the top London travelled to Odsal to take on Bradford in the opening play-off clash but, after performing well for forty minutes, they succumbed 44-22, as the Bulls' end-of-season push continued to gather sway. Twenty-four hours later Andrew Johns was unable to work his magic for a third successive week and, despite their defeat of Hull FC at the KC Stadium a week earlier, Warrington were unable to repeat the dose at home, going out of the play-offs at the first attempt 40-6. St Helens, who were now without lynchpins Paul Sculthorpe, Sean Long and Darren Albert through injury, entertained Leeds in the Qualifying Semi-Final. On a terrible wet night at Knowsley Road, Leeds held on to win a roller-coaster encounter – which included a typically cavalier Jamie Lyon-inspired fight back by the hosts – 19-16 to book their tickets to Old Trafford, Ali Lauiti'iti producing one of the tries of the year. Those who poured scorn on Bradford's chances of success from third place had their eyes opened when the Bulls annihilated Hull FC – winners of the Challenge Cup just over a month earlier – 71-0 at Odsal, with Lesley Vainikolo racking up four tries from his wing berth. That win left the Bulls just eighty minutes away from a repeat Grand Final, but first they had to contend with St Helens. Since the introduction of the play-offs, no team who had finished as league leaders had failed to make Old Trafford. Add to that Bradford's dismal record at Knowsley Road, and the Saints' faithful could have been forgiven for thinking that fate was with them. In fact, the force was in Brian Noble's squad. Rejuvenated by the return of key players in the latter rounds, never had the famed Bulls juggernaut hurtled along with such power and conviction than it did at the business end of 2005. Unstoppable, Bradford dealt with a spirited Saints performance to see off Daniel Anderson's men 23-18 on another grim autumn evening, and set up their own chance for revenge on their previous season's conquerors Leeds.

In the lead up to the Grand Final, much was made of the changes in personnel that had already been announced for 2006. Leeds would be offloading both Marcus Bai and Chris McKenna to the Bulls, while stalwart forward Barrie McDermott would be retiring, Andrew Dunemann was off to Salford and Mark Calderwood to Wigan while the massively influential Keith Senior was out injured. For their part, Bradford would be losing inspirational captain Jamie Peacock to his hometown Leeds, and they had allowed Leon Pryce to sign for St Helens, Robbie Paul for Huddersfield, while Stuart Reardon and Rob Parker (both Warrington), and Lee Radford (Hull FC) were others departing Odsal. Whatever the theorists said, it was to be Bradford's night as they extended their eleven-match unbeaten run. Another capacity crowd was present on the usual wet Old Trafford night to see the Bulls emerge victorious from what was a very similar, tight game to the one the teams had played out a year earlier, only this time it was Bradford who applied the most concerted pressure and reaped the rewards. With former Rhino Adrian Morley a short-term signing from Sydney Roosters to bolster an already strong Bradford six, the Bulls came back from conceding the opening try to Danny McGuire to give Leeds a second-half shut–out and conclude a remarkable run of form by winning 15–6 to take the Super League trophy back to Odsal for a record–equalling fourth time, Lesley Vainikolo, fittingly, claiming the final touchdown of the first decade.

TOP 10 SUPER LEAGUE STALWARTS

1 ROBBIE PAUL (BRADFORD BULLS, HUDDERSFIELD GIANTS)
The Kiwi international was one of Bradford's players of the decade, appearing at full-back, half-back and hooker in 229 Super League appearances, scoring 121 tries and making a tremendous contribution to the club's brilliant off-field marketing drive. A great ambassador and, in the words of Peter Deakin, the Bulls' first and ultimately most influential 'franchise player' he became known as the 'hot stepper'.

2 ANDREW FARRELL (WIGAN WARRIORS)
Already a teenage international prior to the dawn of the Super League era, his ability to score with both deceptive hand and metronomic boot earned him 2,376 points in 230 appearances over the first nine years of the competition. A supreme talent in a variety of positions, the dual Man of Steel was an inspirational leader and an outstanding professional.

3 STEELE RETCHLESS (LONDON BRONCOS)
Carrying a name that was surely made for this toughest of sports, he lived up to his parents' poetic licence by providing the girders around which the Broncos' packs of the Super League era have largely been built. A total of 188 appearances in seven seasons for the capital club, plus an extraordinary world-record statistic of 66 tackles in a match of just eighty minutes, make him one of the decade's genuine, often unsung, heroes.

4 BARRIE MCDERMOTT (LEEDS RHINOS) AND TERRY O'CONNOR (WIGAN WARRIORS, WIDNES VIKINGS)
Bracketed together because of their similarities, the pair were already great mates and had been squaring up to each other prior to Super League but their powerful surges and uncompromising defence quickly became a hallmark of the summer era. Their careers, which encompassed the whole decade, were also paralleled in terms of statistics – McDermott 232 appearances for Leeds, O'Connor 247 for Wigan/Widnes – though McDermott's 28 tries more than doubles his fellow stalwart's 11. Durability in the most physically demanding role of all was merely their starting point.

5 KEIRON CUNNINGHAM (ST HELENS)
One of the few British players to have been genuinely courted by Australia's NRL clubs during the decade. Injuries may have hit his international career, but the stocky, powerhouse hooker has been a major weapon in St Helens' extensive armoury during their run of summer success, making 249 Super League appearances and posting

110 tries. Almost unstoppable from dummy half, his invention around the ruck has terrorised marker defences.

6 MALCOLM ALKER (SALFORD CITY REDS)
A tireless worker for the City Reds' cause since his debut in 1997, he has remained loyal at a club out of the spotlight but merits his place for being the top tackler in three of the past four seasons, including an awesome 1,050 hits in the 2001 campaign. Unlucky to be born in the era of the likes of Keiron Cunningham and James Lowes, or he would probably have picked up a Great Britain cap or two along the way. His 174 Super League appearances yielded 37 tries.

7 FRANCIS CUMMINS (LEEDS RHINOS)
One of a crop of talented youngsters brought into the Leeds squad in the early 1990s, he survived all his peers with an exemplary attitude, instinctive finishing ability and an elegant running style. Versatility was his middle name, playing at centre, wing and full-back, which brought 120 tries in 230 Super League appearances. Set a club record for consecutive appearances at the end of the 2003 campaign with 178. Now on the Rhinos coaching staff.

8 GARY CONNOLLY (WIGAN WARRIORS, LEEDS RHINOS, WIDNES VIKINGS)
Tough-as-teak Connolly had been both victim of and then victor in the great Wigan teams of the immediate pre-Super League era, progressing from full-back to become a world-class centre and then returning again to his original role. Famed for his immense upper-body strength and ultra-dependable, he hardly missed a tackle, and scored 80 tries in 225 Super League outings.

9 ADRIAN VOWLES (CASTLEFORD TIGERS, LEEDS RHINOS, WAKEFIELD TRINITY WILDCATS)
Voted Man of Steel in 1999, the Queenslander provided a determined, ruthless edge in the Castleford pack in two spells at the club. Strong, mobile and with a great pair of hands, the Australian back-row forward or centre graced the competition on 172 occasions in a seven-year stay. The Tigers had no hesitation in calling on him for another cameo stint at the end of 2005 to aid their drive back into the top flight, such was his value.

10 STEVE MCNAMARA (BRADFORD BULLS, WAKEFIELD TRINITY WILDCATS, HUDDERSFIELD GIANTS)
A classy, ball-handling back row, whose introduction to the top flight came with his home town Hull FC in the early 1990s. Played a huge part in Bradford's title win in 1997 and helped them reach Wembley twice, before appearing for both Wakefield and, in two spells, Huddersfield; making 160 Super League appearances between 1996 and 2003. Continues to make an impact as Bradford Bulls assistant coach and is widely tipped for the top as the competition moves into its second decade.

SIX

STABILITY, OFF THE FIELD

'I have long held the view that there is one characteristic more than anything else that identifies the genuine, dyed-in-the-wool rugby league supporter – a deeply held, almost innate sense of grievance.' – Former MP and staunch Wakefield fan David Hinchcliffe

The reintegration of the Rugby Football League and Super League Europe into a single, overall governing body under the lead and direction of Richard Lewis heralded a much-needed equilibrium in the corridors of power to match the unfolding deeds on the green swards. Of almost equal magnitude was the appointment of three non-executive directors, all with specialisms and expertise in key areas of modern sporting business practice. Welshman Ian Edwards, who played for Carcassonne and was involved in the BBC's coverage of the code in the late 1980s, was a key player when the television rights came up for renegotiation in 2004. Former Halifax chairman and leading West Yorkshire entrepreneur Tony Gartland heads the RFL's Internal Audit and Remuneration Committees and Maurice Watkins, who was on the board at Manchester United, is one of the country's leading sport's law-yers. What the new senior management team gave the sport as it began to settle into its new clothes was a transparency of governance, moving it away from the traditional, factionalised in-fighting that had punctuated the course of its chequered and colourful history. Division, resentment and insularity still existed but it was becoming increasingly marginalised, allow-ing the sport to plough a lone furrow rather than having to continually turn back to re-sow its seeds. Despite coming across as somewhat reserved and maybe even introverted, those who work under Richard Lewis point to his resolve and determination as key characteristics that have enabled rugby league to attain a measure of consistency in its decision-making processes. After a period of brash, personality-led leadership, which may have been necessary to drive through so many expedient revolutionary changes, Lewis sought calmer waters through a more arms-length management style that was centred on devolving power to his departmental heads while took care of the direction in which the ship was sailing. One of his greatest assets was that he came into the thirteen-a-side game with an unjaundiced eye, and was therefore able to see it for what it was and, vitally, what it needed to be. 'My perception of the game was based upon Saturday afternoon *Grandstand* during the Eddie Waring era. The sport had lost me a little bit with the switch to summer, I must admit. I remember driving my children back to drop them off at boarding school on light, mid-summer Sunday evenings listening to radio commentaries on matches and not having a handle on when rugby league was being played, and that was very influential to me when starting the job. Equally, I knew that it was a big sport with major events that was strong and with a lot to offer. I was very aware of the existence of London Broncos although not where they played and that they had been around for a long time, and the international element, of England and Great Britain against Australia. I knew it was strong in the North but I didn't think that it was just a northern sport.'

A successful player, international coach and then team manager when Great Britain won a silver medal at the Atlanta Olympics, his first love was tennis. He had been a director of the Lawn Tennis Association but was particularly attracted by the role of executive chairman within the RFL. 'There were two really strong reasons; I play tennis at Wimbledon with the same people every year – and have done for years – and we have lunch afterwards and this was two days before I heard about the job at Red Hall (RFL headquarters). One of the players was someone from the North of England, a former rugby league player, and although we had never really talked about the sport before, he spoke at great length that day about how it was getting its act together and how it had changed and how disastrous the 2000 World Cup had been financially. When I heard about the job I knew that it was something worth looking into because it was a sport that was moving in the right direction. Secondly, the role of executive chairman – the combination of chief executive and chairman into one drill – attracted me enormously because it immediately meant less politics and made sense. I had no real preconceptions about how the sport was administered before I took the job. People said there were strong personalities but I didn't take any real notice of that because there are in all sports.'

He was conscious from the start, though, of a need to move essentially from the benevolent dictatorship of the past to collective responsibility. 'Those are fair words to use, especially stressing independence and the

benefit to the whole sport of working together and finding common ground
when you can. Trying to communicate effectively, bring good order, discipline and processes into the administration and the conduct of meetings, and
openness as well, were the priorities. I was determined to make people feel
comfortable with and part of that decision-making process, rather than have
concerns of being misquoted in the minutes, for example, or stitched up.
When I first started I had an overwhelming impression that a lot of change
had already taken place and that it was a sport that was used to changing
things and almost, in my opinion, doing it too hastily without thinking it
through. I quickly started to espouse stability as part of the management
style rather than deciding policy on the hoof and a whim so at least people
could feel there was some continuity. Equally, if something is wrong I am
prepared to admit that I or the organisation has made a mistake.'

What he saw at the outset was a real potential for the spectacle that was
Super League. 'It was just great, the match-day experience was really good
and what was happening on the pitch was fantastic. I believe television cov-
ers the sport very well but it is even better when you see it live because
of the drama and the constant need to keep your eyes on the action. One
missed tackle and it's either a score or a genuine scoring opportunity, which
is very hard to put across on the small screen. You realise that when you go
to a game. It was heading in the right direction financially; a lot of difficult
stuff had been done before I arrived and, in terms of renegotiating the new
TV contracts, to me we had something that was worth buying and therefore the tactic was to hold out for the right kind of deal, which I think we
got in the end.'

His Davis Cup background in particular made him acutely aware of the
international dimension but he did not find the strength of the sport being
based on a strong and improving club-based elite competition a drawback.
'It's not frustrating because that's one of the things I see as a real opportunity. When you look at something you have to analyse whether it is being
used to the maximum and stretched to the limit or is it a scenario where
you can actually make a difference, and the international game is some-
where where we as administrators can still do that. There are a number of
people at club level who do see the bigger picture and can see the need
to put the international game to the fore. If you want to make your mark
in rugby league administration then the international sphere is one of the
areas where you can do that. So much of Super League is right, I feel. You've
got such a good base to work from, unlike the international game where
a lot of new ground has to be broken and it's a different challenge. There
is now a genuine independence in terms of decision making in the centre

but the big clubs are still very important, they are the bedrock of the game. Leeds Rhinos getting record crowds or Wigan having a difficult season are hugely important to the code and I can't imagine a situation where they or the top players are not at the forefront. For it to be any other way would be a nonsense, unlike in some other sports where the lack of understanding about the issues for the clubs and what they face is a real problem and that is wrong.'

He also found that Super League was rapidly becoming a more mature concept, not least in terms of its growing self-regulation. 'The salary cap was a huge asset when I arrived; I thought it was incredible to have it in place and great for the game, a tool and a mechanism that was not necessarily going to guarantee the future health of Super League but made sure it was pointing in the right direction. Self-regulation and the ability of the twelve individual clubs to look at the collective good is often underestimated. The acceptance of the cap is a good example of that; it does not necessarily work to the advantage of all the clubs but it is something they are not given enough credit for having implemented. Putting into effect a set of minimum standards is slightly different because it's not quite so immediate; it's quite easy to vote for something that isn't going to have an impact on you for the next three or four years or maybe even in the foreseeable future. Where minimum standards help is that they remove the pressure on directors to be seen to be just investing in the team to actually saying we have to make sure facilities are good because of the direction the league is going in. That helps in discussions with local councils and potential developers; the threat of being outside Super League for that reason is a huge negotiating and bargaining tool for clubs, which they welcome. "Framing the Future" was a valuable document that certainly shouldn't be forgotten, a defining moment in the sport's history, but life has moved on a little and now we've got the Super League strategy and National League strategy being launched and the Whole Sport plan.'

With media and sponsorship activities now such a crucial element in the overall funding of sport, most governing bodies would find it difficult to continue to operate in their current form without those huge sources of investment. That made it imperative that the third broadcast rights negotiation of the summer era in 2004 was the right deal. 'It was about value and balance but also the fine detail in the small print. New media is becoming more and more critical so those rights are very important to the game. It was also about territory. It was never a particularly difficult negotiating point but certainly we wanted to just sell the rights to the UK so that we could do more to use and sell the rights around the world and, also in terms of tactics, we took on an agency from the word go. That was, and still is in certain circles, very controversial – a number of people within the sport think we shouldn't use agents, which I find bizarre because it is a very specialised area. To be able to actually work out where things are going in terms of this technological age that we are living in, is incredibly difficult and to be a part timer or amateur on that, someone who only gets involved occasionally, is not the way to do it. Taking on an agency also gives you credibility, not just with the BBC or Sky, but internationally. We get a lot of enquiries nowadays about coverage, almost on a weekly basis – for example we have just sold some rights to the Middle East – and if they say they are interested and how do we go about discussing it with you and we put them in touch with a company that has a worldwide reputation, like Trans World International, it says everything about your sport. It means that you know what you are doing.'

He was equally keen to get benefits from both sides of the broadcasting divide; terrestrial and satellite. 'I don't think the code sold out to Sky originally, I can't relate to that at all. Sky is a huge asset to the sport. I've been involved in a few interviews with regard to cricket now having nothing bar forty-five minutes of highlights coverage on terrestrial television from 2006 and that's a discussion point, but in terms of what Sky has done for rugby league in the way they cover it, two live matches a week and sometimes three plus showing other levels and a magazine programme, it's just a constant exposure that is very beneficial. Rather than saying the sport "sold its soul", I would contend that Sky have been a fantastic partner in taking the game forwards – Super League wouldn't be what it is now without Sky. To be fair to them they do now hold the rights to some major events like the Ryder Cup. They are gaining more and more subscribers – it's up to over seven million now – so their access to the wider community is growing by the month. Fifty per cent of our viewers on Sky each week are from the South of England according to the statistics we get and the game has grown very significantly over the last few years in different parts of the country. That's the result of many things but also because we get very good coverage from Sky and the BBC almost throughout the whole of the year now and that's helping us to grow the sport beyond the traditional heartlands. One of the things we've gained in the last couple of years is an improved package from the BBC. That was a long and protracted negotiation but we're delighted that the corporation are now showing highlights of the end of the Super League season and also the international matches. We feel that between the two broadcasters we have an extensive mix and ironically in some ways that is leading to more and more fans coming to stadiums to watch matches live because they are seeing how good the games are on television. I get frustrated with the BBC sometimes but overall though you have to acknowledge that the major rights are sold to another company. Having said that they could do more with the Challenge Cup, they have a property there that they undersell and under-promote. Is there "institutional bias"? At times I think there is although I don't think it's nearly as great as some people think it is. Straight editorial decisions are made sometimes perfectly validly on the interest in say a Super League match report vis-à-vis another sport, but there are times when the people in London are influenced by who or what they talk about with their mates in the pub on a Friday or Saturday evening and that might be tennis, football or cricket and less often rugby league. There is an institutional issue there that it will be very interesting to monitor if the corporation do move their sports department to Manchester as they are planning. We are still reactive rather than proactive with regards to news management, in particular selling the players to the widest public and merchandising. It's about finding the expertise and the resources and time to go that extra yard in creating news coverage. If you actually analyse what we get say regionally through the BBC or via Sky Sports' network we probably do pretty well on the whole but when you go into the non-sports pages or the feature writers on the sports pages, we probably don't do as well as we should. That's an area we are working on now with the appointment of Simon Malcolm, who has a very important job title; it's not just director of marketing but it's also corporate communications. That to me is about high-level selling of the sport beyond the rugby league journalists.'

In 2004 Lewis was invited to sit on Sport England's National Investment Panel, which provides strategic guidance to the organisation's main board on the distribution of major funding to all sports. As such he is in constant contact with leading politicians and the major movers and shakers connected with other sports. He has found their reaction to Super League to be extremely positive. 'I don't think I've met anybody in all the time I've been in post who has watched Super League either live or on the television and then said that they hadn't enjoyed it. But there are a lot of people, possibly even the vast majority, who do not realise how big the sport is outside of the heartland. When you look at Super League and there is only London outside the accepted M62 corridor at the moment, then you can understand and respect why they come to that conclusion, that's just the way it is. I also think the game has suffered from not having Wembley, big time. As a sport I've found there is a huge amount of respect for the code and for an amazing number of people rugby league is their second favourite sport and is right there among what they enjoy watching and plan their weekend around. That, in terms of growing the game, is where our hunting ground will be – converting that second choice into a first one.'

A progressive image is also important to him. Recent market research undertaken by the RFL in their drawing up of a new corporate identity under the banner 'It's a whole new ballgame', reconfirmed that family values are still at the code's core. 'In rugby league it's fairly easy, you can do corporate hospitality in a way that's family friendly. For example, we had a number of VIP's bring their children to the Challenge Cup final because it was over a Bank Holiday weekend. I think pricing is also very important; we don't price ourselves out of the family market. There are other things that affect our family image that we need to be careful about and that includes anti-doping and behaviour on the field including continued respect for match officials and the eradication of foul play. We need to be very alert about that sort of thing. By and large rugby league is so clearly identified with being a family sport and perfect to take the family to. The sport is so strong in its communities but when we get to something like the Challenge Cup final then the exposure a major event like that gives us is very significant. It creates a lot of extra interest and we are able to run things like the Champion Schools competition alongside it, which has enabled us to grow the sport at that level very significantly. Equally, when you get to the Super League Grand Final – which has sold out Old Trafford for the last few years – that is now a huge moment in the fans' calendar.'

A measure of how Super League has evolved over the decade can be seen by the changing profile of its title sponsor; from JJB through Tetley's – who both had club affiliations – to a finance house. 'To a certain extent that's true but I personally wouldn't overstate it. Currently "engage" are a perfect fit with us – we can do a great job for them and they for us and it is happening – but you just don't know who the next sponsor will be and how long they will be with us. I certainly think in the way the sport has gone over the last few years that it is no surprise that it is a financial services company; it does reflect the way the sport has moved and is positioning itself very deliberately and professionally. If we went with a betting or gaming company or a brewer next time round then I don't think that would necessarily be a disastrous setback, it depends what they are trying to achieve. The government is very pro-gambling at the moment so who is to say that it is anti-social? There are lots of ways to position yourself as a family sport without necessarily having a title sponsor who is particularly family friendly.'

One of his primary concerns has been to move the Challenge Cup final so that it retained it's pre-eminence as a 'crown jewel' event rather than merely becoming devalued as a pre-season tournament in the build up to Super League. 'To have your major showpiece cup final towards the end of the season is of absolutely overwhelming importance. For the passing sports fan, they need to be able to understand the structure of the season very easily and you can do that with rugby league now. If the average spectator – whoever he or she is – can do that then the media are much more likely to cover it because they are reflecting what is of interest out there in the market place. To have a season that culminates with a cup final, the play-offs and then the international season is so easy to explain to anybody and is overwhelmingly logical. The thing that everybody was always concerned about, with having all the big events around at the same time of the year, was if that was affordable for the fans and the answer has undoubtedly been yes it is. I think that having too many matches is one of the great challenges for the game. It is such a long season for such a physically demanding sport that it is obvious we have got to find a way of reducing that. I know we are going in the right direction with things like the salary cap, growing the attendances, improving the sponsorship. All that is going to make the clubs more financially sustainable on a shorter season in due course but we are still quite a few years off.'

One of the other great debates is the value and balance of club versus country, both for players and fans. 'It is easy to have a sport where there is too much emphasis on the international game. Just because the international game delivers big bucks doesn't mean to say that it should be the be all and end all. It is perfectly possible to have a balance between club and country. Arguably for the next ten years or so, if the international calendar has good quality matches at the end of the season and a couple in mid-season that would be absolutely fine because how many other big fixtures or great events is the sport able to sustain. I think France will be very competitive soon but who else in Europe is there who could give England really good, tough matches that generate huge money? It's just not going to happen.'

For continued stability to provide the right springboard for future expansion there has to be a real commitment to youth development. 'The Academy structure is very good and well respected. The quota is coming down although circumstances beyond our control have conspired to make it difficult to limit the number of overseas players, but that is not the fault of the sport, it is legal changes outside of it and the development of young talent is happening. It is one of those elements that is heading in the right direction; we just need to continue that process and make sure it speeds up a bit. The performance department has had a real influence in terms of organisation and the development of talent, but it is a job that is only half done in my opinion. We have retained David Waite as a consultant and we still have things to do that he has pointed out, but we need to go the extra yard if we really want to be the best nation in the world and that is about less matches for the best players. The formation and popularity of the Tri-Nations Tournament is a reflection of the sport's strength, but it's all based upon the success of Super League. That competition is the bedrock and foundation to all of this, in making the Great Britain side so much more competitive. The fact that Super League is now being compared to the NRL – most observers would say that the overall standard isn't quite as good, but it does at least justify comparison – means that we are in there against the other leading international powers with a genuine shout. There are some things we still need to do to be confident that we will be better than Australia rather than just hope for a victory. There has to be sustainability, a position where we expect to win and then continue doing it and if we lose we think it is just a blip, and there is still a way to go before that happens.'

The perceived success of Super League may well have seen international competition enhanced, but there are still critics that see the sport as a perennially northern game, which will always see it held back. 'It's a funny thing but I think Super League as a brand is not thought of as being particularly northern. I think it's when you use the words "rugby league" when that "northernness" comes across. Super League is recognised as a national brand; people have heard about it even if not every general fan would know what sport it was and if we can grow that awareness with Les Catalans coming in or a second London team or a Welsh club then I really do think Super League will be right there to be on the widest national stage. It's almost there now in many people's eyes and once it is that will be the stepping stone to rugby league no longer being seen as a northern sport and in terms of brand positioning that's the way I see it. Rugby league is still that connotation of Eddie Waring, winter rugby and all that but Super League has taken us a significant way away from that. I wouldn't call rugby league a minority sport although I don't think it's as big as some people think. For example, if you look at the number of kids playing the game in school compared to other sports like tennis or cricket, we've got further to go than a lot of people realise. I don't see any reason whatsoever why it can't be a major sport in this country – I can see lots of reasons why it should be and I can't see any to stop it. I think it's perfect for schools and universities and once it's established there you're up and running.'

What he is even more certain of is that genuine uncertainty of outcome – which will speed up the expansion process – is already happening. 'In Super

League X, taking the play-offs, there were five teams who all genuinely deep down thought that, given a fair wind, they could get to the Grand Final and win it. I don't think London, as the other side in the top six, would have ever professed to do that but if you take the plans for Harlequins for 2006, the potential for Les Catalans with their player base and the impact of the salary cap and analysing the trend of increasing spend on teams, then I would say we are actually getting quite close to it, surprisingly close, more so than people might realise. The difficulty will be, over the next four or five years, that there are likely to be a couple of teams who cannot aspire to win Super League because their stadium is not going to be modern enough and they don't have the ability to generate sufficient commercial revenue for players in a given year. However, it is not unrealistic to think that ten out of twelve teams will soon be starting a season with a really genuine feel that they have had an equal chance of recruiting the players they need to have a crack at the Grand Final, and there are very few competitions around the world that could say that. It's not something we should be apologising for.'

His utopian vision again harks back to the need for advanced strategy and forward planning in a sport not renowned for it. 'I think we have changed that perception and most observers would say that there is now long-term planning but there is a balance between saying "this is what we are going to do" and delivering it. You have to achieve a reasonably high percentage of what you intend to; it's acceptable occasionally to miss the mark and set out the reasons why or to be big enough, confident enough and honest enough to change your plans occasionally if you think that a course of action is no longer the right thing to do. The bottom line is that to be considered to be consistent in your thinking long term, you have to deliver a high percentage of your stated aims and objectives and overall we have started to do that. Les Catalans would be a good example; it was a big decision and we've stuck to our guns although it hasn't been plain sailing all the way. They are coming in to Super League with every chance of hitting the ground running, obstacles aren't in their way and they have had every opportunity to recruit a really good squad and to get themselves ready off the pitch. I didn't take a lot of notice of what happened with Paris but as the decision became imminent on UTC before they changed their name, then I was told more and more about what went on in the capital. But that wasn't what dictated my thinking. Of more concern was the logic of how long a club would need to be ready to come into Super League and it was just overwhelmingly obvious that it was more than a few months. What happened in Paris, it seems to me, was a perfectly legitimate reaction to an opportunity and who is to say it was the wrong thing to do? The chance and the money were there and if Paris hadn't happened, people would have said the administrators at the time were unbelievably cautious and narrow in their thinking. At least it was an attempt but in this day and age, to set up and run a professional club and recruit a team, coach and back-up staff cannot be done in few months so the thinking with Les Catalans always was that we had to give them a long lead-in period. To be fair, we originally aimed for 2005 but did not hit the target but in 2006 we did it, which is a good example of honest, long-term planning.'

Beech and Chadwick, in their study of the business of sport, identify the key elements against which a sport like Super League can quantify whether or not it has attained what has been identified as the third phase of its advancement; stability. Product development, which has seen the summer now firmly established as the playing season, is being further achieved with the opening up of the Catalan market in particular. Customer relationship management while maximising sustainable profit is being realised, although a flexible pricing policy will need to be maintained to ensure that the intense loyalty and fervour of the fans is not exploited by making excessive demands on them. Finding the right customers does pose an inherent dilemma for Super League when trying to retain traditional fans and take them on an unfamiliar journey while cultivating and enticing a new kind of spectator. The tangible elements of the product, like the stadium, hospitality, merchandise and programmes have basically reached an accepted and definable norm, as have the intangibles such as the service offered by the arena personnel, overall branding and the actual game itself. The promotion of star players as wider personalities is yet to be fully realised though. The rise of e-commerce has seen most clubs focussing more on supporters' needs with its ease of ticketing and merchandising and provision of exclusive information. The internet is now an established and important part of the sports marketing mix although official message boards, even if extensively moderated, carry potential for litigation with risk management for all businesses now becoming a highly pertinent issue. As Beech and Chadwick conclude, 'As spectators' lives change so must the services offered by the sports industry. To what extent will sport remain popular in the context of proliferating expenditure choices; will customers come to perceive sport as a virtual experience or will the live occasion have an enduring appeal? Sport businesses will increasingly engage in the diversification and development of product portfolios; this will embrace brand building and the extension of sport business franchises. Given the importance of top performers to the on-field playing and off-field commercial performance of sport businesses, there is a need to address the implications of conduct and behaviour on and off the field of play. Players will have to reconcile such competing pressures and their training and development needs may become evident with a need to consider whether traditional agents can continue to provide an appropriate service or whether professional business managers fulfil a more useful role.'

So how does the most important administrator in rugby league assess his premier competition after ten years on the scene? 'If I was to write it a school report,' Richard Lewis concedes, 'it would be, "you've achieved a lot, well done, but you need to keep working hard and you've got some potential that you haven't quite fulfilled yet. Keep behaving yourself, your classroom behaviour is important, it does affect your output but you've improved a lot over the past few years."'

TOP 10 WORST DECISIONS

1 1997 WORLD CLUB CHAMPIONSHIP
Not the concept itself, but the inclusion of every club from Britain and Australia instead of a much more concise, competitive event, which made it embarrasing and at times excruciating. If you were a one-eyed Brit it was a bit like watching Ricky Gervais' anti-hero David Brent in *The Office*.

2 AUSTRALIA *v.* GREAT BRITAIN, SYDNEY, 2002
Given that Great Britain had not won a three-match series against the Aussies since 1970, it was hardly surprising that asking the Lions to fly halfway round the globe and take on the world's best inside a week and with jet lag was commercial suicide. Conceding eleven tries, ten of them converted, made this 64-10 record hammering the worst advertisement for the domestic game in a decade.

3 VIDEO REFEREE, 1999 GRAND FINAL
Presumably not on Christmas card lists of either Michael Withers or Leon Pryce, video referee David Campbell decided that Withers had knocked-on in trying to intercept Paul Atcheson's pass. Pryce's subsequent score was ruled out and the Bulls lost another decider to St Helens.

4 ABANDONING THE 'ON THE ROAD' CONCEPT
Introduced as an afterthought because of a mid-season gap designed to avoid soccer's 1998 World Cup, during which it had been hoped an international league tournament would be held in the southern hemisphere. Instead, every Super League club played an extra match at a neutral venue across the British Isles showcasing the game in non-Super League areas. A great idea that sadly lasted just one season and would have benefited from greater promotion.

5 LOOPY 'LOOP' FIXTURES

The introduction of an extra six fixtures, tagged on to the end of the regular home and away rounds, continues to be one of the negatives of the Super League era. Done with scant regard for the welfare of the players, but instead to swell the coffers of the clubs, the majority of whom have patently not studied the phrase 'false economy'.

6 THE 'SHUDDERSFIELD' MERGER

A nickname thought to have been invented by *Yorkshire Post* journalist John Ledger for the coming together of Sheffield Eagles and Huddersfield Giants in 2000, under the banner of Huddersfield-Sheffield Giants. Aside from being a commentator's nightmare, the merger was unpalatable for both sets of fans – a disaster all ways round.

7 AU REVOIR, MATE

Aside from the numerous other reasons that Paris St Germain lasted just two seasons in Super League, their forced, liberal use of mainly journeymen antipodeans did little to help their onfield cause and, worse, further alienated an already unfamiliar public.

8 EASTER FIXTURE PROGRAMME

At the risk of repeating the words of any Super League coach, you simply cannot have players turning out in four matches in a fortnight any longer. Once again the physical demands placed on players are outweighed by what the club chairmen call commercial necessity, while the second of the fixtures over Easter invariably but understandably short changes the fans on quality.

9 A GLEEFUL PUNT AT LONG ODDS-ON

Inextricably linked with the Easter programme is the type of situation that induced the infamous bets placed by Sean Long and Martin Gleeson on Bradford to beat their St Helens side at Odsal on Easter Monday, 2004. With inside knowledge of how depleted Ian Millward's run-on team would be, the pair backed a loser in the most ill-judged decision either is ever likely to make.

10 THE LOSS OF MARKETING 'GURU' PETER DEAKIN

Rugby league in Britain has only become aware of its commercial value since the advent of the summer era, and the driving force behind its exploitation was the late, great Peter Deakin. With a fantastic track record at Bradford behind him, he was appointed Super League Europe's marketing director in 1997 but lasted only a matter of weeks, complaining that the budget offered to him was less than that at Odsal. 'If my going shakes the clubs up and makes them get serious about what needs to be done, then it might do some good,' he said, but it would have been better if he had been given the tools to do the job.

SEVEN

VIEW FROM THE BOX

'I don't think sport at any level in this country would survive without the revenue from television coverage. The worst disaster is to lose it, to fall out of favour. The importance of top-level sport is the inspiration factor.' – Michael Grade, chairman, BBC

The constant reoccurring theme in any debate about or analysis of developments in modern sport is the inordinate influence of the small box in the corner and, in the case of televised Super League, the large one in the stadium. It has changed from being an inquisitive novelty that a governing body could seek to regulate and monitor to a voracious beast with an enormous, insatiable appetite that dominates the landscape. While rugby league in Britain was in no position to reject the advances of the Murdoch empire in 1995, its decision to throw in its lot with the satellite revolution not only proved to be commercially expedient but also far-sighted and progressive. Television irrevocably changed the sporting landscape after the Second World War, although initially there was some reluctance and scepticism, principally from the clubs themselves, as to how it would affect live attendances, at the time still virtually the sole source of income for the game. Rugby League kept the mounting advance at arm's length; the 1948 Wembley Challenge Cup final being shown only in London and the one between Warrington and Widnes two years later relayed solely in the Midlands. The first live transmission was Great Britain's thrilling 20-19 Second Test win over the Kiwis at Swinton in 1951, contemporary reports noting, 'Here at least is a splendid chance to show the country the best of our matches. We have always suffered from the fact that in the past there have been so few opportunities of taking rugby league to the great towns and cities of the Midlands, London and the South. Now TV is at hand and we shall be fools if its offer is not accepted. The benefits of nationwide television of rugby league will only be reaped if we prepare plans against the time when the country will be ready to receive us. Planned expansion is the next great milestone.' Almost exactly the same debate was still trenchant forty-five years later. Soon after, led by demand to watch the Coronation in 1953, mass sales of television sets meant that millions of people suddenly had access to sport, many of them new or casual viewers. Although there was some ambivalence on behalf of the RFL during the remainder of the 1950s, the code has been associated with some notable television landmarks. In 1954, the inaugural World Cup final was broadcast live on the fledgling Eurovision satellite link from Paris, the first occasion in any sport that a British team had been seen in action on foreign soil in a World Cup decider. The BBC2 Floodlit Trophy was inaugurated in 1965, which precipitated the change to a limited-tackle rule. The BBC initiated the European Club Championship four years later between Leeds and Perpignan, which helped roll out colour transmission, and live coverage of the 1978 'Dad's Army' Second Ashes Test at Odsal was the main feature of the first *Sunday Grandstand*. Not only that but, as John Ford suggested of the code's lowest point in the early 1970s in *This Sporting Land*, broadcast on Thames Television, 'It would perhaps be fair to say that the BBC has sustained rugby league through a difficult period when it could possibly have collapsed.'

The relationship between governing body and principal broadcaster was essentially a cosy one; the sport gaining revenue from the provider and associated sponsors who increasingly wanted to see their name given a greater exposure while the television companies could fill large chunks of their schedules with programming that was relatively cheap, invariably dramatic and had a defined following and market. All that changed with the irresistible and immutable arrival of commercial satellite television, as Garry Whannel reflected: 'By 1985 we had come to take for granted the provision of high-quality live colour pictures relayed around the world by satellite, augmented by slow-motion action replay. Sponsorship had become a major source of revenue for the elite level of sport. In the television era, sport had become an international spectacle, producing vast earnings for elite performers as the brakes came off commercialisation. Much of the impetus for the transformation came from opportunist and maverick entrepreneurs. Satellite sport in the United Kingdom grew slowly at first, hampered by slow dish sales and competition between two providers, BSB and Sky. Once they had merged, the rapidly growing revenue from pay-per-channel services began to give satellite television enhanced scope to obtain the rights to major events. Broadcasting, like sport, became a commodity.' Dennis Brailsford in *British Sport – A Social History* (Lutterworth Press, 1992) concurred, outlining the new dilemmas facing a sport like rugby league. 'A new

multiplicity of television channels raises new problems for sports administrators. In charge of activities that have always tended to be traditionalist,
conservative and cautious in their attitude to change, they have to relate
to a powerful, dynamic medium that has become central to most people's
leisure. Apart from the other effects of television on sport – its treatment of
it as entertainment, as staged drama, its focus on action, conflict and personality – there is the increasing inter-relationship between television and
the popular press. Tabloid dailies are, in fact, virtually incomprehensible to
anyone unacquainted with the latest offerings on the television screen. They
both pick up on the same themes.'

Nowhere was that more true than in Australia where 'favourite son'
Rupert Murdoch knew that to obtain the quickest and most effective return
on his massive hardware investment he needed to buy the exclusive rights
to major, live, indigenous sport. Natural resistance to subscription fees and
dish, box or cable charges was gradually broken down – like with all new
consumer technology – and from being a luxury item, satellite transformed
into a must-have necessity, central to leisure activity. Fans, particularly 'working-class' ones linked to a sport like rugby league, would undoubtedly resent
the additional, unwarranted pull on their already stretched pockets but
the lure of indulging in following their passion was always going to prove the
greater. 'It is significant that rugby league was born and thrived in Australia
thanks to one single factor: money. Rupert Murdoch was, in fact, upholding
the oldest tradition in the game. The big profits in pay television were in
subscriptions, what he needed were the viewers and that meant sport. The
footie got the dish on the roof and the rest followed. Rugby league was an
obvious target and Murdoch was looking much further than just showing the game to its traditional followers. He was now in a position to take
it to the world through BSkyB, Fox in the US and Star throughout Asia.'
(Colman) Even at the time of the announcement that the British game had
thrown its lot in with the new master in April 1995, cultural commentator
Mark Lawson highlighted the dichotomy faced. 'The weekend when true
sporting fans were to be heard bemoaning the power of television – following the take over of rugby league by Rupert Murdoch's News Corporation
– was also the very weekend when true sporting fans were to be found
beached helplessly in front of the set. Rarely has there been a more opportune time for a replay of that great old grudge-match: Television *v.* Sport.
Should we be cheering or jeering?'

One of Murdoch's most dependable and trusted lieutenants, Vic Wakeling,
managing director at Sky Sports for the last twelve years, has played a central role in establishing the new order. He is keen to stress that although

his organisation has become such a dominant player in the market, the relationship between the sport and the company that points its cameras at it was more of a partnership, even from the outset, countering allegations that a soul was sold. 'I think that's really a question for rugby league. Did they think they sold their soul? We at Sky certainly didn't think so. There was a document commissioned by the Rugby Football League called 'Framing the Future', which made certain recommendations, including the switch to a summer sport. We didn't ask for the switch to summer, that was in the document itself. The RFL approached us and told us what they were doing. Maurice Lindsay came down to London and had a meeting with Sam Chisholm, the chief executive of Sky, and myself, and talked about the switch to a summer sport, and would we be interested in renewing – because we already had the old rights of course – and supporting this? There was of course a lot more detail to the chat, because if you remember in those early stages there was some alteration proposed to the clubs who actually made up Super League, and there were some strange names in there like Calder. We looked at all of that and we said yes of course, if you look at our business and the success of our football coverage, we thought that Super League would work for us in the summer. We thought it was an exciting idea and we said, if you make the switch, we will bid for the rights. We would have if it had stayed where it was in the winter, although perhaps we might not have bid so much. I think there was concern from the RFL as to whether we would support the switch to summer, or whether we were happy with where it was positioned, and if they switched to summer, would we say "Thanks very much but we're going to concentrate on cricket, we don't agree with the idea." What we said was "It will work for us, if you're sure it will work for you, we'll definitely go along with it if it becomes a summer sport."'

Twice during the initial negotiations in 1995, the RFL went back to Sky and raised the ante, partly to assuage clubs outside the initially proposed structure that they would not be cut financially adrift. Many assume that it was the conductor who was leading the orchestra down the road of mergers and a broader geographical base to Super League. 'There was certainly never any requirement from Sky's point of view to have a European element to Super League. I think it was far more important that London had a success-ful team. I was there for that first night in Paris, and the initiative for the French experiment came from the RFL itself, because let's face it we have no transmission in Paris, or in France. We broadcast into the UK and Ireland, so a team joining from France didn't really make any difference to us. We'd have preferred it I suppose, if there had been another team in another part of the country, but they felt that because of the interest in rugby league in France that it would help strengthen the league and give it more status, more credibility. That a French team was put into the competition in season one was certainly not at our request, and we would actually have preferred a team to be in Wales for example. That has been discussed many times over the years. We had been covering rugby league having inherited the contract from the old BSB and I think if you look at BSB's early impact, that was the most attractive property they had in Lancashire and Yorkshire, and they had already made inroads. So I think that by the time Super League came around we were already very strong in the North. We actually believed in the sport, that it could appeal to a wider audience and add to their enjoyment. Every sport that we cover, we try to say, okay, we know it has a certain number of followers, loyal followers who will watch everything, but how do we make a sport exciting so that it transcends its fan base? So whether that is golf, cricket, rugby league, rugby union, football, whatever, you hope that you can attract new viewers and therefore new fans to that game. That's what we work on. With rugby league we knew that we had a strong base before Super League in the North of England. We thought that the switch to summer would help to expand that base beyond there and so that is why we backed it. Let's face it, we're a commercial organisation, and everything we do – that's not just rugby league, but everything – is to sell boxes, but within all that we feel that we are able to help to spread sports to a wider audience and build their popularity and we think we've done that.'

Sky's audience may be smaller than that attracted by terrestrial television but their viewers are more pre-disposed to serious sport; after all they pay directly for it, rather than casual watchers who may, for example, have had Eddie Waring on as part of an afternoon's wallpaper filler before checking the football pools. There was quickly a growing acceptance of Sky Sports as the authoritative medium for the enthusiast. Consequently, satellite advertisers have a ready-made, specialised, dedicated niche market available to them, which is another attractive element in the deal for the broadcaster seeking a return on their huge initial outlay. 'I think we do draw a more passionate, committed fan in many ways. We're always trying to grow that base and grow the popularity of any sport, whatever that may be. So, for example, if you're a dedicated rugby league fan, before Sky you'd see the occasional match but now if you subscribe you see at least two matches a week from Super League, at least two matches a week from the NRL, plus we're bringing you internationals, we'll be covering the Tri-Nations Series this year from Down Under, and there are other matches that we have broadcast in addition to all that. They are fans and they want to watch a regular guaranteed diet of their sport. In my first ever meeting with Richard Lewis, one of the first things I said to him was that I would love to see a Tri-Nations Series happen. I'd watched it in rugby union and it worked and I said we should have Great Britain, Australia and New Zealand playing in that sort of tournament once a year and that it was something I thought he and the RFL should be looking at. I think rugby league has traditionally suffered on an international basis when compared to rugby union, and I thought this would be a great chance to build a credible, successful international tournament, and I've been delighted with the way it's gone so far.'

Few would argue that what Sky has done is revolutionise the look of the sport. Multiple camera angles and lush production values reflected in eye-catching promotional videos as well as, on game day, judicious use of vibrant music to enhance the image, have all forced re-evaluation among their competitors. 'When we launched Sky Sports fifteen years ago we knew that it would take a long time to grow an audience. But what we said right from the start as a principle is that we would never allow people to criticise our coverage. They are paying for our services. They expect to see top-class events and they expect to see quality coverage of them. We've put more cameras into stadiums, we've made more effort with sounds, effects and in everything we do, more than other broadcasters have. We scour the world every year to find new bits of kit that we can use, whether it be a new camera, a new relay machine, a new graphics machine and we do that across all our sports. We've got to be good. We've got to earn the loyalty of our subscribers who are paying a monthly fee to watch our services. It's all very well if they are passionate about their sport, but if the coverage isn't good enough they will feel that they are being sold short, so we try very hard to be leaders in every sport that we cover. It is just a case of attempting various things that you hope will add to the production. If we think it works we keep it, if not we don't, or sometimes we might go back to a modified version of it in the future. It's really down to Neville Smith, who at the start of the season will look at his production, give me a briefing, look at what he wants to do and advise me of the cost implications. I'll then tell him whether I agree with his ideas or not, though with Neville I have to say that I agree with most of his ideas. I think he is a very talented producer/director and I think he's done an outstanding service to the game.'

One of the acknowledged innovations has been the installation of a big screen at live matches, to which on-field referees can refer decisions over whether a legitimate try has been scored to a video referee who has all the latest slow-motion, close-up wizardry at his disposal. The images used for his deliberations are relayed to those in the stadium as he undertakes his analysis. There has been some thought that occasionally the release of the final decision is extenuated to enhance the dramatic impact but Premiership soccer referee Steven Lodge extolled its implementation – along with the idea of independent timekeepers – when he said in 1998, 'We've got a long way to go until we catch up with the principles of rugby league.' Additionally Mark Lawson noted, 'No-one can deny television's influence on modern sport. It has changed the nature of spectating. For all the excitement of actually being at an event, you find you want an action replay when something happens.' Vic Wakeling was acutely aware of that. 'I think the big screen has definitely added to the spectacle in the stadium. It's far more important to the people in there than it is to the viewers at home, because they've had the replay facility for many years, but to bring that facility into the stadium as well was very, very important to encouraging people to go along and enjoy the spectacle of rugby league. I'm not sure if they do have a cut-off point regarding video referee decisions. I will say though that the most important thing is to get the decision right, and I think we'd all agree on that.'

The difficulty is that, unlike in Australia, all the matches within a round are not fully televised over here, which means that the screen is not universally applied and, understandably, that is unlikely to change in the foreseeable future as to operate it requires the same hugely expensive need for multi-camera options and a state-of-the-art mixing vehicle with a production team at each venue. Right from the start of its coverage, in the pre-Super League winter days, Sky worked on the premise that those interested would understand the action anyway and so the production team concentrated on targeting and maintaining a new audience with a commentary style based on the promotion of definable personalities. Its principal duo from the outset have been former local radio soccer and rugby league commentator and television producer Eddie Hemmings and ex-Great Britain skipper Mike Stephenson, who cut his media teeth as a summariser on ABC after moving to Australia to play for Penrith in 1973, where he also had a respected newspaper column. There is little doubt that the formula worked, more dispassionate league fans in particular quickly coming to associate their repartee and evident passion with the modern face of the sport. Equally, within the industry, their profile and professionalism is genuinely recognised and much admired. Where there is some disquiet is with the more ardent fan. Just as opinion is divided about the contribution of the immensely knowledgeable and committed Eddie Waring – who was synonymous with the sport and its wider recognition outside the normal boundaries but eventually became a parody that tended to enforce a negative stereotypical image that hampered it being taken seriously – so 'Eddie and Stevo' have been labelled 'hype and tripe' by certain sections of fans in the trade press and on internet message boards. The Sky philosophy of 'I'll call it as I see it' has a tendency to accentuate controversy or incident, which seems to be part of the accepted style and that can lead to an impression of garish superficiality. Sport's media expert Steven Barnett in his influential text *Games and Sets – The Changing Face of Sport on Television* (BFI, 1990) highlights the importance of such tactics in the mediation process. 'The television viewer is a prisoner to sports producers, directors and commentators. In front of the screen, the event is interpreted on our behalf, in ways that can make the living-room experience utterly different from live experience. Viewers may lose out on uniquely atmospheric moments of sporting drama, but their perspective is enhanced in other ways that can make live spectating a humdrum experience. If a match is tedious, even the most sophisticated camerawork cannot instil drama where none exists. Many sports are not consistently exciting. This is acceptable to those interested in the action who will be able to appreciate skill and subtlety. It is less acceptable to transient television viewers who may have only rudimentary knowledge and marginal interest. Enter the commentator – a voice-over accompaniment to describe, explain, analyse and predict the event as well as to contribute an occasional dramatic embellishment that the game itself may lack. Most television sports now have their established "voices" whose characteristic tones are almost irreplaceably wedded to their respective games. No commentator can hope to appeal universally to every member of the audience. The balance between description and embellishment is a difficult one that has prompted much discussion over the years inside broadcasting institutions. Harry Carpenter wrote in 1964: "The cardinal sin of TV commentary is to talk unnecessarily." Much the same advice was advanced by the legendary Brian Johnston who advised that "the commentator's remarks drop like stones on a still pond". Generally speaking, a certain body of knowledge is assumed. There are two very different characteristics of a more pro-active television commentary: the instructive and the entertaining. The descriptive or instructive mode might foster a greater sense of awareness and comprehension among viewers, the dramatic mode often serves only to lift humdrum action into melodramatic excitement. When genuine drama exists, this can constitute a vital element of the programme's impact and enjoyment. But when real drama is lacking, there can be an irresistible temptation to invent it, to contrive a fierce competitive battle in order to heighten artificially a programme's entertainment value. The sports commentators' role as interpreter is seen as more closely resembling an ambassador and enthusiastic follower of the sport than an objective reporter. Given that it is the marginal viewers who represent the difference between ratings success and failure, television channels will want to minimise this audience wastage by emphasising the positive, the alluring and the entertaining. For this reason, there is a constant temptation to exaggerate certain elements of a contest that might serve to heighten tension and evoke a dramatic atmosphere. Benjamin Rader (author of *In its Own Image – How Television has Transformed Sports*) expresses a concern that the heavy emphasis on drama will eventually lower viewers' appreciation and enjoyment threshold. If elements of a match are constantly hyped because the genuine drama is too occasional to enrapture the marginal viewer, the proper focal point becomes gradually eroded and cheapened. It is the long-term consequences of this shift of emphasis that inflict the greatest damage.'

Vic Wakeling is aware of the inherent stylistic tensions, especially as the match callers are also the studio analysts. 'As far as commentary is concerned in any sport we come across that criticism of commentators. I think it's true for all other channels and for all other sports. You can't please all of the people all of the time, but we try to please most of the people most of the time. If I felt that Eddie and Stevo weren't performing to the level I want them to then I'd make a change. I think they love their sport, they have a clear passion for their sport, and that passion comes across and I think that's very important in commentary that people do display that passion because the majority of people listening to them share that passion for the sport. We've also introduced Phil Clarke to the commentary as someone who is, I suppose, much closer to the game in that he's from a more recent era than Stevo, and I think that the contrast of views that we get from those three and the various studio guests that we use provides a good balance and I'm delighted with the team. We do get letters and e-mails about our commentators regularly, and if there was a huge groundswell of opinion against them I would know about it, but I honestly get very few letters of complaint. Apart from Eddie, we only have Andy Gray on football who does studio presentation and dashes along to the commentary gantry and Keith Huewan does it on superbikes and other motor sports events, where he presents and commentates. So it is rare, though not unique. Eddie is a good presenter and a good commentator and if he's good enough to do both then he can do both. Stevo is also good both on the gantry and in the studio and as they work well together it makes sense to have them doing both elements together.'

The danger for both sport and broadcast partner is that if the product on the screen becomes too appetising and appealing in all its associated packaging as an unmissable show, attendances could be materially affected although, in Super League's case, the reverse has proved to be true, thanks to the quality of the live action. 'We're always concerned if we think that there's going to be any impact on attendances. It was the same with football. If you go back to the first Premiership deal in 1992, when suddenly there was a huge leap from eighteen matches from the old First Division on ITV up to sixty matches with Sky. There was concern within football and we said that we would work with the Premiership people to promote the game, and we've done exactly the same with rugby league. There is no point in us putting in millions of pounds into a sport if we're going to knock the attendances because the floating viewer won't watch. What we need is good games, but also great atmospheres. We need packed, noisy crowds, whatever the sport is, because that makes a viewer stop when he or she is zapping around looking for something to watch on a Friday or Saturday night. If that person doesn't see something which has atmosphere, noise and passion surrounding it then they won't stay with it. So it's vital to us in any sport that we do that the stadiums are busy, noisy and generating passion. I think a clear indication of our commitment to the game is the screening of NRL matches, the Varsity match, National League finals, and more. If you look at football we cover the schoolboy internationals, Conference football and I think with rugby league, like football, it's important where you can to give exposure to other areas within the sport. We're not a charitable institution, and if I didn't think that people were going to watch those then I wouldn't show them, but they do have an audience. As far as the TWI highlights are concerned, that's down to Super League. They wanted that as part of the rights deal and we were happy to agree it. I think that's very important for the game because the *Transworld Sport* programme goes everywhere. It's shown around the world. I can't remember the number of territories it's shown in but believe me it's huge exposure for the game as a whole. Having to reschedule games is a tough one. We try and work out and plan and give as much notice as possible, but in those closing weeks of the season when you're looking for the final play-off places it gets difficult. We want to bring the games that really matter and I do understand when there are late switches that it does annoy fans but it's inevitable that we want to show the important fixtures in the build-up to a season's climax. We have a sensible dialogue with Super League about this. Neville has an ongoing debate with them about when decisions must be made about when matches must be moved around those Friday or Saturday slots.'

If Sky has raised the production bar with the arrival of Super League, the BBC has started to follow suit although their decision to screen their high-lights package, the Sunday *Super League Show*, only in the northern regions, despite the undoubted new found national interest in the sport, still rankles. Previously the code could justifiably claim that 'Auntie' had merely paid it lip service, Maurice Lindsay commenting in 1995 amid furore over their diffidence in covering the World Cup, 'there's been a feeling for years, that you have to accept what you are given by the BBC.' The practice of sharing Jonathan Davies as a main summariser between rugby league and rugby union would seem to bear that out, as is the traditionally vapid and cursory review of the season in the annual *Sports Personality of the Year*. Moving the Challenge Cup – one of the nation's protected 'crown jewel' events – to August has reinvigorated the relationship with Pat Younge, head of programme planning for BBC Sports recognising that the size and scope of the market for the game is changing significantly. 'This was an expensive contract that was doing nothing. It had to change for our sake, the viewers' sake and for the sake of rugby league. We want the Challenge Cup to take its place alongside the Super Bowl as a global event.' Presenter Clare Balding has been a breath of fresh air as has the use of more of the code's current, personable stars as studio guests, such as Brian Carney and Kevin Sinfield. However, the sport and its broadcasters still have a long way to go with regard to the promotion of player personalities who abound within Super League. There was a glimmer of the a new guard at the BBC when Great Britain's defeat by the Kiwis in the 2005 Tri-Nations tournament in late October was the lead news item on the main evening news ahead of the Premiership round up. From such acorns... The major success for Super League, right from the start, in its relationship with the BBC has been Five Live and more recently its digital sister station Five Live Sports Extra, which has been a regular carrier of full match commentaries. Even as early as Super League I, much-vaunted commentator Dave Woods stated, 'Rugby league has really arrived on Five Live. Our recent competitions during broadcasts have given us an overwhelming response and tremendous confidence that our coverage is reaching new areas. There is real support out there for the game country-wide, and as far as Ireland.' They are also leading the way in terms of innovation with the trialling at the end of 2005 of a commentator for each side, adding an urgency to match the unfolding drama as possession switches. With the eventual loss of the analogue signal, digital broadcasting is one area that is set to grow. In 1997, perceptive *Yorkshire Post* correspondent the late Robert Mills stated, 'This is a game unashamedly looking to the future in everything it does. Some members of the media with only a passing acquaintance with it continue to be pathetically patronising about it and about our friends in the North. It is not like that at all any more. At the top this is a game showing others the way forward.'

Richard Lewis is acutely aware of that. 'I hope and I believe that Sky will continue to want to show rugby league for the foreseeable future, it is a sport that works for them. I'd love the BBC to do more as a partner but, to be fair to them, the opportunities are limited. They could show more highlights during the season, though. The area that I really would like Super League to grow to make it overwhelmingly impossible to resist in the media is newspapers and the non-sports magazines. For them to take an interest would mean that Super League was so big that it could not be ignored and they would have to give some attention to it. Deadlines are a problem, you can't get away from that. Eight o'clock matches on a Friday night, which works for Sky and a for a lot of the clubs, doesn't work for the printed media. Maybe new technology will help solve that, I know of one newspaper where in a couple of years' time they will be able to cover such games in their first editions, which they can't do now. Bigger crowds and viewing figures would help the process, let's say hypothetically that half to a million people watched games on Sky and ten million took in the Challenge Cup final broadcast. The various other editors would have more of an obligation to cover rugby league because of the attention being paid to it. Those figures are a long way away at the moment but that's what would happen.'

Across the negotiating table when the rights issue comes to the fore next in 2008, Vic Wakeling is equally convinced that the symbiotic relationship between the sport and its chief conveyor will remain strong. 'I think it's very important that the base of the game grows. The heart of the game is still in the North and the strength of the game is still up there. I have queried the Catalan extension to the league. I've asked Neville if they are going to be competitive and attract decent crowds because we're going to be putting a couple of Outside Broadcast units across there, which costs us a lot of money to do, but he feels that he wants to go across and show the expansion of the game. I hope it is successful, but it's more important from Sky's point of view that the clubs in this country continue to do well. I see there's a new club launched in Wales and I would love them to grow up into a Super League club over a period of time. I'd love the Harlequins team to be successful, because that helps me in selling the sport to a British audience. They all know about Wigan, St Helens, Leeds and Bradford, but it would be great to have a Welsh club competing against them in Super League and the new Harlequins club doing well to add that extra dimension. I'd love to see another club develop in another part of the country. With Newcastle, where I'm from, the timing has got to be right. I know Gateshead has a small core following but if they were talking about moving in with Newcastle Falcons then it should be properly planned. I honestly think it is not an easy call up there. They talk about Scotland, but I don't think so. You have to have that base in the first place or the same mistakes will continue to happen. If you're going to expand then you have to be reasonably sure that it's going to work. The people who run the sport have got to investigate the possibilities for expansion in these areas. They need to produce some good studies, some scientific research and be prepared to say "Yes, if we invest we can really make this go". I would love to see expansion in Britain and Ireland, yes, but those decisions are ultimately for the game to make. I'm glad I don't have to make those decisions myself; I'll just stick to pointing the cameras and covering it!

We are delighted with the numbers watching and the returns we get on rugby league, I can assure you. Our contract to cover the game is the longest that Sky has had alongside that with the Football Association. Both have existed in various forms over a fifteen-year period and we're delighted with the figures we get in homes and of course the pub figures. Remember we have 45,000 pubs and clubs who subscribe to Sky Sports. I know that not all those pubs and clubs will watch Super League every Friday and Saturday night, but a lot of them are and we are delighted about that. The old cloth-cap image of the game is certainly not prevalent within the walls of Sky. But it's more important what the people outside of Sky think. But I actually think that what you have found is that the appeal of the game has changed. Without being unkind, in the old Eddie Waring days players weren't as fit as they are now – I know that's the same for all sports – but now in Super League you have a breed of superbly fit athletes playing a game with what I would describe as frightening physical impact and at high speed. I think that everywhere now, and I mean nationwide, people look at these players and admire them. They are in awe of their skill, their strength, power and resilience and very often they are compared very favourably to some very highly paid footballers. Into that you can add when we do interviews, which are very important to our coverage in introducing the personalities in the game, I think that the public at large is impressed by the Super League players we talk to. There are plenty of articulate guys who are happy to give their view immediately after a game, or maybe a considered opinion on *Boots 'N' All*, or in the preview programmes that we do. I think perhaps the Australian influence has helped with that too. When you have people like Shaun McRae, who has done a lot of work for us, sitting in the studio and talking so fluently about the game, I think that does wonders for the image of the sport too. I'm not so sure that this old northern cloth cap, pigeon-fancying image still exists. I don't think it does and the game has to take a lot of credit for that. That's not down to Sky, I think we've played a part, but

I think the switch to summer, getting away from the winter conditions, the mud and that feel of a hard slog and into better conditions for players and spectators alike, I think that has a lot to do with the improved image of the game but that was really the RFL who brought that about.'

When asked about particular success and failures of the partnership over the last ten years, he has little doubt. 'When you've run Sky Sports for as long as I have, you make a few mistakes. The World Club Championship was one of mine. It wasn't my idea; in fact I think the idea came from Australia, although whoever came up with it I have to say that I fully supported it. You make errors of judgement in life, but I thought when I first saw the proposal that it would be terrific, and that it would widen up the game and give it more international appeal. In actual fact I have to say that I think it did damage Super League in my opinion. I'll give you an example that I told Maurice Lindsay at the time. I was in the bar over the road from Sky just before the World Club Championship kicked off. It was a Friday night and I was in there with the Sky football crowd, including Andy Gray and a couple of other commentators, and we were having a drink while the Super League was on. Now this is Andy Gray of Scotland and Aston Villa. I don't know still if he's ever been to a rugby league match in his life, but he certainly didn't come from a rugby league area, and neither did any of them around the table. We were chatting away and Andy and the others were saying that they thought the game was fantastic and how they loved to watch it on a Friday night, how they'd "got into it" and this was the message that I was getting from fans from all over the country at the time; that's how popular the game really is. Then the tournament started and our teams got trounced week after week and I think that did set the game back because the fans that we'd been winning – those that I'm talking about when I say that we try to help sports transcend its fan base – those fans were suddenly thinking "Hang on a minute, we've been told how good Super League is and how good these teams are, and yet these Australians are hammering them out of sight." I think it was damaging for the sport and it actually affected our ratings too and took us a couple of years to recover. So it wasn't my idea but I will own up and say that I fully supported it and I was wrong. One of the greatest improvements has got to be the play–offs. That was my second big mistake, because I did not think that they and a Grand Final would work at all. Being the age I am, I said that it would never be accepted in England. In this country, I felt that first past the post at the end of a league season would always be considered champions. A few people changed my mind. Neville Smith argued against me, Maurice Lindsay obviously did along with Chris Caisley and Gary Hetherington. They all got on the phone and told me I was wrong. They said "Trust us, rugby league fans will accept this principle" and I'm telling them "Guys, it works in Australia, but over there you don't have the entrenched traditions that we have." I think traditions are a strength of British sport but every now and then they hold it back. Remember also that it wasn't part of our contract, so they really did have to convince me, and eventually I said "Okay guys, I'll go along with it." They all know the sport and the fans better than I do and so I was prepared to back them and now I think that Saturday nights at Old Trafford for a Grand Final is a marvellous showpiece for the game. I think it's helped the image of the sport. It's different to the Challenge Cup final, which has always been on a Saturday afternoon in May until last season, but this is in a great stadium in the North – the heartlands of the game – under floodlights with a great atmosphere, packed out, and I think it's been an unqualified success. Those four men convinced me that the fans would accept that change and they were right.'

There will be similar dilemmas in the future as the media world continues to fracture. Sky's monopoly of live television rights has recently been ended by the European Commission, which was on the verge of charging the Premier League with violating the anti-competitive provisions of the Treaty of Rome in an effort to give fans greater choice and value, although they are likely to remain the dominant broadcaster. The top soccer clubs have their own satellite subscription channels and may well be positioning themselves for individual rights deals to maximise their revenue at the expense of the competition as a whole. Super League does not have that kind of pulling power but a dedicated channel to the code may well not be pie in the sky, especially if the output was broadened by showing classic matches from different eras. A pay-per-view element – or electronic turnstile – has been pioneered and accepted by the most committed with linked promotional activity targeted at the smartcard spectator, although again Super League is not yet a broad enough competition to warrant debate as to its merits or otherwise. Other new media issues are also on the forthcoming agenda, which may signal the next era of sports broadcast coverage. As Roy Greenslade, former newspaper editor and now media analyst, has warned, 'The majority of young people now like to get their news for free, whether through computers, giveaway newspapers or mobile phones. That's aside from those who prefer twenty-four-hour rolling news on TV and radio. Internet portals, such as Google and Yahoo, have become the fastest-growing route to news for millions of people. News is ambient nowadays; it can be transmitted so quickly and so comprehensively by a variety of media that everyone seems to hear about events in no time at all. We should see this as the most exciting time in media history.'That prompted Rupert Murdoch to say in April 2005 that, 'There is no greater priority than to expand our presence and properly position ourselves for the internet explosion.' In the meantime, Vic Wakeling is happy manning the Sky ship, although he does see some uncharted water ahead. 'It's a very competitive marketplace that Super League is in. When they are looking for sponsorship for example, and when you look at all the other sports who are out there fighting for money, it's about international success. Cricket received that boost recently when England won the Ashes. If Great Britain had won the Tri-Nations, that would have been marvellous for the guys trying to sell the sport. They could get out there saying "didn't we do well? We've won the Tri-Nations, now give us 'x' amount of sponsorship please." It would be a massive help to have international success. I wouldn't know enough about the business of the clubs themselves to know how they are doing in terms of commercial revenue. There is no doubt that in the papers I read every morning down here in London, that rugby league is fighting for space. I'd desperately like to see it get more because when you look in terms of the crowds and the interest the game really does generate, then the coverage in the southern editions is disproportionately small.'

For those who still think that Sky's commitment is anything other than total, he has categorical reassurance. 'We're in this for the long haul. I think we will look with interest to see what's going to happen over the next ten years. I know there are two World Cups planned in that time and I think it is a very interesting period for the game now. Rugby union's great success is at international level, the Six Nations, that sort of thing. You look at the crowds that flood into Twickenham for every match that England play. Why have a couple of high-profile league players switched codes? I think it's because they want to play in tournaments like that and go on tours with the British Lions. Don't get me wrong, I think it's obvious that they love the club game in Super League. There's no doubt about that, but in union they've raised the bar at international level and it's important now for rugby league to strengthen internationally. For example, how will Great Britain do in the Tri-Nations when they go Down Under this autumn? It would have been fantastic if we could have won it at home in 2005 because the publicity when we go down there probably won't be as significant as it is over here. Then we're splitting into the home nations again and playing as England. The club game is safe and very strong, but even that would receive a huge boost if we had international success. If you look at the history of football, you'll see that for just about every outstanding performance that England have put in, the attendances at club matches rise because it stimulates interest in the domestic game. I think that rugby league is moving in the right direction, we'd all as followers like to see it move faster – and from a business point of view at Sky that's because of the investment we have made – but I really believe that international success is a key goal for the game in the next decade, and perhaps even by the World Cup of 2012. We could do with a lot less of this uncertainty as well about when these tournaments are taking place. There needs to be a structure set out so that rugby league fans and general sports fans know when World Cups and other tournaments are on, so that everyone can understand it and work by it. I have to say that cricket is in a spot of bother with its international schedule at the moment, but football has a calendar, everyone knows that the World Cup is every four years, so is the European Championship, there's the Premiership, the FA Cup, the Carling Cup, a Champions' League, and they have that structure in place. I'd love to see that with the thirteen-a-side game. I remember sitting at Wigan at the old Central Park on the Saturday morning when we announced the new Super League deal. We were still hammering out the details in the club that morning and the press conference kicked off late because we were still arguing over the contract and as a result we kept all of the press waiting. I remember thinking to myself, "My goodness, this is a huge gamble we're taking," but the RFL were also taking a huge risk as well and for their part it was really the move to summer. But what I've found is that the people in the game, probably more so than in any other sport, have this willingness to work with you and try a few things. The spirit of co-operation is excellent, because without it, if the clubs didn't help Neville Smith on a week-by-week basis I think the coverage would suffer as a result. But I feel that we've built a good partnership with the game in helping it to move forward in the past decade. It's been a very exciting ten years; I think we at Sky have shown that we are not here today and gone tomorrow. We will continue to work with rugby league because we believe that the game has got a great future and we're looking forward to the second decade of Super League.'

As Stephen Barnett notes, 'Throughout the developed world, at almost every level beyond recreational parks and back gardens, television considerations have influenced, often dictated, the progress of sports. Prize money has escalated. Rules have been changed. Events have been tailored, rescheduled or abandoned. Amateurism has almost vanished in all but name. Decisions on which sports, at what times of day, for what duration, with what sort of investment… can have extraordinary effects. They can provide a financial lifeline for one sport, or devastate another.' Super League is an almost perfect sport for satellite television. Bright, sometimes brash, always athletic, colourful and exciting, its summer slot has been a scheduler's dream as the need for ever-more reliable, regular, rolling output increases with the advent of each new specialist channel. In December 1996, as the dust settled on the opening season, Vic Wakeling was quoted as saying, 'I've no doubt that something is really happening with the way people react to rugby league. It's a sport that always deserved a bigger audience. I live in Hampshire and when I go down to the pub on a Sunday lunchtime and hear people talking about the Super League game they have seen the previous Friday night, I know Sky and the rugby league are getting something right.' Ten years later he stands by that conviction.

TOP 10 TRIES

MARTIN MOANA: HALIFAX BLUE SOX *v.* CASTLEFORD TIGERS
THE SHAY, 9 APRIL 1996
An extraordinary, intricate move that began in their own '20' and saw virtually the whole Blue Sox team play a part before Moana finished off underneath the 'black dot'.

PAUL STERLING: LEEDS RHINOS *v.* ADELAIDE RAMS
HEADINGLEY, 18 JULY 1997
If ever there was the perfect response to conceding a score, this was it. The Rams had just touched down, but made the mistake of kicking off to Sterling. The Rhinos winger took the ball on the full behind his own line and proceeded to part the Adelaide defence and scorch his way along the South Stand touchline for a sensational try.

JASON ROBINSON: WIGAN WARRIORS *v.* LEEDS RHINOS
OLD TRAFFORD, 24 OCTOBER 1998
The inaugural Grand Final was the defining moment of the season, and when 'Billy Whizz' danced through the Leeds defence and went, jet-heeled, to the line, the outcome was decided.

DARREN ROGERS: CASTLEFORD TIGERS *v.* HUDDERSFIELD GIANTS
McALPINE STADIUM, 7 APRIL 1999
Another spellbinding team try down the Castleford left-hand side, with the ball reaching Rogers, who chipped over the top and re-gathered, handed on to Aaron Raper, and then popped up on the inside to take the final pass and plunge over the line.

CHRIS JOYNT: ST HELENS *v.* BRADFORD BULLS
KNOWSLEY ROAD, 22 SEPTEMBER 2000
There can have been few tries as dramatic as this in the whole history of the sport. A

Sean Long cross-field kick – deep inside his own half – started it, and after Kevin Iro, Steve Hall, Sean Hoppe, Hall again, Tim Jonkers, Long, and then Dwayne West all handled, Chris Joynt beat James Lowes and raced fifty metres to touch down and snatch victory for Saints with no time left on the clock for a riposte. 'It is unbelievable!' screamed Sky Sports commentator Eddie Hemmings and no-one could argue.

TONY STEWART: ST HELENS *v.* BRADFORD BULLS
KNOWSLEY ROAD, 2 JUNE 2001
Not quite déjà vu – this was well before the final hooter – but another breathtaking score, begun by Sean Hoppe on his own line, involving Kevin Iro, Paul Sculthorpe and Paul Newlove and ending with Stewart spinning out of two tackles and racing in from halfway.

STUART SPRUCE: WIDNES VIKINGS *v.* LONDON BRONCOS
GRIFFIN PARK, 11 MAY 2002
The former Great Britain full-back was in the twilight of his career but turned back the clock, getting on the end of a marvellous handling move involving six men and including a mesmeric forty-metre burst from centre Adam Hughes.

BRIAN CARNEY: WIGAN WARRIORS *v.* LEEDS RHINOS
HEADINGLEY, 10 OCTOBER 2003
An individual effort showing the pace, evasive skills and sheer opportunism of one of the finest wingers of Super League's first decade. The Irishman picked the ball up from dummy half within ten metres of his own line, bounced off two defenders, evaded Wayne McDonald, and sped the rest of the way to score between the posts. A magnificent 'pinball wizard' try that inspired a play-off win for his team.

DANNY MCGUIRE: LEEDS RHINOS *v.* WIGAN WARRIORS
HEADINGLEY, 19 MARCH 2004
A last-tackle gem as Leeds ran Wigan ragged on the power play from inside their own half. McGuire initiated some exquisite handling from four of his teammates, and his support skills were never better exemplified than when popping up for the third time in the move to post a remarkable four-pointer.

ROB BURROW: LEEDS RHINOS *v.* CANTERBURY BULLDOGS
ELLAND ROAD, 4 FEBRUARY 2005
The last of five tries in a sensational first-half performance by the Rhinos, with ten men involved in handling that bewildered the Canterbury defence, before Burrow's rapier thrust pierced his opponents' line. A try befitting the occasion.

EIGHT

VIEW FROM THE PITCH

No-one takes liberties with Brian McDermott. The ex-Marine made his name as a no-nonsense, permanently grafting, uncomplicated prop forward who was frequently referred to as the cornerstone of one of the toughest, most unforgiving packs playing the most physically demanding of games. From rugby league stock, his brother Paul had a distinguished career principally at his home town club Wakefield, then at Sheffield and York. He came to the professional game in his mid-twenties, carving out a reputation as one of the genuine hard men. Appearances, though, can be deceptive and the colossus on the field was one of the most assiduous students of the changing sport from the inside. After 251 games with his sole club, Bradford Bulls, during which time he won every major honour in the code – including 4 caps for his country in 1996 – he joined the coaching ranks with Huddersfield and then Leeds; playing a key behind-the-scenes role in the Rhinos' first title win for two generations. His career began in the dying embers of winter rugby and he became the epitome of the modern professional in the summer era in a playing position that changed the most as a result. Fiercely proud of the sport he graced and continues to serve, he is never short of an opinion or a willingness to continually learn and adapt. Once, when answering the question, 'If you could change one rule in rugby league what would it be?' he replied, 'No refs and we would go with what the crowd said because they are never wrong.' By his own admission, he reckons that he came into rugby league at the perfect time, having signed from amateur outfit Eastmoor Dragons in 1993/94. He played 5 games on loan for Doncaster that season, scoring 3 tries and serving a vital apprenticeship before stepping up at the Bulls just at a time that the code was considering the need for full-time professionalism. 'There was already some agitation for it, that was the ideal everybody wanted. How it was going to come about nobody, especially the players, knew. We knew Wigan had an advantage but until you become full time you don't realise how great a benefit that is. In many ways, wrongly, personally I saw Wigan as a prima donna type outfit, where they didn't really need to be full time but it looked good on their CVs. Probably naively I didn't think we were lacking, way off or missing out that much. Looking back, obviously we were because once you've experienced it, the difference is massive. I don't think the game was stagnating as such, Bradford had come joint-second in 1993/94, missing out on the title on points difference and Leeds had gone close the following year. Maybe there was a bit of inevitability about matches against Wigan but the challenge was let's see who could get closest too them.'

In the lead up to it, as Super League burst on the scene, the seemingly indiscriminate awarding of 'loyalty payments' threatened to split dressing rooms apart. 'There wasn't any resentment on my behalf. I didn't get anything but then I don't know if I deserved anything. I do agree there was a haphazard way of doing it, it seemed as though it was just a case of whoever's name was in the paper on the Monday morning got the payments, but there was some panicking going on. It was a crazy eighteen months where some people made a lot of money, there were some very poor decisions and a few good ones but I don't think any of them were well thought through. It was just a case of being scared to death of losing all our stars to another body so let's keep them here without giving it any prior thought, but I also take on board that I don't know if there was enough time to plan either. It all happened so quickly, there was no real sniff and then it was announced. I actually remember when I was told about the decision to go full time and move to the summer. I was in my amateur club and I hadn't heard too much about it prior to that. I knew there had been some suggestions of going full time but one of the guys came up to me and said it had been decided for the following year and it just seemed like everything had changed overnight. That's when the panic set in. I know I'm going to be called naïve but if somebody wants to go to jump ship for money, let them go. If you love rugby league you stick with the sport that has given you so much. I was twenty-four at the time and only playing loose forward because Dave Heron was injured – I was a prop in a back-rower's shirt! I couldn't wait; it was just a case of at last we weren't going to be playing in mud. We knew that was wrong, playing in conditions where your extremities didn't work – when they shut down it's the first stages of hypothermia, I know because I've done some time in Norway and I used to think "this can't be right". So when summer rugby was announced I was very excited knowing that we were going to be playing on top of the ground instead of six inches under it.'

Bradford's Odsal ground, the historic cavernous bowl that still holds the record for the largest British crowd at a game when officially 102,000 but more like 120,000 crammed in to watch Warrington and Halifax re-play the 1954 Challenge Cup final – and that despite a bus strike – went from being the most inhospitable environment to one of the most lively and atmospheric. That experience mirrored what was starting to take shape out in the middle. 'Moving to summer allowed the sport and the athlete to become more explosive and the game as a showpiece to become more dynamic. When somebody made a break it was probably because of power, pace and strength rather than a defender slipping over in the mud. We paint a picture that in the old days it was always twenty-six men covered in mud, it wasn't always the case but there were a multitude of reasons why play-ers missed tackles; the cold, the wet, their hands slipped or studs weren't deep enough. The other major factor for me was that we had Brian Smith take charge at Bradford at the beginning of Super League, so not only was it a shock to the system that we had switched seasons but also that we were exposed to a totally different type of coaching. All of a sudden we were breaking down every single facet of the game; how you carried the ball, where you grip it, how you tackled, how you passed, where to defend at marker, how you defend in a line – it was all taken down to scratch, shown to you and then built back up again. You had the time to do all that under full-time professionalism, you didn't mind being out on the field for two or three hours at a time and the coach had you when he wanted you. I'd not been shown that before and I reckon that ninety-five per cent of the Bradford squad hadn't either. The era of coaches had dawned and that of the old-type managers put to bed. We'd had conditioners before but all of a sudden they became the head coach's right hand, whereas in the past he had either been the warm-up man doing the same drills over and over again or the person you were sent to during a session while the manager regained his composure and thought about the next stage of training. Even for the players, "Bullmania" made a huge impact. I knew we had something special right from the opening game in Super League in 1996 against Castleford. I thought that this was not just summer rugby; there is something more here, something a lot bigger than had been suggested by the initial move. The addition of Peter Deakin on the marketing staff was a massive boon for the club and he was the guru. In many ways you could argue that the Bulls are still living off what he implemented now.'

The impact of the ten-metre rule around the play the ball began to take full effect, with coaches exhorting their smaller, faster players to 'run at the big men' to move them around and tire them out, leading to the greater tactical use of substitutes as a key counter. 'More space to play allowed for a lot more attractive rugby league and put a bit more skill on show. In the winter era there wasn't too much of it, there was a bit of brawn but you weren't able to see the strength and power because of the conditions. The ten-metre rule allowed players to ramp up against each other; there was a lot more flair, a lot more collision, a lot more impact. I still think it's taken some time for people to realise that it is now a seventeen-man game and that if A.N. Other's got 17 on his shirt that he's probably not as important as say number 13. Slowly they are starting to understand that those on the bench are invaluable and that some players actually suit the role better. That makes them no less important and in fact in some ways it makes them more significant, coming on after the cannon fodder that starts the game and the initial biff and bash has blown itself out – and everyone has got their aggressiveness out of the way, especially the ones who have tried to prove a point in the opening stages. Then you can bring a strike player off the bench after ten or fifteen minutes to carve the opposition up.'

Concentration on reinventing the club game at the same time that the Australian domestic campaign was in disarray had massive repercussions on international rugby at a time when McDermott was coming to the fore. Inevitably, the players were caught up in the crossfire. 'One of the arguments is can you have both a good club competition and be strong at international level? Rugby league in the early 1990s competed really well against the Aussies and Kiwis yet at club level only one team was really winning. Super League came in and all of a sudden Bradford were a force with St Helens and Leeds then a few years later London, Hull and Warrington and now it genuinely is a top six, teams are winning from everywhere but we seem to be struggling at Test level. The governing body have got to take some flak for that in the early stages; they didn't think things quite through when appointing coaching staff of Great Britain teams and how it was run. I was a victim of being sent home from a tour in New Zealand because apparently it had run out of money. I'm not bitter about that but I'm very angry that what should have been one of my proudest periods of my life ended up being one of the saddest. I just don't know if there was as much thought put into the international set up as there had been at club level, which was a shame.'

A measure of compensation for him came in the domestic season in 1997 when the Bulls stampeded their way to the title, dominating the competition from the start and, in the last pre-Grand Final campaign, winning it by a commanding seven points. The portents, though, had been coming. 'We ran everyone close in 1996 when we came third. I remember that year we beat Wigan at home even though Jeremy Donougher got sent off early on and when we won that game we realised that we were one of the main players in the competition now, not just an invite to the party. The pre-season in 1997 was one of the most arduous times in my life, one of the toughest I've ever done. I don't know if it was the smartest because we started early November with only a few weeks off after the previous season had finished but we began the next campaign like a house on fire and we just carried that on. What we were ultimately were big, extremely fit – because of Carl Jennings – and immensely strong players with some very smart pivotal people in there like Jimmy Lowes, Steve McNamara, Graeme Bradley and Glen Tomlinson who marshalled fellas like myself around the field. It was a great combination as well as being Matt Elliott's first season as head coach. He had a bit of extra enthusiasm to prove himself and everything seemed to click that year for us.'

The 20-12 victory over Wigan that he refers to, like Paris on the opening night, is regarded as a seminal moment by those connected with the Bradford club. A crowd of 17,360 meant the highest gate at a league game at Odsal since 1950 and, as Brian Smith commented at the time, 'the era of Wigan's total dominance is starting to wane'; it was also the night that Bradford Northern died. If there was a criticism of Super League in those early stages it was that too many games were being won by wide margins and that was seen as a contributory factor as to why traditional fans were becoming more discriminating about their involvement. It was estimated that on average a try was being scored every seven minutes as the speed of the game increased dramatically with it becoming increasingly difficult for defences to regain their feet, get back in position and repel the next advancing wave. The better sides were capable of getting on a remorseless roll if their opponents faltered and nowhere was that being felt more than in the position of prop. Rudi Meir, a noted lecturer in Sports Science at the Southern Cross University in Sydney, who spent time on secondment with various Super League outfits, researched the dilemma, concluding that the emphasis for the big men had changed dramatically. He calculated that, on average, a front rower would cover approximately six-and-a-half kilometres during the course of a game and may be required to move forward over eighty times in one forty-minute half of play, causing a huge amount of energy and heat to be expended with the constant stopping and restarting because of their greater mass. Suddenly prop forwards who were used to being on the whole game were playing in defined spells, which was physically and psychologically difficult to adjust to. As McDermott recalls, 'It's how it's sold to you, that's the big issue, especially if you're used to doing eighty minutes and making thirty-five tackles with people slapping you on the back and telling you how well you'd worked. All of a sudden you're getting coaches looking at what you do in that time and what type of tackles you've made and so if he then says I want you to go out there for twenty-five minutes and absolutely empty your tank and do your best, and he puts as much worth on that as the eighty-minute prop, then I think you've got no problem with it. If you get dragged off after a spell because you're not up to scratch there's the problem.'

Just as the Bulls looked to be setting a new standard in Super League II, the convoluted World Club Championship came as something of a shock to the British fans, the champions-elect failing to win any of their matches and taking some decisive beatings in phase two over in the southern hemisphere. 'It wasn't so much an eye-opener. I just found it really disappointing. Personally I didn't play to the level I should have done and I reckon a few more in the squad could say the same if they were honest. We competed for long periods in the home games; we should have beaten Penrith and the Auckland Warriors at Odsal but then we went out there and got a shellacking in two of the three matches – we had our moments at Cronulla – but the whole series was a let down on our behalf. We didn't step up and we underperformed. If we'd played at our best and still got thrashed I'd have said we still had a lot of work to do to catch the Aussies. Someone looking from the outside in would think he's bound to say that, and I don't blame them for that, but I do know for a fact that we never showed our best in all the games.'

The distance by which Bradford took the spoils in 1997 was one of the catalysts for the instigation of the Grand Final and the principal of the last match being the most important. Despite Saints denying him twice, he has the memory of victories over Wigan in 2001 and 2003 to savour and the idea appears to be a winner with the players. 'I love the Grand Final, the whole concept of it; I think it's great; they've got the right balance now. Again I just don't know if the initial idea was thought through properly where the team that comes first past the post needs to be awarded something for their efforts. I was in a side in 1999 where we were four points clear at the end of the regular season and were very dominant and ended up with nothing, which is wrong. Now there's the League Leaders Shield and then I suppose it's up to the club how much worth and celebration they put on that. I'm a big fan of the question the Grand Final idea raises of which squad of players can be nursed through a season and conditioned and coached the smartest so that they are in the best physical and mental state to perform for the last task, the ultimate hurdle. I've had some disappointments in Grand Finals but I tend to think that I'm just glad that I got there and was involved in some great games. I also think that St Helens are a tremendous team and if Bradford had lost as many deciders against different sides then the problem would have been with us. Saints were superb on both occasions and I was just unfortunate that I played in Grand Finals where they appeared as well.'

Like so many in the game, he is eager to see the event as a showcase for the best British talent but acknowledges that there is a need for balance with overseas signings. 'You've got to be careful. If we had twenty-six British players appearing in the next Grand Final that would be superb but if we allowed that, what standard of spectacle would we have? You've got to be smart. I just don't believe there are enough British players playing the game over here so there isn't enough cream on the top and the bottleneck of those tying to get through isn't as harsh as it should be. I've been involved recently at Leeds in talking to some very good youngsters about coming on board at Headingley and endeavouring to sign them up. I should have been trying to persuade fifty of those types of kids rather than five. The Players' Association is in the background, I don't see anything of it. I find it hard to comment on, it's not in the headlines or a part of any decision-making processes. The only time I notice it is when it's asking me for my four pounds a month.'

The toughest decision for a player is when to call it a day and how to fill the void that comes with leaving the unique atmosphere of the dressing room craic. Keen to stay involved at some level, he renewed his association with the famed Smith dynasty, arguably the most influential in the modern era for finding and developing backroom talent, coming under the tutelage of Brian's younger brother, Tony. 'I went to Huddersfield as a conditioner/coach, a dual job. Initially when I packed in playing I had talks with Tony and he asked me where I saw my career going and I wasn't sure myself. He suggested coming on board to do both roles so that I could find my feet. Within two or three months at the McAlpine it became apparent to me that I wanted to be a coach and I wasn't as excited about being a conditioner as I thought I might be. Either way, the transition from playing to becoming a member of the staff is underestimated, it's a massive thing.'

In such an environment, his thoughts on how the game should be played were honed and slightly antithetical to the modern call for multi-skilled players whose primary asset is versatility, which has become the maxim. Conversely, his early apprenticeship taught him that a coach has to be a psychologist, biologist, scientist, nutritionist, disciplinarian, teacher and psychiatrist to name but a few. 'The best teams are those that have a definite stand-off and a definite hooker. The ones who try unaccustomed players in those positions tend to struggle. Until the laws are vastly changed, which I don't want to see happen, a prop will always be a prop. I disagree that second rowers can now just play at prop. There is a certain mentality needed to play in the front row and it's hard to make somebody into one. My uncle Michael, who has a very smart rugby league brain, told me one thing I'll never forget; that you can't invent a scrum half, they're born and I believe that to be true. You can get somebody to play better than they are in that position but the natural feel for it has to be there. There is some multi-tasking, which is not a bad thing, but personally I'd stick with the specialists. If I was head coach, I'd want a say in everything. You can accuse me of being a control freak and I'd accept that but I'd struggle being held accountable in areas my team was deficient in terms of skill or conditioning, for example, if I'd not overseen it. If you are going to go about it right, you must have some knowledge of everything and if you haven't got it, get it. Ultimately, even when you're playing, those who want to coach know they do as a twenty year old so that when they overhear a conversation at dinner between the conditioner and his assistant, they lend an ear to it. To start learning about conditioning when you've finished playing is probably too late, you should be doing it as you go.'

Statistical gathering and an intimate knowledge of available information technology have also become prerequisites for the expanded Super League staffs at club level, but they are viewed as progressive, indispensable aids. 'It is vital; we have a stats system that would blow your mind. I couldn't use a computer, I didn't even have a mobile until I stopped playing and now I've got everything and it does make your job easier. I've been under a coaching system that has used back-to-back videos where you're trying to edit and cut tapes from dual recorders and you're kidding yourself if you think you can come up with the same degree of quality. Now we have a high-tech editing system where frames are captured and put into different positions. I think it adds mystery; you can show players six or seven clips of a trait within ten minutes on a raw tape and then they can walk out the room certain of what it is they do or may be facing. Under the old system of forwarding and rewinding that whole process could take a day, by which time the players have fallen asleep and you've nullified their interest. You can come up with more slants in previews of the game.'

Such detail coupled with heightened expectation and profile adds to stress levels, which are further ratcheted up by the intense focus of the camera looking for a reaction in any given situation. His views about that are as forthright as the hit ups he used to make with such regularity out in the middle. 'I believe it's a bit of Britishness to be honest and a weaker side of society. I don't think its rugby league or sport, just that we're all being bred to be ambulance chasers at the moment. I vehemently disagree that when a team is scored against the focus is on the coach's face to see if he's in pain. People are then watching and portraying sport for the wrong reasons. When Lee Smith, say, scores a try does anybody focus on what hand he put the ball down with or on the type of pass Ryan Bailey gave to set him up and, more to the point, who he put it on against, or do they just look at the coach's face? If they're doing the latter then they're looking for the wrong emphasis. Give us a set of reporters and media that know that Mark Calderwood favours a left-foot step but scored that try off his right and isn't that a great piece of skill no matter who he's gone round, if they continue to focus on the coach's reaction – that's *Coronation Street* and they'd be better off tuning into that. The media leads the way and unfortunately when something happens in this country everybody goes to the tabloids to find out how we must think about it. Sky is a powerful product and those watching at home would be just as or even more excited by them identifying and then following different trends and skills of the players, never mind what the coach is doing. Coaching is a stressful job if you want it to be. If you go in there expecting not to have some nervous times – and nerves and stress are two different things – then you will be stressed. If you think everything is going to be hunky dory and the players will always do as you ask, then you are going to have some stressful times. If you go into coaching knowing full well that you're going to be banging your head against a brick wall for a lot of the time, that players are not going to do exactly what you say, that you will lose some games – and more to the point that you want to in order to go through that experience as quickly as you can and put your head on the chopping block – then there is a lot worse in life.'

Having been on both sides of the playing/coaching divide, he is uniquely placed to comment on the wisdom or otherwise of salary caps, agents, freer player movement and fixture scheduling. 'For the good of the game I understand why there is a salary cap in place. Some clubs would argue – like say Bradford who have come from being journeymen to big hitters – that if they are prepared to generate their own income they should be allowed to spend the money how they want. If fifty-one per cent of what you generate or £1.8 million is the bench mark then fair enough, but don't tell us how to spend it. I believe you can't have the salary cap and the 20/20 rule, that is too restrictive. Some clubs can't operate like that, they would end up with a full team of mediocrity without having one or two stars in there and ironically that hurts the lesser clubs rather than the big ones. I never once had an agent, I had a very good and fair relationship with Bradford and I think that if players are honest with clubs and don't ask for loads of money before they deserve it, they can't go far wrong. But I also believe that clubs need to bear the brunt of some of this and have a pay structure in place that won't allow somebody to come into the club who hasn't produced as much on the playing side and be financially well above another already there who has: that's where the upset starts. If a new signing who isn't an international can only be paid a certain amount that allows fairness at the bottom end. If you have got a decent structure then at the top end, if you do get to play for Great Britain or are producing consistent quality, you will get all your money back and the due rewards for it. The danger of player burnout due to the overload of the repeat fixtures and lack of recovery time associated with that is massive. In 1996 we only played twenty-two games, then we added the extra six, the play off series, then the Challenge Cup and the international games. I'm not sure how many different ways it has to be said. I've been reading since I don't know when quotes from players and coaches about how you can't play that many matches at club level and ask for quality. That then has an impact on the intensity week in, week out and is translated into the performances at international level. It's not rocket science.'

Prior to the 2005 Super League campaign, the Rhinos hosted the England rugby union squad at Headingley in a unique link up that tacitly acknowledged that Super League was at the cutting edge of the coaching art in the oval ball codes. It was welcomed by all as a valuable experience. 'We pride ourselves at Leeds on being very innovative and always looking for a better way of doing things, not particularly new but better. We're not going to fix anything that isn't necessarily broken but when Andy Robinson came up with his coaching staff, in the explanation of what we do, it really rammed home the point to ourselves actually. It was a tremendous buzz to coach the World Champions at another sport for a couple of days and to see some of their big men improve. Personally I thought there would be some reserved fellas in their camp but not at all, they were open to learning and improving, especially on a skill level.'

It served to illustrate the principle philosophy stressed by coaches in modern sport that performance rather than result must be paramount for worthwhile sustainability, which sets up a contradiction with the passionate fans for whom winning, no matter how ugly, is all that matters. 'We are getting back to the debate about where do we want the camera directed. If, as a fan, you come to games and all you want to see is your side winning, then I don't believe you are a proper supporter. Surely deep down a true fan wants to watch twelve sides who are as good as each other and that there is true and real competition as a result. Nothing too much hinges on the result if you are working on your performance. If you haven't got that, you will ultimately fail. By performance we mean that a player may have a particular trait to his game that needs to improve because at some stage come the latter end of the campaign that he will need to be strong, the weakness will need to have been fixed. In the early stages of the season if we can monitor certain improvements in that area, that is a great performance. It might be a different facet for each of the seventeen players but we are looking for week-to-week improvements. If the fans are honest with themselves, they have to put worth on what they have seen and hopefully they do want to see skills regardless of whether the guys have just lost by a couple of points.'

More of a danger for Super League could be that because it is now so hard to play at that elite level it may put all but the most talented of the next generation off trying, which would breed a similar scenario to American football, that you either play or watch and there is a lessening middle ground to develop or nurture talent. 'You've always had that, even before Super League and playing in the dry conditions. It's always been far easier to have jumpers for goalposts and play soccer. What I do get excited about is that when I go past a council estate or a patch of grass there are a lot more kids playing touch and pass in their spare time and, because of the better marketing strategies by the clubs, in their favourite team shirt. I take on board that it is a tough sport for an eight or nine year old. I've coached from aged eleven upwards and it can be cruel, especially in those age groups where a youngster can be a yard taller, ten metres faster and over a stone heavier than his teammates or opponents. I daresay it does turn away late developers, including some good athletes, but that has always been the case.'

With the rewards now higher at the top level, risks taken to achieve them become greater. Coaching staffs are again in the front line and face a dichotomy in the fight to educate about and combat drugs while at the same time stressing the need to enhance performance. 'In terms of food supplements and isotonic drinks, once you spend any length of time at the top flight, the proteins and carbohydrate shakes contained in them are for recovery and help players do it quicker so you can get back to training sooner. We're only talking a matter of hours here, the difference between say Tuesday morning and afternoon. I disagree with drugs completely, either performance-enhancing or leisure ones, I think you're kidding yourself if you take them and dishonest to the root of you. If you can step onto a field knowing you've taken something and play against those who haven't and maybe pick up the Man of the Match award and stand there in front of the cameras saying how tough you are and how you did it for the boys, it sticks in my throat. I can't understand how people can do that. It's something that sport, not so much rugby league, needs to look at. There is an air of the king and his birthday suit in sport in general, where you know for a fact that someone has taken drugs but nobody dares say anything. My black and white answer is that there should be no drugs and anyone caught should not be allowed to play the sport; maybe that is unrealistic and perhaps I am the kid stood on the pavement saying the king has no clothes on, but I stand by that.'

TOP 10 COACHES

1 BRIAN NOBLE
The Great Britain coach and former international skipper emerged from his role as understudy to Matthew Elliott in October 2000 to mastermind the club's memorable Grand Final successes in 2001 and 2003 and a remarkable assault on the competition in 2005, plus a Challenge Cup victory in 2003 and World Club Challenge wins in 2002 and 2004. A truly outstanding record of achievement.

2 IAN MILLWARD
The man they call 'Basil' led St Helens to two Super League titles, two Challenge Cup wins and a World Club Challenge success in five outspoken seasons at Knowsley Road before he was sacked and switched his allegiance to Wigan of all places in 2005 – and they say there are no characters left in professional sport.

3 SHAUN McRAE
Team meetings must have been interesting when the talkative 'Bomber' was asked a question. A journalist's dream, McRae usually had a smile, always had a quote, and was a good enough coach to lead St Helens to the Challenge Cup-Super League 'double' in the first season, with a second Wembley win in 1997 before club-building spells at Gateshead and Hull FC, eventually returning Down Under to resuscitate South Sydney in 2004.

4 MATTHEW ELLIOTT
Having served an apprenticeship under coaching guru Brian Smith, he presided over the Bulls' magnificent 1997 Super League championship charge when his troops overwhelmed all the opposition. He was also victorious in the Challenge Cup in 2000 before returning to Australia with Canberra Raiders.

5 TONY SMITH
Did it tough at Huddersfield, eventually making them highly competitive before moving on to Leeds, where he plotted the club's first title win for thirty-two years in 2004, backing it up with a World Club Challenge success over Canterbury Bulldogs three months later and taking the club to two further finals in 2005.

6 ELLERY HANLEY

The enigmatic former Great Britain skipper and finest player of his generation returned from a spell in Oz to inspire his St Helens players to 1999 Grand Final success, despite being suspended by the club at one stage during the season, but remaining the people's champion. Six months later he was sacked.

7 JOHN KEAR

Former England coach who has never possessed a squad with the strength in depth to win a Super League title. Instead, his renowned motivational skills have come to the fore as commander-in-chief of Sheffield's astonishing Challenge Cup win over Wigan in 1998, as an assistant at Wigan in 2002 and Hull FC's smash 'n' grab success in 2005.

8 GRAHAM MURRAY

If Tony Smith ultimately delivered Leeds fans with the championship they so craved, then Murray's stint at Headingley in the late 1990s had regenerated some credibility for the sleeping giants. A narrow defeat in the inaugural Grand Final to Wigan plus a record-breaking Challenge Cup win were the high points of the coach's two-year term of office. He also led Sydney Roosters and North Queensland Cowboys to NRL Grand Finals and novices Hunter Mariners to the 1997 World Club Championship decider.

9 TONY REA

The first coach without a trophy to his name, he makes the list for his belief in and pioneering of the London Broncos cause, both on and off the field. Played the first full Super League season before becoming chief executive and then, in 2000, head coach. His unruffled, easy-going style appears to perfectly complement a club that has never been too far from its next crisis. Looking to do it all again with Harlequins.

10 PAUL CULLEN

Notoriously uncompromising on the field, where his career lasted until Super League I, he cut his coaching teeth at Whitehaven before returning triumphantly to rescue the Wolves from relegation in 2002, improving the squad to reach a play-off place twice in the next three seasons. Also proudly picked up county coaching honours with Lancashire.

NINE

CASE STUDIES

SOCCER

'Still tenacious, still compelling, rugby league has disguised its brutish appeal in a coating of Disneyland. Perhaps sports that think themselves superior should come and learn. The razzmatazz brings a family audience… the new rules keep the sport flowing to a pitch that demands total concentration from players and spectators. Is football too arrogant to learn?' – Soccer writer Rob Hughes in *The Times* (May, 1997)

As the original, quintessential working-class sport, rugby league has always had more in common with the ethos and values of soccer than rugby union where, at times, the only similarity has been the shape of the ball. Northern Union may have grown out of, and been the cousin to rugby union, but the real sibling rival was the round-ball game. Comparisons are valid because of historical precedent, the early heritage of both sports being intertwined in the North of England at the end of the nineteenth century. As eminent sports historian Mike Latham noted, 'A decade or so after its formation the Northern Union was facing huge problems in its hinterland, with many junior clubs struggling or having gone to the wall, unable to meet the costs of the new professional game. Of those that survived there was another major worry, the increasing popularity of association football, whose spread was rapid, particularly in areas that were traditionally strongholds of the oval ball game.' Nowhere was that better exemplified than at Valley Parade where, at their 1903 Annual General Meeting the committee of the Manningham club – which had the distinction of being the inaugural winners of the Northern Union Championship in 1895/96 – voted to change codes and become Bradford City. Not only that but their accession to the new ranks was hastened when they were invited to join the Second Division even before they had kicked a ball in anger, because the new Football Association were desperate to cash in on the growing appeal of their sport by putting a club into the heart of NU territory.

The initial hostility soccer faced as it grew in favour bore direct resemblance to what the Northern Union was also struggling to achieve. 'In the late 1870s some northern clubs such as Darwen, Blackburn Rovers and Blackburn Olympic were taking a more serious approach. Cup matches attracted crowds, but to achieve success good players were necessary and they were increasingly semi-professional, enticed (often from Scotland) by offers of better-paid jobs and pay for time off work with expected compensation from 'gate money'. As the Lancastrian 'professional' teams succeeded, traditionalists, North and South, portrayed their tactics as unfair, ungentlemanly, tricky and deceitful.' (Huggins) The only major difference was that where one governing body quickly recognised professionalism to keep its code together and make it stronger, the other sub-divided and its national standing and popularity was severely and, perhaps, irrevocably diminished. Even in terms of style of play in the early days, there were distinct parallels. Eric Midwinter in *Fair Game – Myth and Reality in Sport* (Allen & Unwin, 1986) charts, 'Changes were made in the rugby league (Northern Union) laws but they were relatively marginal. What is interesting is that they corresponded to the revisions wrought in soccer under the influence of professionals. The wider strewn pattern of football, with its specialised players, careful passing and clearer formation was matched by the rugby league's concentration on the 'play the ball' rule and man-to-man passing. Both were, of course, consciously designed to exhibit the individual player and to quicken the flow of the game.' Even soccer's oldest club, Notts County, were formed following a meeting at their own George Hotel.

Coming to the turn of the twentieth century, both sports again underwent profound shake ups as a result of ceding power to the top clubs in combination with vast income predominantly from satellite television companies; soccer's Premiership coming into being in 1993, three years before Super League. Like it has done with so many other lesser-profile sports, the Premiership could have (and in its early days very nearly did) swamped Super League but the move to summer, away from direct competition, halted the shifting sands and gave rugby league's shop window a chance to glint in the sunlight. As Super League celebrated the end of its tenth season, the Premiership was beginning a new campaign in the midst of deep introspection. Despite still being the overwhelmingly dominant sport in the country, dwarfing the schedules and column inches, football's golden egg was seemingly coming home to roost. The traditional ethics and associations, many of which ensure long-term sustainability rather than transient fashion, were seen to be being eroded or undermined. Soccer stands accused of having lost its roots while one of the reasons for the apparent continued success and growth of

Super League has been its ability to at least recognise and incorporate theirs. The problems seemingly affecting soccer's Premiership at the start of their 2005/06 season, namely static or falling club attendances, paucity of product due to negative tactics, lack of promoting young local talent, fractured links with the community, over-inflated entry prices, diminishing identifiable role models, lack of respect for authority, higher incidence of gamesmanship, predictability of outcome, tumbling television ratings, alleged managerial bungs and massive overall debt linked to unsustainable and incomprehensible players wages, are all those that could easily have afflicted Super League as it celebrated its first decade in existence. However, virtually every one of those measurable variables show the exact reverse despite the immense upheaval the sport has undergone. In soccer at the top level, fans no longer make a direct contribution to the sport; they merely provide background fodder by way of an increasingly muted atmosphere. Part of the reason for that is due to all-seater stadia and the continued need for segregation post the Taylor Report, following the tragic events at Hillsborough in 1989, but also because exorbitant ticket prices have changed the complexion and make up of the fans. Even their chanting, so long the breeding ground for black humour, biting wit and poetic adaptation has been blunted by an excess of transient foreign players who wear the shirt, often as a badge of convenience and about whom it is virtually impossible to create a song. In contrast, Super League's more compact grounds and involving pre-match theatre have embellished the spectacle. Although contract lengths have generally become shorter in Super League and testimonials are rarer, the gladiators are still an integral part of the communities they represent. Those who stay at a club for ten seasons are rightly feted, unlike in soccer where, because of the almost obscene sums being earned in comparison with those watching, testimonial events have been turned over to charities in an effort to show that there is still some sense of altruism left in the game. According to soccer magazine *FourFourTwo's* editor Hugh Sleight, when unveiling the sport's rich lists, 'In 2005, Rio Ferdinand and other top players earned four times as much every week as the average Brit earned in the entire year.' Sports Minister Richard Caborn has called for a European-wide salary cap to be introduced in soccer with the money saved by the clubs being given back to the fans by way of lowered prices. Super League may not have been his model for that but it could have been. He was backed up by Dave Whelan, the JJB Sports mogul who has masterminded Wigan Athletic's remarkable rise to the Premiership – the 2005/06 surprise package in that they commendably managed to hold their own after being promoted – who also has his hands on the tiller at the stadium-sharing Warriors. 'There's only one way to guarantee healthy

competition in the Premiership and that's why I'm calling for a salary cap to
be enforced in the top flight. I'm not knocking Chelsea but if they continue
dominating and win the title for another three or four years, then the entire
Premier League runs the risk of being ruined. Too many clubs would be
left simply making up the numbers by a one-club monopoly. Rugby league
has seen the benefits of enforcing a salary cap and soccer should take note.
[Because of the unhealthy dominance of Wigan RL] The interest fell away
and football could go the same way if we aren't careful. Rugby crowds have
come back but now football's attendances are being hit. If we don't look at
our finances, our great game will have major problems.'

One of the key tenets of sports marketing is finding common areas of
interest between the sport and its supporters and a primary influence is geography; not just the desire to associate with and support the resident team but,
crucially, local players within it. Soccer has its academies but rarely promotes
its incumbents whereas the 20/20 rule has at least made Super League clubs
invest more in their up-and-coming home-grown talent. Tactically there
are other interesting parallels. In soccer, particularly at Premiership level,
losing is no longer an option for clubs because of the money attached to
every point gained. Managers need results not just for their own job security – which at times seems to be about three results before the knives come
out – but to keep the financiers at bay, which leads to a pervading tendency
towards caution. At the start of the 2005 season, prompted by the success of
Greece in the European Championships the summer before, debate centred
on the ability of lesser sides to stifle those with flair by adopting a negative
4-5-1 formation, with away teams especially happy to soak up pressure by
putting the maximum number of bodies behind the ball and looking to
counter occasionally on the break. That tends to lead to contests being suf-
focated of skill and excitement almost before they have begun. As a result,
the goals-per-game ratio and consequently entertainment value and television ratings continued to decrease at a time when admission prices spiralled.
Predatory England striker Michael Owen, on his return to the British game
at Newcastle in 2005 commented, 'There is not so much attacking and it
is difficult to score a goal. It is a slightly different Premiership I have come
back to from Spain… maybe that is of some concern.'

Conversely, at the end of the 2005 Super League season, Leeds Rhinos,
finishing in second place, registered the highest number of points and tries
scored in a regular season campaign. To most soccer observers Chelsea
– whose position of money-injected dominance is comparable to Wigan's
in rugby league through the mid 1980s and 1990s – had wrapped up the
2005/06 Championship virtually within two months of the start of the sea-

son, building an unassailable lead to the detriment of the neutral fans' interest. At the turn of the year, barely halfway through the campaign, all sections of the media desperately tried to build up interest in the clash at Highbury between Arsenal and Manchester United, the other two 'challengers' among the Premiership's really 'big three'. Despite £90 million worth of predominantly foreign talent on the field, no more than a half chance was created, the sterile game finishing 0-0 to essentially hand Jose Mourinho's monied men their second successive title. Former Manchester United star Ray Wilkins confessed that his former team, 'seem to have accepted that coming second is the limit of their ambition.' It used to be like that in rugby league until the advent of Super League. Even the Old Trafford club's principal sponsor Vodafone had negotiated their way out of the link up. Alongside the regular tactical sterility, Wigan Athletic's manager Paul Jewell honestly admitted that 'simulation' was now an accepted part of the soccer game. He went on to explain that if his side needed a win and had a chance of getting a penalty, he would expect his player to dive in order to get one. That sort of blatant cheating not only devalues the game, and it has become increasingly part of it with the introduction of more foreign players from leagues where such a ploy is the accepted norm, but it short changes the public and shows increasing disrespect for the officials – as does clubs appealing to have virtually every red card doled out rescinded. Rugby League players and fans pride themselves on how genuinely tough their sport is; it is integral to the game and cannot be compromised. It is probably not worth asking them what they think of players rolling around in so-called agony when contact has been, at best, minimal. The intrusive, multi-angled, prying camera captures every facial expression while in Super League the referee's open mike allows each word and, importantly, aside to be heard. If the general and committed public feel increasingly alienated by the wages their soccer idols receive then sympathy is hardly likely to be regained if their heroes appear spoilt and petulant. Most of the invective and sardonic gesticulation is directed at the men in the middle but such dissent has been conspicuously absent in the more arduous league environment. The additional potential punishment of an extra ten metres in a game so ruled by territory is a sufficient deterrent but there is nevertheless a genuine bond of mutual respect in the relationship and appreciation of the difficulties of each other's tasks that money has not tainted. Interestingly, soccer eventually acceded to the same ten-metre rule in an effort to 'clean up its act' but subsequently found it unworkable and surreptitiously dropped it.

For many neutral fans that jumped on the Premiership bandwagon, the elite soccer league has become boring and predictable. Outside of three or four clubs who have ostensibly become the playthings of big businessmen or at the whim of multi-national owners or shareholders whose love or passion is for an economic return rather than the inherent qualities of following a team, survival is paramount. Being in the Premier League, by virtue of associated television handouts, guarantees existence for most while for others not being in the Champions League signals a disaster; a competition that has in itself been devalued by being opened to sides that have not won a domestic championship to qualify, all for the sake of television. Even some celebrities who grew up with a love of soccer have switched their allegiance and all-important endorsement. The best example is Ricky Tomlinson who, despite a brilliant portrayal of fictitious England soccer manager Mike Bassett, has swapped his Liverpool replica shirt for that of St Helens and a seat at Knowsley Road – alongside fellow thespian Johnny Vegas – ironically at about the same time he brought out a book called *Football, My Arse*. In his brilliantly constructed study *The Beautiful Game? Searching for the Soul of Football* (Yellow Jersey Press, 2005) one of the sport's top investigative journalists David Conn outlined the dilemmas facing the national game, few of which afflict Super League in the same way. 'The difference between fans before the grounds sat down and the prices went up doesn't seem to be predominantly class, but age. You can see the odd teenager but not groups of them consumed by the football… the commentators still scream at the style and panache of the hammerings that Chelsea dish out, desperate to justify the "product" the TV channels pay millions for… post-Premiership implosion, the bust it fashioned from the years of boom… even the bonanza at the top has been misspent, as it has been distributed to reward the already rich and therefore concentrated success in the hands of the winners… [quoting Graham Taylor] "The players are on enormous wages and I can tell you that many of the foreign players, particularly, don't care about the clubs and the local pride at stake – they are difficult to motivate." Do the clubs, football people, ever stop to think through what the business is in which they are involved; what sport is, what it could do, what's its place, its true heart, its purpose is or could be, in society?… Ticket prices are punishingly high; professional football is pricing out the poor and the young – although the absence of the next generation has not been adequately recognised by the clubs.'

Maybe, as Kevin Keegan pointed out on leaving Manchester City, soccer has reached saturation level, that it is too much under the microscope and has lost its mystique and there is a void for another sport to expand in to if it can see and seize the opportunity. It would be churlish to claim Super League bears direct comparison with the avaricious, all-pervading, media-obsessed and ceaselessly courted Premiership, not least because of the spectre of the cash cow that is the Champions' League, a dimension rugby league simply does not have. Equally,

Super League is not totally a paradigm of virtue. Where there is an analogy, is in terms of perceived underlying qualities. Hewn from the same seam, their respective paths taken in the advanced capitalist state of sport are becoming increasingly divergent. Rather than perhaps trying to aspire to match its much bigger brother, maybe Super League should take some quiet satisfaction from the fact that it has managed to retain a considerable modicum of the integrity that actually brought it about in the first place and, as a result, has not completely lost sight of its core worth. Ironically, it knows its sense of place in its communities while continually struggling for recognition outside them.

SHEFFIELD

'The fan. They're the people you don't want to alienate. While he or she might not be paying the total bill I would hate to go to any contest where there is no-one in the stands except for the corporate boxes. Fans create the atmosphere so important to players.' – Wayne Bennett, legendary Brisbane Broncos and former Australia and Queensland coach

Above all else, St Helens-supporting Ian Swire is a passionate fan of the sport, regularly scheduling holiday breaks around the French domestic league programme. By virtue of his commercial position, he has also been able to make a contribution to it. In March 1996, just as Super League was coming on stream, he was appointed to the board of the Amco Corporation, a conglomerate PLC that provides specialist construction and engineering services and is engaged in property development, mining, structural steel fabrication, and plastics manufacturing. Having graduated from Sheffield University, the former chartered accountant, now finance director, had remained in South Yorkshire and gradually became more tied-in to the fledgling Sheffield Eagles. Come the new era, his company were already sponsors at the Don Valley Stadium and he could see the instant benefits. 'It was the exposure side of it more than anything, moving it to summer and taking it away from competing with football that added value and interest. It was difficult to see how Super League was going to develop but the lift in the profile was going to be good from a sponsorship point of view. Gary [Hetherington – chief executive at the Eagles] was always looking at new proposals. He got people involved, there were sponsor nights to try and explain what was going to happen. In the early days it was mooted about a merger with Doncaster to form a South Yorkshire team, which fell away. I don't see what they would have brought to it as such, Doncaster people would have stuck to supporting their side going on their way. There is a lot of rivalry between the two – it's the big-brother city overshadowing the local towns. You see it in football in places like Barnsley and Rotherham against the big Sheffield clubs. I still think that's the case now even though the relative positions of the Eagles and the Lakers have effectively been switched. They've got a new stadium on the way but I still don't see any mileage in a merger. Obviously we can work together on various things like junior development in the service area but the clubs remain independent. Mergers disillusion people – it's not like a Tesco and a Sainsbury's where if one closes you move to the other, sport doesn't work that way. Even as a sponsor, a South Yorkshire side didn't have an appeal.'

The opening night could not have worked out better for an aficionado of the French game, with Sheffield drawn to begin the proceedings in the Paris springtime. 'We went independently and made a weekend of it. It was just a great occasion with the crowd and the atmosphere in the stadium, it all worked very well but you didn't really get the impression in greater Paris itself that anything was going on. It was only near the ground that people started appearing. As you went back into the city late at night I don't think anyone was remotely aware what had gone on but it was certainly looked a good starting point. To be honest, knowing the way rugby league works in France – and you could see there were a lot of buses there from the south – you wondered how sustainable it was in the capital. I'm not convinced there was ever a real opportunity there. It should have been Toulouse from the start for me personally.'

By the start of Super League II, Sheffield were the sport's first PLC with LG Electronics head Paul Thompson having bought the club and floated it, although not to universal approval. 'It wasn't a way ahead any more than it is for football; PLC's in soccer don't work. It was the in-thing at one stage but I dare say virtually every club has failed to benefit from being quoted – and the spectre of Manchester United being back in private hands raises major questions about them putting themselves in the public sphere like that to be taken over. In the scale of rugby league it was never really a viable option to do that. I don't think very much was raised, I think it probably cost more than it was worth and it was a mistake. It was something Paul Thompson liked doing, taking companies to the market. He was an accountant by training and he'd got a couple of larger PLCs that he had been involved with but I never saw any great benefit to come out of it and I don't think anything did. Gary was so personable; he was just about irreplaceable anyway with that enthusiasm. The guys who came in before the Paul Thompson era tried and kept the show on the road. After that, Paul put some money in and employed professional marketing personnel but it all became very impersonal, very much a commodity. It wasn't the same. Rather than being cajoled and persuaded into helping, suddenly you had people ringing you who felt that you were almost honour bound to do it and it lost something. Their background was in the Sheffield Sharks basketball side, in which the PLC had also taken a large stake and eventually failed. They knew basketball and there was an element of cross-sponsorship but sometimes you wondered who their true master was. They were trying to sell a product but they weren't rugby league people.'

Nevertheless, 1998 brought on-field success of an historic nature, beyond the wildest dreams of anyone associated with the club, when the mighty Wigan were defeated in the Challenge Cup final at Wembley. The question is, in the new commercial era, did the club make the most of the ideal marketing opportunity it had created? 'They missed their chance after the semi-final. The attitude was "right we've got there, the people of Sheffield will flock in, we don't need to do anything to get them there" and they sat back and waited for the rush, there was never a doubt in their minds that they would sell their allocation of tickets. Consequently they made no effort to market them and just expected queues around the block to pick them up but the reality struck them a few weeks later that that wasn't happening and it wasn't going to but, by that time, a valuable opportunity had been lost. They missed the chance to get the sports fans in the city down there and, in hindsight with the result, the possibility of getting a lot more people hooked on rugby league. As it was, a number of people in the city watched it on TV and there was a big cheer at the Sheffield Wednesday game when the score was announced but that was it; not many saw it live or videoed it or really appreciated the scale of the upset. There was a big crowd the following week for the game with Wigan in the league but then it seemed to slip away in a case of after the Lord Mayor's parade. Afterwards, there are conflicting tales, you'll hear that the cup was never in the office, it was out on the rounds of the schools or wherever but whenever I was in it always seemed to be there, there was never much evidence of it being used to promote the club but it's difficult to know what they could have done.'

After that, there was a sharp decline, with the PLC looking to extricate itself from its commitments as the following season wore on. 'Paul was a very private person. I never particularly knew him at all while he was at the club, although I've spoken to him a little bit since. I don't know where his interests were. He had an involvement in football prior to the Eagles – he'd sponsored the shirts at Sheffield Wednesday and Southampton and became chairman of West Bromwich Albion soon after he left the Don Valley. I think he may have been a bit disillusioned that people weren't coming to watch the Eagles and expected a return on the investment he'd made and, knowing the parties involved, which he probably paid over the odds for and which was never realistically going to be there. Some of that might be down to the size of the stadium and the distance between the spectators and the action – British sporting fans are not used to athletic tracks around their pitches – which leads to a lack of atmosphere and provides a reason for not going. I don't know what triggered the decline but there did appear to be a slight disenchantment among the management generally, coupled with the money it was costing, and then Super League gave him the chance to actually get out of it altogether.'

That came about with the surprise announcement that, with incentives available to reduce the number of teams, Sheffield would merge with Huddersfield. The most dreaded word in the Super League vocabulary was back on the agenda and no more popular or considered than when it was first mooted in 1995. 'You looked at the finances here, the crowds, the Sky money and what they must have been paying to recruit the players and it didn't stack up, so there must have been an element of subsidy coming from Paul Thompson. How sustainable that was depended solely on that one person and a similar situation seemed to be the case at Huddersfield with Ken Davy bankrolling the club, which the accounts proved. The major concern at Sheffield was if, as had been indicated, Paul Thompson wanted to pull out, what course of action would then be open? Would the club accept the seemingly inevitable prospect of relegation and what that would bring, or grasp at straws and see what would happen? It's before my involvement, there are very muddy waters; there was lots of talk of Huddersfield putting a team into the First Division and the Super League side being above it, but I'm not sure quite how that would have worked. Whether that was actually a genuine, serious suggestion I find it slightly difficult to believe. If that was ever the intention, if Huddersfield were happy to take their place in the NFP, then why bother merging with Sheffield? I have doubts about that one to be honest. Once it became apparent that Huddersfield were going to effectively take over the regime, you had to wonder what future there was for rugby league in Sheffield given that Huddersfield had the more apt venue and the lack of expectation that existed. It seemed that the whole operation would move up there, which is what happened within twelve months. The option to involve local Sheffield businesses was never there. I don't know if anyone would have come forward but the club was never advertised as being for sale. Arguably there was nobody there when Gary Hetherington stood back three or four years earlier apart from Paul Thompson, but then again until you test the water and put out the appeals you don't know. I think they had painted themselves into a corner looking for a way out and then Super League opened the door behind them and they stepped through it. The people running the club weren't necessarily Sheffield supporters. They were given an easy opportunity and they took it. Had that not arisen it would have been interesting to see what would have happened. I'm not convinced anybody would necessarily have stepped forward to sustain it at Super League level but we'll never know. One part of me thought that it was a decent move to keep Super League rugby on the face of it in the area if it was going to be a genuine fifty-fifty partnership, but as I got more involved on the Sheffield side I could see that it was never going to be. You could tell that Huddersfield-Sheffield wasn't going to be sustainable and it became important to keep something going in the city because, the way I saw it, there wasn't necessarily that intention. I'm sure they would say that there was and that we pulled the rug from beneath their feet but I've got to question that. I'm not convinced there was a master plan; it certainly didn't come across that way. It didn't seem sensible having expanded the year before to take Gateshead and the whole of the North-East into the equation to then suddenly pull the plug after one year and then contract and drop two clubs. I don't know what the initiative behind that was. It certainly wasn't extra money for all the other clubs initially because what Sheffield would have got went to Huddersfield and what Gateshead were scheduled to receive went to Hull, so no-one else stood to benefit from it. It caused a lot of bad feeling, especially among the supporters of both clubs. To be fair Huddersfield lost a lot of fans through it who didn't want it any more than the Sheffield ones did, and it has taken a long time for the Giants to win those people back. People still begrudge it on both sides and I don't see that anything whatsoever could have been gained by doing it. If Sheffield couldn't afford to continue at Super League level and were relegated then so be it, people would have stood by it and maybe they would have bounced back, or possibly they wouldn't. Who is to know? I don't see what was gained out of it at all, I don't know why Super League dropped the clubs or why they play these extra fixtures now. The logical thing is surely to get back to fourteen clubs and play twenty-six games and that is apparently the long-term plan, so why drop to twelve in the first place? I didn't understand that at the time and I don't now.'

Watching events at arm's length, the man who had formed the Eagles, Gary Hetherington, was similarly non-plussed by the whole merger option. 'I was involved in a sense because I was on the board of Super League and I was first approached by David Lloyd to tell me that Hull were sinking and could I do anything in my position to try and save it? So I was acutely aware of their perilous situation. I wasn't a supporter of the merger concept, I don't think that fundamentally there is one, it's not a merger it's a takeover but when you get a situation where clubs are facing the possibility of extinction or retaining some form of survival then it becomes a different thing. Hull were very, very close to folding; David Lloyd had put a lot of money into the club but had taken a lot of bad advice and become impatient and just wanted to pull out. Gateshead had had a raw deal. They were admitted to Super League but only on restricted money. They got some £350,000 less than everyone else, which was a ridiculous decision by the then SLE. They built the crowds up to about 3,500, which was quite respectable, but nevertheless that first year they lost around half a million pounds, which left their chief executive Shane Richardson in a difficult position financially. When the Super League clubs decided to revert to twelve clubs from fourteen and offered a financial incentive to do so, then it became inevitable that some unlikely clubs would seek to get together. There was an element of opportunism for Gateshead to take over a sleeping giant at Hull, it was effectively a reverse take over, and then it was a strategic decision for the game. The initial strategy of the merged outfit was to stay in Gateshead as a Super League side but to resurrect and maintain Hull as a First Division club, but that division voted not to accept them in membership, which was not in the best interests of the game. That posed an ultimatum to the new owners to choose one or other location and that forced a decision to be made in favour of Hull, particularly with the prospect of a new stadium in the city. When you look back there were some solid reasons why that happened and what shaped it and of course now we can see that at least some good has come out of it because Hull have re-emerged a strong club in a vital area. On the down side, I still remain convinced that support for rugby in the North-East would have gravitated towards Gateshead. Even though it is a football area, the Newcastle Falcons have had five-figure crowds and I'm sure that would have made Thunder a viable entity. Huddersfield and Sheffield was somewhat different. The Eagles had won the cup the year before but unfortunately simply couldn't generate enough interest in the city to maintain a Super League presence and that had always been a fear of mine. The club had moved away from the community element and had embarked on a fairly lavish spell of spending, which had put them in a bit of financial difficulty. Huddersfield weren't progressing and it was a bit of opportunism on behalf of the two owners, Paul Thompson and Ken Davy, who were both losing money and decided to cut their losses. There was no real support for a merged club and everyone could see that it was essentially a move to Huddersfield but, unlike Hull, where you were fairly certain that if things could be turned around there would be the backing, there was no certainty that either Huddersfield or Sheffield would be able to build to that level of success and indeed there hasn't been. That was a sad, messy merger.'

Rather than sit back and accept that Sheffield would cease to have a presence in the code, Ian Swire set about re-forming the club as far away from a business principle as could be imagined, with a refocus on what the Eagles originally did best, working with the community. 'It was difficult to know at the time what was going on; I was very sceptical as to whether it would be possible to form a club in the NFP, certainly with no money coming through from Sky. We looked at the numbers and felt that we could put a side together with the backing of the supporters and corporate sponsors. It was a lot of people coming together and putting a little bit in that enabled us to move forward. The opportunity to achieve Super League has always got to be there on the horizon. It's not in our short-term thinking – we've got to move into National League One and establish ourselves there and build our gates up to an extent that we can put a decent business plan together to not only get into to Super League but to actually add something to it once there. It's a distant dream but it's still achievable. From a city profile Sheffield is big enough and we've re-engaged the business community, which had been let slip with the reintroduction of luncheon clubs, gentleman's dinners and golf days where you actually get to talk to the corporate people who have no obvious interest in rugby league and persuade them to come to a game. From that, if they like what we're doing and the people they're deal-ing with, the community feel and what we're doing in schools and the area, they might put a few thousand pounds' worth of sponsorship into the club. That tends to stay year after year so we gradually build up our portfolio. If we can continue to bring the kids through generally, we fit the bill and we'd have as much right to look at Super League as anyone else.'

How far the 'new' Eagles can go in the future may well depend on the promotion/relegation debate, the likelihood of franchising again rearing its head. 'There are so many pros and cons, I can understand why they would want to give clubs time to establish themselves. They've seen what's hap-pened to the likes of Leigh putting a team together in such a very short time and then struggling badly. On the other side, you look at Castleford. Did being relegated do them a favour? They kept their fans and community programmes together but then lost a lot of their leading players who got them back up, and are following the Leigh route for recruitment. You look at Halifax who three or four years ago got themselves into chaotic financial problems and to have propped them up for another couple of years in Super League would not have been a sensible option when there were teams out-side of it like Widnes who had got their act together, spent a few years in the lower reaches sorting out their finances and rebuilding the stadium and were ready and willing to take their place. To have deprived Widnes their chance and now Castleford theirs would have been wrong. At the end of the day if people are willing to stake their opportunity they should be able to even if there are casualties along the way. There are no rights and wrongs. Overall Super League's been a success; it's difficult to see where the game would have been without the Murdoch money, especially with the spectre of rugby union going professional. You look at the effort and commitment the players put in at all levels and without the Sky deal we could not have rewarded them or possibly even held onto them. The razzmatazz wouldn't have been there with the gates increasing to a now self-sustainable level at many of the top clubs. Overall it has been for the benefit of the game. Things move on; we couldn't have turned down the money at the time – and which other sport would have? – but we had to dance to the piper's tune and maybe we do that a little too much at times. A lot of tradition has gone and some traditional clubs are on their uppers, but that's the nature of the way things operate. It has been good, it's a changed game, a different game but times change and people change and their outlook on life changes. If the sport had stayed where it was it would have withered away.'

SCHOLARSHIPS

'To have young players already good enough to beat Australia at youth international level as the England Academy team did in 2002 is testimony to how far the game has come at this level in the Super League era.' – Dean Bell

The opening decade of Super League has unleashed some players with exceptional skills but enthusiasts of the sport are always craving for more. If the media is guilty of anything in this respect, it is merely to speculate as to who will be the next great star, perhaps even helping to form such a player through their own promotion. For the clubs, however, the true creation of future talent is a much more pragmatic exercise and on that score the production line has undoubtedly gathered momentum since 1996. Dean Bell, forever synonymous as a commanding presence in the great Wigan teams of the late 1980s and early 1990s – and one of the very few in the code to feature on *This is Your Life* – has been at the forefront of such activity since making the switch to head of youth development in 1997, during his second spell at Leeds. As a man who has played and coached at Super League level, and who has since carved his own niche in helping to shape the futures of stars such as Kevin Sinfield, Chev Walker, Gareth Hock and Sean O'Loughlin, the former New Zealand Test star is ideally placed to assess the impact of the summer switch and full-time professionalism on the generations that hold the sport in their hands. 'There's no question that the move to summer has been good for the game as a whole and for youth development. We're now producing a lot more skilful players who can show all their talents. We're getting better coaching as well, because the weather allows coaches to spend more time doing the things they should be doing with players, instead of just running around kicking and passing the ball. We now have more coaching staff at Super League clubs than ever before as a result of going full time and that transmits right through the club. Instead of finishing work at 5.30 p.m. and being on the training field at 6.00 p.m., it allows players to remain fresh and it also allows the coaches to develop themselves. I can't see any negatives as far as youth development is concerned since Super League began.'

So what really has changed then? In the days of professional winter rugby league, clubs would appoint scouts who would scour the local parks and beyond, looking to recruit the next Shaun Edwards or Garry Schofield. Once they had spotted that talent the clubs could trial them, sign them and discard them or, if they were unsure and dawdled, they might lose out to another club and risk the wrath of their own fans if the player made it to the top. Edwards would be a prime example of the old system, signing as he did for Wigan live on television at exactly midnight on his seventeenth birthday in 1983 for a then record fee for a schoolboy. The transition can be traced back to the early part of the 1980s with the introduction of the Colts League and, for the first time, there was a feeling of long-term structure when a fully fledged academy and scholarship system was born around ten years later as the ideal proving ground. Even so, the game was still part-time and played between August and May, and although improving standards were apparent, it was the introduction of Super League that truly got the ball rolling. 'One of the key things is where you draw your players from. Wigan is a rugby league area that is very strong as far as quality of players is concerned. But what really changed was that you have to put structures in place so the young players have a pathway on which they can develop, and mine was a pretty simple philosophy, to concentrate on the core skills, the simple things about the game. So at Leeds I'd have the guys continually working on those basic aspects aligned with a good strength-development programme. From there I think that players can take their game forward, and the summer era has definitely helped to do that more so than in the past.'

Despite leaving Leeds as long ago as 1999, the fruits of Dean Bell's labour at Headingley have come to blossom since the turn of the century. 'The rewards for me are to see a significant number of them come through that youth system and go on to reach first team, or even international football. I watched the 2005 Grand Final and I think I counted eleven players who had come through the youth system that I'd been involved with at Leeds. Don't get me wrong, I'm not claiming that I've had a huge influence on them lately, but I did play a part in helping them to get where they are now. Actually, the Leeds youth system was already well established when I went to Headingley, and really I just fine-tuned a few things about it. But when I came back to Wigan there was more to do. Obviously there were some good things about youth development at the JJB Stadium at the time, and it would be wrong to say there weren't. But, for example, one of the big things was that you can't learn things sitting on the sidelines and, along with Brian Foley, I started a scholarship scheme as well, which had worked really well at Leeds. I guess we were really the pioneers behind that sort of thing. From there, the Rugby Football League has adopted the system for the whole of the sport in Britain now.'

Scholarships were a mere pipedream in the pre–Super League era but, as Rupert Murdoch's money facilitated a more all-embracing professionalism, clubs were able to take care of much more than just the odd training session for their youngsters. 'In terms of scholarships we are talking about the elite kids who are aged thirteen through to sixteen. I quickly realised that when you have talent, you can't wait until they're fifteen years of age before you start to work with them. The sooner you get hold of them the better. A lot of it is about getting them to realise what they can achieve by having a good attitude and to focus on what they should be doing because, as with any fifteen or sixteen year old, there are distractions in life. So it's about focus and getting the players to believe that they can achieve and that with self-belief and hard work they can get to where they want to be. Those are lessons I learned as a youngster myself. I wanted to see how far I could go with the ability that I had and that is what I try to say to the young guys. There can be no worse thing in life than to look back on your career and wonder what might have happened. There are no guarantees that through hard work they will achieve, but what they will get is the satisfaction of knowing that at least they tried. I can handle a lack of talent but what I can't accept is a lack of desire. People with not a lot of talent can achieve if their desire is strong enough, but it rarely works the other way around. So it's not just about rugby league skills, these are also life skills that will stand them in good stead in other areas. We try to formally educate them and encourage the guys to do well in that respect so that they have something to fall back on. We don't sell them any dreams of making it as a rugby player. What we do is deal with the immediate things, making the most of your education, working hard in your development as a player and emphasising the rewards will come if they do. We generally take on twelve players in each age group and you'll find that most Super League clubs who run scholarships do the same. Kids sometimes develop at different ages. One of the toughest jobs is telling a youngster that you can't have him back on the scholarship the following year. If you have to let a thirteen or fourteen year old go, then at fifteen or sixteen he could still develop into a very good player, so you have to have an open mind about that. You're not saying that the player isn't good enough, but you've got to make a judgement and I think if you're honest with people, and I think that's one of the things that I've always been, then they respect that.'

A small number of talented players have probably always slipped through the net, and that may still be the case today, but the Wigan rugby executive is clear in his view that the past decade has not meant simply a mad rush to get to the best young players first, but equally as important is how those players are managed once they are taken under the wing of a club. 'Finding the players is the easy part; we're not a massive national game that's got them up in the Orkney Islands or wherever, that you're going to miss. In youth rugby league, everyone knows who the good players are, but it's what you do with them and how you treat them that moves things along. I believe that if you treat people fairly then when they do make it they pay you back in that respect, but if they don't make it then they should still have enjoyed their time with you, and that's the key.'

Bell learned how to play league in his homeland during the 1970s and, reflecting on what was happening then and how young players are nurtured today, he says there is no comparison. 'There have been massive advances in youth development since I was coming through the ranks in New Zealand and even since I was playing the game over here. Lots of things have happened and continue to happen and that's not just down to people like me at Super League clubs, but right through to the amateur clubs things have got better. Youth development is not a headline-grabbing subject, you're not always hearing about it, but I can tell you that I've been working in this part of the game for about seven years now and I've seen some great things happening that I don't think would have happened quite so quickly or efficiently if it hadn't been for the switch to the summer game, and that bodes well for the future of rugby league at all levels. For example, we were a long way behind the Australian system ten years ago, but we've put in lots of work in that time. BARLA and the RFL are starting to get together now, which they weren't before, and that was always a big issue hampering youth development because it didn't allow the continuous stepping stones that players needed and there were a lot of questions about whether the professional game was doing enough for the amateur game. Now that things are starting to come together you can see an improvement. It's not perfect yet, but that's not going to happen overnight. We can't sit here in our nice stadiums and produce Super League players off a conveyor belt. Where it really happens in the first place is at the grass roots. The government is worried about obesity with kids and they want to get more people active, and rugby league or sport in general is a great way to do that. As far as the amateur game is concerned I think the clubs are definitely becoming more professional in their approach and their coaching methods for the kids have improved. But what we in the elite clubs are not giving the amateurs is enough of our time. At Wigan we spend as much of it as we can with the local clubs; we run coaching courses, we help coaches develop, and we have a good rapport with the amateur clubs in the area. That's the only way the game is going to go forward. At the end of the day they want their players to do as well as they can, and we want as many players to come through with a chance of making our first team as possible and that's a win–win situation. Over half of our 2006 first-team squad is from local junior amateur teams. It's impressive, but I'm not getting carried away with it because the real question is can they stay there? We can give them the opportunity and then I want to see them take it.'

A supreme athlete during his own playing career, Dean Bell is positive when questioned about the heightened fitness levels of players in the Super League era and, with the trend of players retiring slightly earlier than in the past, that it is a sport with even more appeal and opportunity for the young at the very top level. 'The game is faster nowadays and the players are definitely more athletic than they used to be, even ten years ago. I know here we are talking about youth, but there will always be room within the game for experienced players. You can do lots of things with a young player to improve his game. You can coach better skills, you can build better strength, even help him with speed, and of course help to shape his attitude, but the one thing you cannot give him is experience. That's how our youth learn some of their best lessons, by watching the older players, and that's where higher up the ladder, in first-team rugby league, you have to get your balance right.'

While that will be pleasant reading for the thirtysomethings who can still cut it at the elite level, there remains ongoing criticism over the quantity of overseas players involved in Super League, with a number of international defeats at the hands of Australia and New Zealand being blamed partially on a perceived lack of young talent in key areas of the Great Britain team. The expediency of signing a ready-made, relatively cheap import often outweighs the time needed to nurture talent or is an indictment of the elite clubs' inability to produce sufficient young quality, depending on which view you take. As an overseas quota player once himself before gaining residency qualification to be exempted, Bell is well placed to judge this issue. 'I've said for years that the number of overseas players in the British game is holding back development of home-grown talent. British teams struggle to put together a top international side nowadays and at the moment there are so many loopholes in the system that clubs are exploiting. I know there are human rights issues involved, but I don't like the Kolpak system. I know I'm from New Zealand, but this is where I've chosen to live, this is where I earn my living and I want what's best for the British game. I think that overseas players do have a part to play, an important part, but we're overrun with them at the moment. I'd like to see a total limit of about three per squad really and that way it will ensure that we only have the best players, and also it will allow the youngsters here to be given the opportunity, which at the moment is blocked in certain positions. It's up to the decision makers in the game to do something about it. It's nothing new. It's always been an issue and I realise it's not an easy situation to get out of.'

Given the lower profile of his role as far as media interest is concerned, Dean Bell will doubtless always be best remembered for his on-field contributions in the immediate pre-Super League era. He may no longer throw too many passes in anger, but he still gets a kick out of watching those he has helped develop make it to the top. 'I was particularly proud of being involved in youth development when the British Academy team beat the Aussie schoolboys a couple of years ago, especially as some of the players have already kicked on from there. Although the British game keeps improving, strength in depth is still a bit of a problem, so to have young players already good enough to beat Australia is to their great credit but there is still much more work to be done.'

SNIPERS – THE 1997 WORLD CLUB CHAMPIONSHIP REPRISED

'Anyone who is interested in sport of any kind should be there to witness something very special and to be able to say that they were part of something truly historical. In that sense the results don't matter.' – Maurice Lindsay (June 1997)

One of the landmarks in rugby league in the past two decades has been the World Club Challenge, where the British champions take on their Australian counterparts. Originally sporadic and hastily arranged, since 2000 it has become a well-organised annual event, showcasing the best two clubs in each hemisphere. Maurice Lindsay, then in his first spell as chairman at Wigan, is the man credited with the initial idea of a one-off challenge match to decide the very best in the game back in 1987 and, on a memorable night at a jam-packed Central Park, his emissaries astonishingly beat Manly in absolutely gripping fashion to set the seal on the idea. It was the type of bold move for which Lindsay made his name, and its longevity is an indicator of its success as a concept, certainly as far as the British viewpoint has been concerned.

Ten years on from that first official contest (Eastern Suburbs had beaten St Helens 25-2 in an unsanctioned match in Sydney in 1976) the world game embarked on one of the most ambitious projects it has ever undertaken, a World Club Championship involving every team from the top flight in both Australasia and Europe. On the face of it, it appeared to be every British supporter's dream; the chance to follow your own club to the other side of the globe and then watch the best in the world back on your 'middin'. The one major drawback was that the clubs involved in the European edition were always likely to struggle playing more than a one-off match against sides from Australia. Despite the war having split the game between the old ARL and Super League Down Under, it was universally acknowledged that the depth of talent available in the southern hemisphere made their competition stronger, despite its apparently watered-down appearance at the time. That theory was subsequently borne out when the Australian Super League team defeated Great Britain 2-1 in a series held later in 1997. Even the most optimistic Brit must have approached the fixture schedule with both excitement and dread in equal measure after they had read the words of Brian Smith, then coach of Parramatta after leaving the club who were to go on and win Super League in 1997, Bradford Bulls. 'I can't see the English clubs competing with the Australian clubs. When Aussie supporters see a couple of results where English clubs have been hammered over there, it isn't going to ignite interest in the visit here of the likes of Oldham or Halifax.' Esteemed journalist Dave Hadfield was similarly bemused by what was likely to unfold when he wrote in *Open Rugby*, 'So here it is then. This great convoluted, confusing – but ultimately compelling – thing called the World Club Championship. I don't imagine I was alone when I first heard of the plan in wondering what substance the people who devised it had been on. Flying Salford across the world to play Adelaide, for heaven's sake. What will they think of next?... It really is a ponderous mess of a thing, full of byes, quirks and dark back-alleys. We are not even guaranteed a Britain-Australia final at the end of it. We could finish up with two Aussie sides playing off in Sydney. Or even – if you want to contemplate the truly bizarre – two British clubs… The question then will be how well the British clubs will fare in the competition. There are two competing theories about this. One says that Australia still has far greater depth of talent and that, with one or two exceptions in our own hemisphere, we are going to get well stuffed. The other says: "Hang on a minute. Have you seen some of those Australian Super League highlights on Sky? They've forgotten how to defend and we've got a great chance."' The benefit of hindsight showed the first of those theories to be alarmingly accurate. The clubs were split into Pools A and B based on their final league position the previous season, roughly, with the former comprised of Bradford Bulls, Halifax Blue Sox, London Broncos, St Helens, Warrington Wolves and Wigan Warriors, while the Australian contingent was to be Brisbane Broncos, Canberra Raiders, Cronulla Sharks, Canterbury Bulldogs, Penrith Panthers, plus New Zealand's Auckland Warriors. That left Castleford Tigers, Leeds Rhinos, Salford City Reds, Sheffield Eagles, Oldham Bears and Paris St Germain representing the European Super League in Pool B, while their Aussie opponents would be Adelaide Rams, Perth Reds, North Queensland Cowboys and Hunter Mariners.

The competition was never really user-friendly, in that not everyone played everyone else in their pool, and it was also to be split into three distinct phases. Phase One was played in June, where the British clubs in Pool A travelled Down Under while the Aussies from Pool B played in Europe, and then Phase Two in July/August, where the reverse occurred. Finally, there would be quarter-finals, semis and a final in October. In addition to that there was some bizarre structuring that meant that four clubs from each hemisphere would make the quarter-finals, ensuring that, no matter what the disparity in results, both hemispheres would be equally represented. For some of the Australian clubs it must have been as frustrating as when your parents make you lose a game to your brother or sister just to make them feel better. 'We can all be proud that the tournament is here,' Maurice Lindsay said at the WCC launch. 'No longer can we be accused of being a sport whose ambition is limited to the M62 corridor.' The opening night saw Brisbane Broncos beat their London namesakes 42-22 in a credible encounter at the ANZ Stadium, while British champions St Helens were on the wrong end of a 14-42 humiliation at home to Auckland; the words 'omens' and 'ominous' being used together for the first time. Halifax conceded the first of two record scores in the tournament, when thumped 70-6 in Canberra two days later and, after defeats for Warrington, Bradford, Leeds, Salford, Castleford and Paris St Germain, only Wigan could provide some British cheer with a tremendous 22-18 success away at Canterbury Bulldogs that had the media wires home buzzing again but only briefly. Round Two was as bad, with only Sheffield Eagles' 26-22 home victory over Perth Reds in the plus column for the northern hemisphere clubs. By the time Round Three was over and done with it was no longer such a big surprise that the Australasian clubs had picked up the points from all the matches, save for Paris St Germain's 24-0 defeat of luckless Perth Reds. The knee-jerk response from the RFL was immediate, with technical director Joe Lydon appointed to head a team to stage an in-depth analysis of both playing and coaching standards in the British game. The inquests from the media and also those within the game began in earnest, with seemingly bewildered St Helens coach Shaun McRae commenting, 'I have never known anything like this in my entire career, and it will be the same for the players. We go on about how good our club sides are, but now I am not too sure that the gap has closed, in fact it may be wider than ever… But I suppose we have got to put everything in perspective.' Supporters were finding perspective difficult to come by, and braced themselves for what fate might befall their club in Phase Two. They had a little under a month to wait, and once on-field hostilities were resumed things began to look up for the British clubs. Warrington's thrashing in Penrith was followed by home wins for Leeds (22-14) against Adelaide, when Paul Sterling scored a memorable, oft repeated, solo try; London, who stunned Canberra with a 38-18 success at The Stoop and, more surprisingly, for Oldham against North Queensland Cowboys, 20-16. Perhaps our clubs had learned quickly from the previous phase of matches and were beginning to compete? That was partially true, but sadly those victories proved to be a false dawn, as all the remaining Round Four matches went the way of the southern hemisphere teams. Round Five was virtually the same. Wigan became the only British club to win two matches in the whole tournament when they did the 'double' over Canterbury, emerging victorious 31-24 at Central Park, but all their fellow clubs from the north were beaten, St Helens going the same way as Bradford had earlier in the tournament, suffering an almighty and alarming hammering (70-6) by the Auckland Warriors. Again, only one British club – this time Salford City Reds, who defeated Adelaide – managed a victory in the sixth and last round of the group matches, and the final tables did not make pretty reading for supporters of the European clubs. Wigan topped European Group A with four points, while London, the only other club to have secured a win, were also assured of a place in the quarter-finals. Three teams from that group qualified by right, so there was then the laughable situation of a team with no wins from six matches – Bradford – going into the last eight of the competition, while in Australasia's Group A, Penrith had to miss out on points difference to Brisbane, Auckland Warriors and Cronulla, despite all four clubs achieving maximum wins. Because the Group B teams in their respective hemispheres had finished lower in the ranks in their previous domestic season, only one place was allotted to the four Australasian teams, that going to new club Hunter Mariners, who had a one hundred per cent record. Meanwhile, the top team in Europe's Group B had to play off with the fourth club in Group A for a place in the quarter-finals. With a trip to face the Brisbane Broncos as the 'prize' awaiting the winners, it was sarcastically suggested that it was a game that neither Paris St Germain, the Group B winners on points difference, nor St Helens, who had emerged point-less but still qualified from Group A, wanted to win. The Paris team selection suggested that they least craved victory and St Helens duly prevailed. The quarter-finals opened in Auckland, where for the second time in the competition the Warriors put more than 60 points past runaway Super League leaders Bradford Bulls, while Wigan could not make the most of home advantage, going down 18-22 to the Mariners in a real cup tie. The following night Brisbane again embarrassed British opposition, this time annihilating St Helens 66-12 without expending undue effort and Aussie Test centre Steve Renouf scoring 5 of his team's 12 tries, while Cronulla Sharks completed the rout with a 40-16 success against a spirited London Broncos, at an atmospheric Stoop. With at least one of the semi-finals scheduled to be held in Europe (or hemisphere finals as they were originally known), there were more red faces now that the Australian competition had produced all four protagonists and with hasty rearrangement, both matches took place Down Under – one of the more sensible decisions associated with the overblown structure. The Aussie interest in the competition was reflected in attendances of only 9,686 at the ANZ Stadium as Brisbane defeated Auckland 22-16, and just 5,214 at Cronulla, who went down 18-22 to surprise packet, newcomers Hunter Mariners. With Auckland Warriors out, there was little Kiwi interest in the final, which took place at their home ground, Ericsson Stadium, and the greatest club tournament in the history of the sport drew in around 12,000 spectators to its decider, which saw the competition's original 7/4 favourites Brisbane cruise home 36-12 against Graham Murray's Newcastle-based interlopers. 'This is a long-term project to bridge the gap in standards,' Australian chief executive John Ribot was reported to have said, yet even his supreme optimism would not be enough to ensure that the tournament would be repeated in its 1997 format, as the game again reverted to type and withdrew.

The competition drew both derision and stinging criticism from supporters and the media alike, with the organisers and the standard of the European game arousing the most vociferous of it, but only the most naïve could really have expected the European clubs to win many more games than they actually did. Reflecting on the tournament, Dave Hadfield – so often the voice of reason and reflection – wrote, 'The tragedy of the World

Club Championship is that it laid bare our self-deception. In varying degrees, we have all fallen for the party line that the game has improved out of all recognition since we called it Super League, moved it to summer and staffed it with full-time professional players. The impression that has been given is that the British game is in a state of precipitous decline. This is not necessarily the case. Our tenth-best team would, as long as I've followed the game, always have been thrashed by Australia's tenth best. We just weren't daft enough to set up a competition to prove it.' Others were less measured in their assessments, and it was not on the admittedly mystifying format of the championship but the results that they focussed. The fallout was that the competition was deemed to be unworkable on an all-club basis, at least until there appeared to be a genuine closing of the gap in intensity between the two competitions. Even Maurice Lindsay, one of the sport's great expansionists and optimists admitted, 'We should take a painful lesson from this and reassess our game and what we have to do.' Considered with the benefit of hindsight, the tournament should have at least been given a modicum of credit for a number of reasons. Firstly, despite its intricacies, rugby league had proved at short notice that it could stage a truly global event. There were no snags on that front, with teams flying all over the world and everything scheduled going according to plan. In addition, the competition was attractive enough for it to draw in a worldwide, if admittedly eleventh-hour, sponsor in Visa; a new, multi-national name to give it that globe-trotting feel. On the field, while there were just 8 wins in the group matches for European teams, there were some terrific performances from the 'expansion' clubs, with Paris the only European club to 'nil' Australasian opponents and London Broncos producing a remarkable, Shaun Edwards-inspired fightback to turn defeat into victory against Canberra on a memorable night that showed the real potential the capital has for the code if the event is enticing enough. A sell out in the return 'battle of the Broncos' next up at The Stoop further illustrated that. Wigan maintained their standing as a true force in the club game by twice beating Canterbury, Leeds Rhinos effectively entered the Super League era after a rusty start with their success against Adelaide Rams on a night Headingley came of age as a summer venue; and wins for perceived 'smaller' clubs such as Sheffield, Oldham and Salford seemed to get steamrollered in the surge to criticise those who should have done better.

There were other mitigating factors involved in the performances of the British clubs who had, by the time the tournament kicked off, afforded their players only a few weeks' break in almost two years. That was due to the back-to-back nature of the centenary season bridging 1996 and the transitional move from winter to summer, Super League I kicking off virtually straight away. Adjusting to full-time professionalism and playing anyone after so little rest would have been difficult enough, but taking on clubs who played at a higher intensity was a task that some players must have felt shattered just at the thought of it. As Rudi Meir pointed out at the time, 'Competing against Australia in more recent times hasn't been easy for the British but trying to compete against them in the new era of professionalism is a bit like throwing Shaun Edwards in against Mike Tyson. The fact is that the majority of teams in Australia have operated on a professional basis for at least the past five years. With each passing season the skill and fitness of players in Australia has improved and along with it so has the quality of the coaching and training support. Research has shown that the average Australian player tends to be faster, more agile and stronger than the average English player. This just didn't happen overnight. Australian clubs have been the beneficiaries of a sophisticated system of player development put in place by the ARL and it has clearly served the game well. The weekly intensity of competition in Australia is substantially more demanding than in England. Gone are the days when the lower-placed teams were simply considered cannon fodder for the top teams in the Australian premiership. This is not the case in England. The top three or four teams are only tested when they play each other. With teams flying halfway around the world and arriving in Australia, as some did, just four days before their first game, this was simply asking too much from players who were still learning to cope with the new professionalism expected of them. Some English teams have a long way to go, but if nothing else the WCC has hopefully accelerated the game's progress in England.'

In trying to take the game to the world but being ruthlessly exposed from a European point of view, the need for the expansion of grass-roots rugby league in Britain had become more apparent than ever. The RFL needed to do something to spread the sport within these shores, so that future generations would produce more players in a more widespread and vibrant game. Perhaps more by accident than design, the World Club Championship did eventually contribute to the grass-roots expansion of the sport with its soul-searching ramifications being an indirect link to the introduction of the Rugby League Conference in 1998, which the RFL subsequently endorsed. Not only that but, in spite of the results, British supporters willing to see the bigger picture were able to marvel at the skills of some of the world's top players. Anyone who had told a Halifax fan in 1995 that two years later he could turn up at Thrum Hall to watch Hazem El Masri play in the colours of Canterbury, or that the great Brisbane Broncos team, containing Darren Lockyer, Steve Renouf, Wendell Sailor, Allan Langer and Gorden Tallis would be popping over to entertain them would have been led away in a straitjacket. Yet that is what the 1997 Visa World Club Championship allowed. Its overall impact on the sport was a negative, but it was one of the catalysts that resulted in an improvement in professionalism in Super League, though it may still have to play 'catch-up' for some time to come if international results are a reliable yardstick. As the one responsible for the control of the British game at the time, Maurice Lindsay's subsequent comments have – perhaps understandably – been an attempt to distance himself from the organisation of the much-maligned tournament. On reflection, however, perhaps his opening stand was much nearer the mark. In a sense the results did not matter.

TOP 10 SIGNINGS

1 JAMES LOWES (BRADFORD BULLS FROM LEEDS, 1996)
For both his qualities as a player and the longevity of his stay, this has to rank as the greatest signing of the Super League era. Incomprehensibly allowed to leave by Leeds, who had signed young hooker Mick Shaw, Lowes came back to haunt the Headingley outfit time and again in a magnificent career until his retirement in 2003. Probably the finest exponent of the crucial dummy half art in the modern era.

2 PAUL SCULTHORPE (ST HELENS FROM WARRINGTON WOLVES, 1998)
Perhaps the last great thing Sean McRae did before parting with Saints was to help beat off competition from Wigan and bring 'Scully' to Knowsley Road. Subsequently a dual Man of Steel Award recipient and Great Britain captain, it is hard to imagine St Helens running out on the field without him at the helm directing operations.

3 KEITH SENIOR (LEEDS RHINOS FROM SHEFFIELD EAGLES, 1999)
At the time it was the worst-kept secret in rugby league. Leeds wanted a powerful, pacy centre and chief executive Gary Hetherington knew where he could get one: at his old club. Senior has terrorised defences with 99 Super League tries from 166 appearances in blue and amber while becoming the competition's elder statesmen, appearing in a record 258 rounds by the end of the decade. Great value for money.

4 LESLEY VAINIKOLO (BRADFORD BULLS FROM CANBERRA RAIDERS, 2002)
If you've got a pack with a strong reputation for steamrollering your opponents, why not add a winger who can do the job just as well while possessing the pace of a sprinter? Brian Noble liked what he saw, but not too many of the opposing players did, and the 'Volcano' scored 102 tries (including a competition record of 6 in a match against Hull FC in 2005) from 95 appearances, by the time Super League X was concluded.

5 IESTYN HARRIS (LEEDS RHINOS FROM WARRINGTON WOLVES, 1997)
Although it all ended acrimoniously with the Rhinos, Harris relished playing under the guidance of coach Graham Murray, who gave him a free rein, switching him between full-back and stand off for maximum impact. Dominated the Leeds team of the late 1990s and had a major impact in skippering his men to Wembley glory.

6 JAMIE LYON (ST HELENS FROM WEE WAA, 2005)
Described by then coach Ian Millward as, 'the biggest signing for St Helens since Mal Meninga', Lyon fled the pressures of the NRL and Parramatta to play lower-grade league in Australia, before being enticed to these shores. A masterstroke from Saints, as the former Kangaroo centre had as big an impact as any overseas signing in a decade. Undoubtedly the supreme entertainer of Super League X.

7 MICHAEL WITHERS (BRADFORD BULLS FROM BALMAIN TIGERS, 1999)
Few British fans knew much about Withers (a.k.a. 'the Ghost') before he arrived at Odsal, despite him being an Australian 'Junior of the Year' in 1994, but this highly versatile member of the backline has been involved in all the successes enjoyed by the club in the past seven seasons, haunting defences with 83 tries in 135 Super League appearances and, because of Irish descent, nearly commandeered to play for Great Britain.

8 SHAUN EDWARDS (LONDON BRONCOS FROM WIGAN WARRIORS, 1997 & BRADFORD, 1998)
By the time he moved to the capital Edwards was thirty, but his brilliance was the driving force behind the Broncos' best ever Super League finish (second) and a thrilling World Club Championship campaign in 1997. His return after an abortive spell at Bradford saw him grace Wembley for a record eleventh time in a Challenge Cup final, when London made their one and only appearance at the old stadium. Most importantly, Edwards' capture gave the capital side much needed credibility.

9 STEVE RENOUF (WIGAN WARRIORS FROM BRISBANE BRONCOS, 2000)
Many wondered how the Warriors afforded the man who broke British hearts by scoring the winning try for Australia in the 1992 World Cup final, but whatever they paid the reclusive, ostrich-loving Renouf, his influence on the Wigan side was worth it. Forty tries in 55 appearances over two seasons was some strike record for a centre.

10 JASON SMITH (HULL FC FROM PARRAMATTA EELS, 2001)
The gravel-voiced Queenslander was the signature at The Boulevard that announced to everyone that Hull FC were serious about returning to the top echelon of the sport. An Aussie international, his stay bridged the move to the new KC Stadium and his sublime, creative influence in midfield inspired the Airlie Birds to their best ever Super League finish of third in 2001.

TEN

GROWTH: THE NEXT TEN YEARS

'We still keep bumping into the same old problem that's inherent in our society. We loathe change. I can't for the life of me begin to understand this reluctance to acknowledge success. There are many positives that have proved Super League will work if it's correctly managed.' – Peter Deakin

Principally through Super League and the switch to summer, the sport of rugby league is enjoying a resurgence that, on 29 March 1996 looked, if not impossible, at least implausible. Full houses at Old Trafford, a Challenge Cup that – having been paraded around Britain – is on its way back to Wembley, the return of the Euro-dynamic with Les Catalans Dragons, a club – in Harlequins – playing off the branding of the Rugby Football Union, the strengthening of links with the amateur game, improved youth development, a game more widespread than ever before thanks to the Rugby League European Federation, the Conference and the Student Rugby League and inclusion in the government's top ten sports for Sport England funding has even converted some of those dyed-in-the-wool followers of the game who said they would rather see hell freeze over than go with the Murdoch dollar. From the stability that came with the administration of Richard Lewis, backed by a more holistic approach at both governing and individual club level, the platform has been created for the growth – and the fourth phase of the regeneration cycle – that was always promised but has never yet been quite achieved. After a year of analysis, the RFL unveiled its 'Super League Strategy' in May 2005, setting out its aims for the elite competition until 2008. The most important of its proposals were:

To consider expansion of Super League to fourteen teams in 2009, if appropriate; to strengthen Super League membership criteria and amend the method by which teams are promoted to the competition

To make a full assessment of the season calendar and the resulting player workload

To place a positive emphasis on developing club business, the ongoing support for junior player production and coach education programmes

To have employed match officials by 2007

Richard Lewis announced, 'The strategy aims to deliver a competition that attracts greater levels of investment, can successfully expand and is the driving force behind rugby league's vibrant and successful future.'

By 2009 then, we could again see a fourteen-team competition, which would also satisfy the governing body's aim to help reduce the number of fixtures that players compete in. In this case, it would drop from twenty-eight to twenty-six matches in the regular rounds of the season. Lewis added that any plans for expansion of Super League were unlikely to take place until after the current television deal with Sky Sports expires at the end of 2008 – as the nature of the current broadcast contract is built around a twelve-team competition. All Super League clubs would undergo an assessment in 2006, and it was hoped that the half of them who were failing to achieve an annual turnover of £3 million would soon hit the target. The business model was actually outlined prior to the start of Super League III by James Dow, author of a KPMG report into the state of the clubs' finances. 'The real dilemma for rugby league is increasing its supporter base. This is the key to helping to pay the players and to bring in more revenue through areas like kit merchandising. You need a minimum of 10,000 – ideally 15,000 – supporters attending regularly in order to develop a viable income stream.' Hopefully those figures will be realised at every club over the next ten years.

Franchising was again back on the agenda, although this time with a more sustainable, achievable, longer-term vision behind it. Alongside Lewis at the strategy launch the RFL's operations director Nigel Wood said, 'The reality is that we've got to work on the quality. Five years ago we had one club spending their salary cap money, four years ago it was two and there are now six out of the twelve clubs are spending the limit of their salary cap expenditure. That is because those businesses have been growing and we've got a better-balanced competition because of that. If in four years' time you have all twelve clubs spending at that level then there's more and more uncertainty of outcome.' The code has been looking to expand since 1895 and 2006 represents its latest incarnation. Les Catalans Dragons are now on board with a sufficient lead-in time and a charismatic on-field talisman in skipper Stacey Jones to realistically think they will more than hold their own in battle. By basing themselves on a fiercely proud and passionate region – something the sport is historically good at – rather than their principal town, Perpignan, they can appeal to a wider, new and uncatered for market. Moreover, by playing selected matches over the border in northern Spain, they immediately open up the prospect of further expansion within the newly created European Federation structure. Although it sounded like fanciful bravado in 1995, there is now a genuine reason to believe that Super League in franchised big cities across the continent could be more than a pipedream – remember Barcelona. At least a start has been made, Catalan look a much safer bet to survive and flourish than their French predecessors Paris St Germain on the basis that they can draw upon the strength of the heartlands of the French game and there is clear potential for further growth in Britain and beyond. Celtic Crusaders, born out of the Welsh Division of the Rugby League Conference and debuting in the National League Two in 2006, were created with a clear intention of creating a viable, grassroots-led Super League club in the Principality. The central principle of bottom-up development rather than imposed-down has been established. Scotland and Ireland both have domestic structures in operation with local talent experiencing the joys and challenges of the sport at a rapidly rising standard. With careful nurturing and little competition for attention in the summer, both countries remain realistic targets, especially as domestic Scottish Rugby Union appears to be in perpetual decline while Dublin is still crying out for a fully professional enterprise that will represent the city's acknowledged sporting fervour. Similarly, with nations such as Russia, Georgia, Serbia, Holland, Germany and Estonia making strides, maybe 'Super League Europe' was actually a nomenclature ahead of its time. Richard Lewis, though, is guarded about the prospect in the immediate future. 'Not in the next decade, I don't think. One of the reasons why Les Catalans are coming in is that we are tapping into a traditionally strong rugby league area and if there was a second French club the same would apply, but I'm not sure that French rugby league in the foreseeable future could sustain more than two full-time fully professional clubs. If we were to create other franchises around Europe without a strong base in that area I would frankly be very sceptical about whether it could work. That's why I'm much more optimistic about London, which is now a very big rugby league-playing area, and South Wales, which is developing and clearly can tap into rugby union as well.'

London took its most significant step yet towards a secure and prosperous future when rugby union club Harlequins invited London Broncos on board as Harlequins RL, the partnership offering a much-needed lifeline to the ex-Broncos who had seen administration or closure as a very real possibility three weeks into Super League X. Not everyone was happy that the old club effectively walked away from its debts without the sanction of a points penalty but, for once, the good of the game prevailed over self and that sets an encouraging precedent. The Harlequins brand can firmly establish league in the capital, a decent drop kick away from the Twickenham home of the opposition that would have preferred it to be starved at birth. Times and attitudes are changing with the advent of professionalism in both sports and, as can not be stressed too much, the change in competitive seasons now sees them as strange, unlikely but plausible bedfellows. Drawing on support from its existing Super League fan base and with the opportunity to tap into the club's fifteen-a-side supporters (and players), Quins RL's return to The Stoop, where they enjoyed their finest Super League years, could be their making. The portents were good then as Nigel Wray, the benefactor behind Saracens, noted. 'It's confusing. London Broncos with a game that is not played in the south go to Harlequins and within a few months draw bigger crowds than the Quins with all their stars. Why?' Provided the partnership, based on the dual arrangement that has been a success at Leeds, works – and it will never have a better opportunity – then there could be serious intent to make similar expansionist moves in other places. Newcastle would be an obvious start, given that it already draws in decent crowds, has good facilities, and is just up the road from existing National League club Gateshead. Leicester has staged Super League matches and would be another likely to consider joining the thirteen-a-side ranks, and then there is Cardiff – which would already be in a far better position to consider a franchise given the development work done there since they were last mooted as a potential club. Richard Lewis has stated his wish for London to have two top-flight clubs and perhaps Wasps, with Shaun Edwards currently at the helm, might be an option, while existing National League Two club London Skolars are also looking to maintain their structured progression through the rugby league pyramid – another major addition to the sport's structure since 1996. In the past rugby league has too often been reactive rather than proactive in identifying the geographical areas it wants to be in strategically. 'Planned expansion is the next great milestone in rugby league. Once clubs have come into being in different parts of the country, we shall be faced with an organisational upheaval as faced the 1906 legislators. If only our plans are well conceived, the future should be radiant in the game. We have reached greatness through the efforts of noble pioneers.' That homily was written in the *Rugby League Review* in the letters of Uncle Bill, on 6 December 1951. *Plus ca change.*

The Super League Strategy message in 2005 seemed to suggest that franchises would be a reality from 2009 onwards, although history over the last decade has told us not to hold our breath. Nevertheless, the current RFL plan is to scrap promotion and relegation in its current guise and award Super League membership based on different criteria – a bit like 'franchising the future'. Clubs such as Leigh Centurions, who finally and desperately experienced the joy of promotion in 2004, only to suffer immediate, ignominious relegation from the top flight twelve months on, will no longer be given only four months to prepare themselves for a Super League challenge and, crucially, all that comes with the move from a part-time to a full-time business. Furthermore, under new and far more sensible proposals, clubs will now have the chance to set out a longer-term plan of how they will cope with the step up in standards, both on and off the field, and once they are promoted they will have three years to prove themselves in the top flight. An ongoing quality control review will then be made on all clubs at the end of each three years of their tenure, and those who do not meet the required standards in terms of playing, business and facilities will find their Super League place is in jeopardy. While there is still the potential problem of meaningless matches that a lack of relegation in particular brings, the decision is surely a sound economic one. The sport's finances have been in a parlous state for long enough – including since Rupert Murdoch declared an interest to the tune of £87 million – and as the latest club to make a short stay in the top flight, Leigh have been well placed to advise precisely what a drain on resources such Super League brevity can bring. Established Super League clubs have got so much more financial clout than those in the National Leagues that four months' preparation is simply not enough for those aiming to make the transition, and those lower league clubs are now accepting the reality of that. Richard Lewis expanded on the underlying rationale. 'I think it's going to be a huge opportunity for the League and it will develop a culture of no excuses. I really do believe that if a club is given three years in Super League to plan and deliver then nobody can turn round and claim they haven't been given every chance in my view. If they are not drawing the crowds and not producing a decent team on the pitch, where are they going to look apart from at themselves?'

Yet again, rugby league may well be in the vanguard, the first sport brave enough to face up to commercial reality. As David Conn has pointed out with soccer, there are 'catastrophic financial consequences of relegation. The Premier League clubs have a duty to ease the financial impact of relegation, so that their clubs are no longer going down and going bust, leaving a trail of miserable creditors unpaid,' while for Richard Lewis, 'The British way may not be the right way, we have to learn through experience what is best for this sport and there is a better way. Super League is a really strong business entity that demands decisions that keep driving it forward and when something isn't right, such as arguably the difficulties facing teams being promoted and the short-term decision making that relegation forces upon clubs, the energy of the competition means that's addressed.'

Perhaps there is even another way of looking at the potentially divisive dilemma of scrapping an institution that is part of the sporting culture here. Why set a limit on Super League clubs? If, in the future, there are for example two National League clubs and two 'expansion' clubs who all have strong cases for inclusion, and those already in the top flight continue to merit a place, why not include them all and simply split the clubs into conferences, as has been successful in American football? Limiting Super League to fourteen clubs may in the first instance be prudent, given the lopsided nature of previous competitions when rolled out to that number, but if the sport is to truly expand then it should be actively encouraging new franchise bids while nurturing those already in. That represents real growth, so that the next generation of followers of this great game might not all speak using flat vowels, but those who do will be around to tell them what it was like 'in't' first decade. It is a scenario that Gary Hetherington has given much thought to. 'I made an ill-fated statement back in the first year when I said that if in ten years' time we've still got, for example, Castleford in the Super League perhaps we've not succeeded. Anybody who knows me is aware that I am from the area and that was the team I supported through boyhood so if I have an allegiance to anybody it is probably them and I used it merely as an example of a small-town team. The point I was making was that, as we go forward and develop, teams like that would not be able to sustain themselves and the competition would need city-based sides throughout the country and if we did not have them then we wouldn't have progressed. Now, especially because I'm with Leeds, everyone in the town thinks I conspire against them every week but the code does still need to expand and become more of a national sport, although that is starting to happen. Having embraced the French, the only other part of the country that has a heartland and tradition is Cumbria. That area has its own problems with regard to population and facilities but if there was a solution to that then we would at least have a Super League presence in all the rugby league areas. The challenge then is to create new teams and rugby league centres and it's not always the obvious ones where you are going to find the big audiences. In rugby union, for example, Worcester – with no heritage – is now drawing sell-out crowds because that area was ripe for a new professional sport. Rugby League needs to be a bit cleverer in terms of its strategies and in the targeting of areas where it can become the primary sport; in these days of such competition that is a major consideration.'

Richard Lewis is conscious of the various directions Super League could take. 'One of the reasons why we announced fourteen teams was because we wanted to show expansion to more teams rather than less. There had been one or two campaigns for cutting it down to ten and we wanted to make sure nobody thought that. It was also important that people realised we were talking about more opportunities for clubs to be a part of Super League and clubs from outside it to still aspire to it. If you go to fourteen, and they are all really strong, it is not a quantum leap to keep growing the league and coming up with different structures for how the competition is run. If all the clubs are strong then they are not going to be relying on playing Leeds or St Helens or Wigan each week for a viable business. They are going to say that no matter who they play they are going to get the crowds, the television coverage and the sponsorship and you can be flexible. Fourteen is an aspiration to grow to but it's not the end game at all. The clubs would really have to work hard to maintain that community link but I do honestly believe they would do that because it is so much built into the heritage and core of the sport and I would be absolutely staggered if they lost sight of that. They would have to be very aware that they shouldn't try and become something that they are not.'

Looking at the longer term, the strategy outlined plans to introduce central contracts for international players and repeated its undertaking to continue working with clubs to relieve the workload on those who ceaselessly provide the entertainment, with Lewis admitting, 'The elite players are involved in too many matches, which impacts on playing standards at international level and career longevity.' The idea of central contracts for elite players has, of course, proved highly successful with the England cricket team who, until their 2005 tour of Pakistan, had enjoyed a unprecedented run of success, including pulling off an Ashes win that their rugby league cousins would love to emulate. How such a system would work in Super League is unclear, though the idea does have undoubted merit. County cricket is administered differently and watched by a minority and, although it is still possible for a player to turn out for his county while centrally contracted, they tend not to because of the heavy international fixture load that ultimately pays all the domestic bills. Given that rugby league is not as strong internationally, maybe central contracts would not adversely affect its core strength, the clubs. Less Test fixtures would mean much more time for a centrally contracted player to turn out for his club and so fans should not be too disconcerted to see the likes of a Paul Sculthorpe or a Stuart Fielden missing from the ranks for any more than the odd few games during a season, provided the system is equitable. Rugby Union has already experienced the kind of problems associated with such a scheme. Three weeks into the 2005 season the governing body was at loggerheads with senior clubs

Sale, Wasps and Leicester for playing British Lions players during their apparently agreed rest period – despite the consternation over such a large squad
being taken to New Zealand in the first place and a number of the players
leaving there frustrated at having had little game time. The RFU withheld
monies despite the clubs' contracts being with the Lions and the governing body merely being the paymasters, their chief executive Francis Barron
commenting, 'We need to manage the elite player resource.' In response, Ian
McGeechan, director of rugby at Wasps countered, 'We need to look at the
way the season is structured. There are too many competitive requirements
put on the players. There is a huge investment put into the players by the clubs
and if central contracts were going to come in then it should have been at the
beginning of the sport going professional.' It is a dilemma Super League needs
to avoid. As Brian McDermott hopes, 'It may be a sacrifice worth making but
it would have to be a well-debated, well-thought-through process. It's good
that a club coach is the Great Britain supremo because any such decisions are
going to be reflective of each dimension, but we do need to compete consistently at international level.' Perhaps a central contract could place a limit
that, for example, a player could only miss up to a maximum of four matches
during a season – excluding injuries – at the behest of his international coach.
That, coupled with the intended reduction in the number of regular-season
games, would help for international training camps, internationals themselves,
or simply resting the players so that they are more able to channel their energies in big, intense matches such as play-offs and finals. Admittedly this idea
does not look like being implemented immediately, and it would also need
careful thought. For example, given that Great Britain looks likely to be dis-
banded in the near future – with the exception of playing as a touring team
– would the central contracts only affect players in the England squad, or
would Scotland, Ireland, Wales and France follow suit? There would soon be
uproar if Les Catalans were able to field a full-strength team every week but,
say, Bradford Bulls could not because they had a squad packed with England
internationals. But whatever the whys and wherefores, the clubs themselves
would need to buy into the concept for the good of the game.

As well as the players, there has been a growing call to make the officials full
time as their performances have come under even greater scrutiny. The sport
is now played at a relentless pace and pressure so the fitness of the men in the
middle – and on the touchlines – is critical. With access to close-ups, ultra-
slow-motion replays and multiple camera angles the audience has become
better educated and the man in the middle more isolated and open to cen-
sure. A move to greater uncertainty of outcome with closer, better-balanced
matches puts even more invidious pressure on the arbiter with clashes more

likely to be decided by a single crucial incident. The money now involved means that mistakes have never been so costly, not least for the security of tenure of coaches. What any of those in charge of sides would call for is consistency, not just within matches but in interpretation from week to week. Having greater access to referees is what is needed with more quality time for them to train alongside local clubs and undertake performance analysis on video. For Richard Lewis, who anticipates having six such contracted officials by 2007, 'It depends what you mean by full time. Our aspiration is to have match officials whose primary source of income is from rugby league so that they can train or rest when they need to, but in any given week there will be spare time to do other things that do not affect their preparations or abilities and I think that is perfectly possible. We've got some now and I don't think it's any coincidence at all that, in the 2005 season, Ashley Klein and Phil Bentham have had good campaigns. They are eating, drinking and breathing rugby league in their various roles as employees of the RFL. It's no surprise that they have improved on the field as a result. I think we can get there very quickly but I don't think the answer is for them to be full time to the extent that they are sitting around three days a week just waiting for something to happen.'

On the international front, the 2008 World Cup is on the horizon, and will revert to the highly successful 1995 format of ten teams. It is hoped that the sport will be able to reflect on the success of that tournament, and another one besides, by the time the Super League XX trophy has been lifted, with the consequent rise in prestige and profile for the whole game. London stages the Olympic Games in 2012 and, with no other major sport other than rugby league scheduled to hold a cyclical world event in that year, it would be the ideal way to pick up on what will undoubtedly be sports fever in Britain by staging our own World Cup on these shores in late summer and early autumn. Sports aficionados, journalists and other competitors from all over the globe will be congregating here in readiness, and what better way to cater for their recreation by staging an extravaganza featuring some of the world's finest, most underrated athletes? Whether the sport has the confidence in its international strength to plan that far ahead is not entirely clear, but if the seeds were sown sooner rather than later and younger nations consequently have a chance to plan ahead – a bit like with regard to the franchising debate – maybe a return to a sixteen-team tournament by 2012 may not be out of the question. Just prior to the announcement of Super League in January 1995, *Open Rugby* published its world rankings; there were eighteen nations listed, another case of the sport not inventing the new but trying to do the old better.

There is further opportunity for future development simply by virtue of the fixture schedule. With virtually all Super League clubs now having ditched the traditional Sunday afternoon 3.00 p.m. kick-off for Friday or Saturday nights, mainly because of the demands of television and corporate convenience, the National Leagues can take the old centre stage unhindered. Not only would that give ardent rugby league followers the chance to see both their own Super League club plus other locally based, community cherished matches, perhaps, more significantly, it would avoid National League clubs having to compete at the turnstiles with the elite level and give them a proper platform for attracting the twenty-first century business investment that has become essential. Most importantly of all, it would showcase the fiercely contested competition and, in the days when media is a bigger sporting god than any collection of players could ever hope to become, it could ensure better coverage and include the possibility of a bespoke National League television deal. The changing demands, economics and essential nature of major top-class sport means that egalitarianism can no longer be the case. If Super League needs to be European for the code as a whole to prosper on the widest stage, then there is little option but to create and concentrate resources on a true elite. The alternative is to remain a respected minority sport struggling for real funding and exposure. By the same token, for the peak of the pyramid to work, it must have solid foundations underneath. Many so-called community clubs in the traditional areas cannot realistically be expected to compete at Super League level. So many have tried to buy their way into the upper echelon that, even when they have succeeded, the effect has only been to temporarily dispel bankruptcy. Finances and public interest are finite; if Super League is now beyond them, a competition that pits them against similarly structured and financed clubs that they are capable of beating has to be given added value. Taking away the pressure of unrealistic aspiration may even give such outfits a new lease of life and purpose. The appointment by the RFL of a National League 'Tsar' would also be of benefit in furthering the cause of its clubs at the decision-making table.

A subject causing much concern at the end of Super League's first ten years continues to be the surfeit of overseas players in the top flight. This issue clearly needs self-regulating by the clubs themselves so that they do not continue to exploit loopholes in the law, in particular the Kolpak ruling, to enable them to strengthen their squads at the expense of home-grown talent. While the salary cap has undoubtedly saved the game from itself, there is mounting criticism from within some boardrooms that the 20/20 rule is becoming too restrictive. Ian Millward believes that it should be withdrawn. 'It is an old rule that needs abolishing. Our aim should be to make Great Britain the best team in the world and anything that restricts a young player's financial and skills progress needs to be looked at.' Perhaps the mistake has been not to make it index linked, so that by 2006 it was a 20/25 rule, the increased amount better reflecting financial reward that will upgrade a young player's contract and keep him within the club structure that nurtured his development. The ultimate example of a salary cap system working is in the NRL in Australia where they have produced seven different winners of the competition in consecutive seasons; some, like Penrith and 2005's best Wests Tigers – showing that the right sort of mergers can work – coming from being also-rans to champions. The reason is because of comparative spends, with the cap amount being flat across all the clubs. That raises an interesting philosophical question about the essence and nature of sport. Should there be and can there be such a notion as a totally even competition unless, like American Football, which instigated a truly equitable franchise system from scratch, all the clubs are of a similar size and have access to comparable catchment areas? For the foreseeable future, Super League cannot totally discount its geographical history; Castleford cannot be expected to match Bradford in that respect. Unrealistic artificiality can reward mediocrity and penalise enterprise, be a disincentive to building a club and instead merely spread the jam thinly, in effect a levelling down of standards.

Uncertainty of outcome that retains the romance should be the goal but, in the interim, a system that encourages talent to be shared by the constant promotion of juniors is the way to grow, which is why the 20/20 principle is such a key regulator. In saying that, during the decade the quality of overseas players in the competition has risen, while the average age at which they have chosen to play over here has reduced, and the old theory that they come over to these shores for a retirement pension is no longer valid. Tonie Carroll (Leeds) and Lesley Vainikolo (Bradford) were both internationals in their early twenties when signing for their respective clubs. Currently Iafeta Palea'aesina (Wigan) is another in his prime – there are more besides – while ageing imports such as Allan Langer, whatever his contribution to Warrington Wolves, are now more the exception. British rugby league should continue to welcome quality overseas players who raise the profile and the standard of Super League, but it should dispense with journeymen and look to the talent that its own youth development programmes continue to yield. The signing of Aussie Test star Andrew Johns, who played just three games for Warrington in 2005 in a blaze of unprecedented publicity, raised the profile of the club and the sport, as did the return to Britain of Adrian Morley, who made twice as many appearances for Bradford, and ultimately became one of the few in the sport to possess Grand Final winners' rings in both hemispheres. For their part, the Wolves went on record as saying that they got full value for having Johns around for a few weeks, but they felt it unlikely they would repeat the dose. By 2016, Super League may be good enough to attract Johns' successor as world number one for a full season. Now that would be a sign of real progress in the competition. By extension, with the 2006 Tri-Nations and 2008 World Cup both set to be staged Down Under, there are tremendous opportunities for the best players to again experience the unique bonding that comes with being part of a touring squad. That can only be good for the sport and, importantly, its fans; sports tourism now being that industry's fastest-growing area. Super League was always supposed to be a global game.

One other thorny issue that continues to blight not just rugby league but many other sports and society itself, is the use of drugs. Already players had been named, shamed and banned before the summer era but in the past ten years others have felt the need to improve their performance beyond accepted method. In 2006, rugby league has done all it can to make the sport clean, satisfying the Sports Council with its guidance and procedures, and working with Sport England to allow out-of-season drug testing in addition to random tests in-season. If the code is to be at the forefront of vigilence regarding this unsavoury aspect of sporting life in another decade, then it is now up to the players themselves, albeit a small minority, to take the responsibility of cleaning up their own acts.

Whether Super League has been an unqualified success or a case of casting adrift the extended family depends on whether you are a Bradford Bull or a follower of Featherstone Rovers. What can not be denied is that, after ten years, the young generation knows nothing other than Super League and summer and they love it in increasing numbers. The speed, colour, noise, atmosphere and ceaseless action are a perfect metaphor and canvas for their world. Surely securing that future is all that matters. Super League, like comparisons between the greatest players of varying eras, is not necessarily better or worse; there never are golden ages, only different ones. Qualitative judgements are impossible to make, not least because of changes in rules and the athleticism of players under full-time professionalism. All a sport can do is adapt to make the best of the forces that shape it and Super League is starting to do that after a furious, fascinating and formative ten years. The diversified audience today would not tolerate the days of seventy scrums per game, as was the norm when crowds flocked partly because there were no other counter-attractions. Then the players were in servitude. In 1966, when the limited-tackle rule was introduced and the game speeded up immeasurably, critics heralded it as being the end of the sport, just as some did in 1995 when Super League changed the landscape immutably. Every epoch is perceived to have lost something from the previous one but, like in all walks of life, history is often recalled through rose-tinted spectacles. As always, the credit for the game's continual survival and revival must go to the players and the fans. Alongside them some visionary administrators and far-sighted marketers saw the bigger picture and cashed in on it.

For Gary Hetherington, undoubtedly one of the prime movers, Super League still offers significant opportunity. 'There is a real interest in and respect for the game and we are getting a much broader mix of people following its fortunes – not necessarily paying to watch every week – but admiring it. If we could achieve success at national level that would elevate us even further; we are moving into new markets and new territories. I've always had eternal faith in the game, even in my darkest hours at Sheffield. The game was the thing that always gave me inspiration and hope and I think we've done a good job with it. The players and coaches are the ones who've elevated the quality of the product. They deserve the most credit. The sport has grown significantly and we are in a very healthy position. Ten years ago I'd have been very happy with where we find ourselves now; the financial stability of the clubs, a significant improvement in facilities and above all else the development at grassroots level, which gives real potential for future expansion from a proper solid base. The transition to summer in ninety-five per cent of people's eyes has been accepted as a good move with the opportunities that creates. Ten years is a short time in a sport's history, a long time in many other ways, but it has been a terrific journey that has not been without its pain and mistakes and, at the end of it, we are much better prepared to go into the next decade. I said two or three years ago that we are on the verge of a golden era for the game and I still think that is the case. There are still some major challenges but there is a new-found credibility that the sport has never had, respect for its disciplines and a growing audience both on the terraces and in front of the television. The possibilities are there to really enhance it.'

The final word must go to those who have invested so much into making the modern chapter of the illustrious sport a success, the gladiators. Brian McDermott is unequivocal. 'It's been a great concept. I love it. Super League is the best sport in the world bar none and I've got the second-best job. I can't play anymore and if I could I would but if I can influence others on how to play it I can't ask for anything more. I might sound like a starry-eyed kid but the game has everything; honesty, integrity, toughness, skill and speed and I don't know any other that can combine all those qualities. 'Privileged' is the right word. I recently met up with a friend of mine from my amateur club who is a couple of years older than me who I hadn't seen for two or three years since I started coaching, but was a big influence on my rugby league life. I showed him round the facility at Kirkstall and talked to him about the stats system and the exciting potential of the players coming through and gave him a brief outline of what we aim to do and it blew his socks off. He said to me "you are one lucky man" and, although luck isn't the right word because I have worked too hard, I am extremely fortunate to be in this position. There are knockers within the game. I went to a sportsmans' dinner where a true star of yesteryear ripped Super League apart and told the audience it wasn't as good as when he played. If that's his belief then he should shut up and keep it to himself because we don't want to hear it.' Super League, like rugby league throughout its long and glorious history, has never quite sought or received the credit it warrants. Rupert Murdoch said it in 1996, 'The game deserves unsurpassed marketing support and promotional excellence. We intend to surprise the world with rugby league.'

FIRST & LAST TEAMS

Only six clubs have retained their status in the elite division throughout the ten seasons of Super League. The names contained within their first and last sides that top and tail the decade are a testimony to all those who laced a boot in what has been a unique time for a sport that was prepared to adapt and essentially re-invent itself.

BRADFORD BULLS
(*v.* Castleford Tigers at Odsal, won 30-18) Paul Loughlin, Gary Christie, Matt Calland, Graeme Bradley, Jon Scales, Robbie Paul, Glen Tomlinson, Brian McDermott, James Lowes, Karl Fairbank, Jeremy Donougher, Sonny Nickle, Simon Knox. Substitutes: Jason Donohue, Paul Medley, Carlos Hassan, Bernard Dwyer.

(*v.* Leeds Rhinos at Old Trafford, won 15-6) Michael Withers, Leon Pryce, Ben Harris, Shontayne Hape, Lesley Vainikolo, Iestyn Harris, Paul Deacon, Jamie Peacock, Ian Henderson, Stuart Fielden, Paul Johnson, Brad Meyers, Lee Radford. Substitutes: Adrian Morley, Jamie Langley, Joe Vagana, Robbie Paul.

LEEDS RHINOS
(*v.* Warrington Wolves at Headingley, lost 22-18) Anthony Gibbons, Jim Fallon, Kevin Iro, Phil Hassan, Paul Gledhill, Francis Cummins, Graham Holroyd, Neil Harmon, Mick Shaw, Harvey Howard, George Mann, Matt Schultz, Adrian Morley. Substitutes: John Riley, Marcus Vassilakopoulos, Nick Fozzard, Barrie McDermott.

(*v.* Bradford Bulls at Old Trafford, lost 15-6) Richard Mathers, Mark Calderwood, Chev Walker, Chris McKenna, Marcus Bai, Danny McGuire, Rob Burrow, Ryan Bailey, Andrew Dunemann, Danny Ward, Gareth Ellis, Willie Poching, Kevin Sinfield. Substitutes: Barrie McDermott, Ali Lauitiiti, Jamie Jones-Buchanan, Matt Diskin.

LONDON BRONCOS
(*v.* Halifax Blue Sox at Thrum Hall, won 24-22) Greg Barwick, Junior Paul, Keiran Mayer, Evan Cochrane, Bernard Carroll, Tulsen Tollett, Leo Dynevor, Tony Mestrov, Tony Rea, Gavin Allen, Darren Shaw, Sean Keating, Terry Matterson. Substitutes: Russell Bawden, Justin Bryant, Darryl Pitt, Duncan McRae.

(*v.* Bradford Bulls at Odsal, lost 44-22) Zeb Luisi, Jon Wells, Tyrone Smith, Paul Sykes, Nick Bradley-Qalilawa, Feleti Mateo, Luke Dorn, Steve Trindall, David Highton, Mark Tookey, Solomon Haumono, Lee Hopkins, Carl Ablett. Substitutes: Rob Purdham, Joe Mbu, Danny Williams, Karl Temata.

ST HELENS
(*v.* Workington Town at Derwent Park, won 62-0) Steve Prescott, Danny Arnold, Scott Gibbs, Paul Newlove, Anthony Sullivan, Karle Hammond, Bobbie Goulding, Apollo Perelini, Keiron Cunningham, Andy Leatham, Chris Joynt, Simon Booth, Andy Northey. Substitutes: Phil Veivers, Vila Matautia, Ian Pickavance, Derek McVey.

(*v.* Bradford Bulls at Knowsley Road, lost 18-23) Paul Wellens, Ade Gardner, Jamie Lyon, Willie Talau, Ian Hardman, Jon Wilkin, Scott Moore, Nick Fozzard, Keiron Cunningham, Paul Anderson, Lee Gilmour, Mike Bennett, Vinnie Anderson. Substitutes: Mick Higham, James Roby, Maurie Fa'asavalu, James Graham.

WARRINGTON WOLVES
(*v.* Leeds at Headingley, won 22-18) Lee Penny, Mark Forster, Chris Rudd, Salesi Finau, Mateaka Mafi, Iestyn Harris, Mike Ford, Mark Hilton, John Hough, Gary Chambers, Ian Knott, Paul Cullen, Paul Sculthorpe. Substitutes: Toa Kohe-Love, Mark Jones, Kelly Shelford, Mike Wainwright.

(*v.* Hull FC at Halliwell Jones Stadium, lost 40-6) Brent Grose, Henry Fa'afili, Martin Gleeson, Toa Kohe-Love, Chris Bridge, Lee Briers, Andrew Johns, Chris Leikvoll, Nathan Wood, Paul Wood, Logan Swann, Paul Noone, Jon Clarke. Substitutes: Mark Gleeson, Ben Westwood, Mark Hilton, Danny Lima.

WIGAN WARRIORS
(*v.* Oldham Bears at Boundary Park, won 56-16) Kris Radlinski, Jason Robinson, Va'aiga Tuigamala, Gary Connolly, Martin Offiah, Henry Paul, Shaun Edwards, Neil Cowie, Martin Hall, Terry O'Connor, Scott Quinnell, Mick Cassidy, Andy Farrell. Substitutes: Kelvin Skerrett, Simon Haughton, Rob Smyth, Andy Johnson.

(*v.* Huddersfield Giants at Galpharm Stadium, won 36-22) Brett Dallas, Brian Carney, Kevin Brown, Sean Gleeson, Chris Ashton, Danny Orr, Dennis Moran, Jerome Guisset, Bob Beswick, Danny Tickle, Stephen Wild, Joel Tomkins, Harrison Hansen. Substitutes: Wayne Godwin, Dave Allen, Danny Sculthorpe, Lee Jewitt.